The Political Economy of Water and Sanitation

Routledge Studies in Development and Society

The Political Economy of Water and Sanitation

Matthias Krause

Routledge
Taylor & Francis Group

LONDON AND NEW YORK

First published 2009
by Routledge

2 Park Square, Milton Park, Abingdon, Oxon OX14 4RN
52 Vanderbilt Avenue, New York, NY 10017

Routledge is an imprint of the Taylor & Francis Group, an informa business

First published in paperback 2012

© 2009 Taylor & Francis

Typeset in Sabon by IBT Global.

Library of Congress Cataloging in Publication Data
Krause, Matthias.
    The political economy of water and sanitation / By Matthias Krause.
        p. cm. — (Routledge studies in development and society)
    Includes bibliographical references and index.
    1. Water utilities.   2. Water supply.   3. Sewage disposal.   I. Title.
    HD4456.K73 2009
    363.6'1 — dc22

ISBN13: 978-0-415-65256-8 (pbk)
ISBN13: 978-0-415-99489-7 (hbk)

Contents

viii *Contents*

Boxes

Figures

Tables

Acronyms

AC	Average costs
ADC	Administrative costs
ANDESCO	Asociación Nacional de Empresas de Servicios Públicos Domiciliaros y Actividades Complementarias e Inherentes (National Association of Enterprises Providing Public Utility Services)
BL	Amount of money billed
BOT	Build operate transfer
CAR	Corporación Autónoma Regional (Autonomous Regional Body)
CCC	Corporación Cívica de Caldas
CDCS	Comité de Desarrollo y Control Social (Committee for Social Development and Control)
Cf.	Confer
CL	Amount of money collected
CODHES	Consultoría para los Derechos Humanos y el Desplazamiento (Consultancy for Human Rights and Displacement)
CORMACARENA	Corporación para el Desarrollo Sostenible del Área de Manejo Especial de la Macarena (Regional Body for the Sustainable Development of the Special Management Area of Macarena)
CORPAMAG	Corporación Autónoma Regional del Magdalena (Autonomous Regional Body of Magdalena)
CORPOBOYACÁ	Corporación Autónoma Regional de Boyacá (Autonomous Regional Body of Boyacá)
CORPOCALDAS	Corporación Autónoma Regional de Caldas (Autonomous Regional Body of Caldas)
CR	Collection rate
CRA	Comisión de Regulación de Agua Potable y Saneamiento Básico (Regulatory Commission for Water and Sanitation)

CPE	Comité Permanente de Estratificación (Committee for Stratification)
DIH	Derecho Internacional Humanitario (International Humanitarian Law)
DANE	Departamento Administrativo Nacional de Estadística (National Statistics Department)
DNP	Departamento Nacional de Planeación (National Planning Department)
DEA	Data envelope analysis
Etc.	Et cetera
EICE	Empresa Industrial y Comercial del Estado (State-owned corporation)
EAAV	Empresa de Acueducto y Alcantarillado de Villavicencio
E.g.	For example
ESP	Empresa de Servicios Públicos–Sociedad Anónima (Enterprise for Public Utility Services–Stock corporation)
FCC	Fomento de Construcciones y Contratas
FENALCO	Federación Nacional de Comerciantes (National Traders' Association)
GDP	Gross domestic product
GTZ	Deutsche Gesellschaft für Technische Zusammenarbeit (German Agency for Technical Co-operation)
HRSE	Heteroscedasticity-robust standard errors
IC	Investment costs
IDEAM	Instituto de Hidrología, Meteorología y Estudios Ambientales (Institute of Hydrology, Meteorology and Environmental Studies)
I.e.	That is
INFIMANIZALES	Instituto de Financiamiento, Promoción y Desarrollo de Manizales (Institute for Financing, Promotion and Development of Manizales)
INSFOPAL	Instituto Nacional de Fomento Municipal (National Institute for District Promotion)
JAC	Junta de Acción Comunal (Committee for Community Action)
KfW	Kreditanstalt für Wiederaufbau (German Bank for International Co-operation)
MDG	Millennium Development Goal
MAVDT	Ministerio de Ambiente, Vivienda y Desarrollo Territorial (Ministry of Environment, Housing and Development)
No.	Number

n.a.	Not available
OC	Operation costs
OLS	Ordinary least squares
ODA	Official Development Assistance
OECD	Organisation for Economic Co-operation and Development
PPI	Private participation in infrastructure
PPIAF	Public Private Infrastructure Advisory Facility
PPP	Public–private partnership
PRS Group	Political Risk Services Group
PSP	Private sector participation
QR	Quasi-rents
RAS	Reglamento Técnico para el sector de Agua Potable y Saneamiento Básico (Technical Regulation for the Water and Sanitation Sector)
RC	Reference costs
RR	Robust regression
SC	Sunk costs
Std. Dev.	Standard deviation
SSPD	Superintendencia de Servicios Públicos Domiciliarios (Superintendency of Public Utility Services)
T	Tariff covering full costs of service
UFW	Unaccounted-for water
UN-HABITAT	United Nations Human Settlements Programme
UNICEF	The United Nations Children's Fund
UNRISD	United Nations Research Institute for Social Development
US	United States
VC	Variable costs
WB	Quantity of drinking water billed to customers
WDI	World Development Indicators (annual database published by the World Bank)
WP	Quantity of drinking water produced
WHO	World Health Organization
WS	Water and sanitation

For the abbreviations and definitions of the variables used in the regression analyses, cf. Tables A4.1 and A5.4.

Acknowledgments

Many people contributed to the making of this book, and I thank all of them. Special thanks go to all my interview partners for their patience and their kind willingness to contribute their time to this study. Thank you also to my employer, the German Development Institute (*Deutsches Institut für Entwicklungspolitik*) in Bonn (Germany), that fully backed this work. Many thanks to *Comisión de Regulación de Agua Potable y Saneamiento Básico*, *Superintendencia de Servicios Públicos Domiciliarios* (both Bogotá, Colombia), GTZ (German Agency for Technical Co-operation) in Bogotá, and the Inter-American Development Bank in Washington, DC, for providing data and logistical support.

I am particularly grateful to the following individuals: Tilman Altenburg (for supporting and always encouraging me to get ahead with the work); Jörg Faust and Stefan Leiderer (for sharing their ideas with me and inspiring me to use econometrics); Prof. Hans-Rimbert Hemmer (for his valuable comments on an earlier version of the study); Rubén Avendaño (for motivating me to choose Colombia as a case study); Michael Rösch (for his hospitality and support in Bogotá); Carmen Lopera, Yves Margon, and Laura Höcherl (for helping me to organise the data); and Astrid Dorn and Ina Klemke (for their excellent help with the manuscript). Despite this great support, all the remaining errors and omissions in the text are mine.

Matthias Krause
Bonn, November 6, 2008

1 Introduction

According to recent estimates, by the year 2004 more than one billion people were not using safe drinking water services, and more than 2.5 billion were not using appropriate sanitation services in developing countries (World Health Organization [WHO] and The United Nations Children´s Fund [UNICEF] 2006). Every day, around 6,000 people, mostly children under five, die from diarrhoeal diseases caused by inappropriate water and sanitation (WS) services (United Nations Human Settlements Programme [UN-HABITAT] 2003, 59). Increasing the coverage with appropriate WS services can, therefore, be considered a priority for development that is also acknowledged in the WS target set in the Millennium Development Goals (MDGs).[1] Meeting this WS target will require substantial efforts in terms of mobilisation of financing and in terms of reforming WS sectors.

Increasing the coverage and improving the quality of services to reduce the burden of disease is not the only pressing issue developing countries are confronted with in the area of WS. Rapid urbanisation and increasing pollution due to lacking wastewater treatment go hand-in-hand with an escalating stress on the resource water in several regions of the developing world, boosting social and political conflict. The need to adapt to climate change poses additional challenges for governments in the area of water management. In many cases, poorly managed WS service providers and lack of finance for investing in WS infrastructure compound the situation. This book focuses on developing countries because the magnitude and the urgency of these problems are especially great in this group of countries. Governments, civil society, and the private sector need to find ways to increase the coverage and quality of WS services and, at the same time, to manage the natural and financial resources in an efficient and sustainable manner. Successful WS sector reform along these lines is critical for advancing human development in a great part of this world.

During the 1990s, the mainstream approach in development cooperation with respect to WS sector reform was private sector participation (PSP)[2] in order to tackle the double challenge of (i) increasing investments in developing countries and (ii) reforming an industry characterised mainly by financially strained and inefficient public WS service providers (cf. e.g.

Finger and Allouche 2002). By the beginning of the new millennium, this view has changed due to several reasons: Popular protests and political opposition to PSP are an issue in several developing countries;[3] the private sector has shown a relatively low engagement to invest in WS services in developing countries,[4] and the research literature has not found a conclusive empirical evidence concerning the actual benefits of PSP.[5] This change of attitude toward PSP in the WS sector becomes evident in the following citation taken from a report of the Operations Evaluation Department of the World Bank (2003a, 21):

> [PSP] is not a panacea to deep-seated problems and cannot be expected to substitute for decisions that only governments have the power and obligation to make. PSP is better likened to a sharp tool. A capable government can use it to great advantage to improve the water supply and sanitation situation but an inept government can make matters worse through an injudicious use of PSP without providing clear quality and price regulation and lending strong and sustained support to PSP.

At present, development agencies do not follow a clear policy paradigm regarding WS sector reform and there is a debate in the policy-oriented literature on second-generation approaches to infrastructure reform in developing countries.[6] This study intends to contribute to this debate by shifting the attention towards the importance of governance.

In this study, the term *governance*[7] describes the elements that shape policy-making and public decision taking. Institutions[8] are crucial elements of governance because they shape the behaviour of the actors responsible for policy-making and public decision taking. The approach followed here distinguishes between the general political governance of a country and the specific governance of the WS sector (WS governance). The key elements of political governance are the institutions that shape the relation between citizens and government actors (electoral systems, political rights) and the rules that determine the organisation of government (separation of powers, checks and balances). Crucial elements of WS governance are the articulation of the actors responsible for policy-making, regulation, and service delivery and the institutional boundaries between them as well as the institutions for user participation.

This investigation sets the focus on analysing the influence of political governance and of WS governance on the performance of WS services in developing countries. It does so because the focus on private versus public providers, which has dominated the political and the academic debate, seems too narrow in order to explain success or failure in the provision of WS services. Due to the equity[9] implications of WS services, their widespread use and the market failures associated with these services, public actors driven by political incentives play a more important role in the WS sector than in many other sectors of the economy (Spiller and Savedoff

1999), irrespective of whether the private sector is involved in service delivery or not. Therefore, the characteristics of the political institutions that shape the actions of public officials and the characteristics of WS sector institutions that shape the actions of regulators, providers, and users seem especially important for understanding the performance of WS services.

The neglect of these governance factors in many empirical studies could be one reason for the inconclusive evidence in academic literature regarding the effects of PSP on coverage expansion and on efficiency improvements of providers.[10] In several countries, inappropriate political or WS governance could dominate or go against the expected benefits of PSP. On the other hand, it can be argued that the relatively good performance of some purely public WS service providers—e.g. in Chile before privatisation—is related to the good quality of the political and the WS sector institutions.[11] Therefore, here it is supposed that the quality of the political and WS governance of a certain country is a crucial factor that strongly influences the performance of WS services. This main supposition contrasts from the bulk of research work that has concentrated on the consequences of the delivery model (PSP versus purely public) for the provision of WS services.[12]

The effect of governance on the provision of WS services has not been systematically investigated in quantitative empirical research. However, there is some evidence from the quantitative research literature supporting the hypothesis that governance affects the provision of other infrastructure services. With regard to the effect of political institutions, Henisz and Zelner (2001) find that more checks and balances in a political system have a significant positive effect on access to telephone services. With regard to sectoral institutions, Cubbin and Stern (2006) report a statistically significant effect of higher quality regulatory governance on electricity generation capacity.[13] This study adds to this body of empirical research by presenting evidence for the influence of governance on the access to WS services and on the efficiency of WS service provision.

In line with the main supposition previously stated, the purpose of this study is to answer the following main research question:

> How does the quality of political governance and of WS governance affect access to and efficiency of WS services in developing countries?

This main research question is mirrored by a complementary enquiry that asks the conventional question addressed in the research literature: How does PSP affect access to and efficiency of WS services? Enlarging the focus of the investigation to include this complementary question serves to learn about the relation between governance and PSP, as well as about the relative importance of these two dimensions for the performance of WS services. Evidence with respect to this aspect seems especially relevant for practical policymaking. It could, for instance, give an orientation to policy makers whether priority should be given to improve governance or to introduce PSP.

The determinants of widespread access to WS services are an obvious subject of research, because the lack of access is a pressing problem in developing countries. In addition, it is asked for the determinants of the efficiency[14] of WS service provision because neglecting this aspect would mean to risk wasting scarce natural and financial resources. This way, the environmental and economic sustainability of the provision of WS services and thus, ultimately, the widespread access to these services would be compromised.

The main and the complementary research questions are analysed conceptually and empirically. The **conceptual part** of the study (Chapters 2 and 3) develops a heuristic framework that offers an explanation for the influence of political governance and WS sector governance on two desirable attributes of the WS service industry: widespread access to services and high efficiency. The heuristic framework combines a normative economic perspective and a political–economic perspective.

The normative analysis in Chapter 2 develops the categories necessary for judging the state of affairs in the WS sector and deriving desirable WS policies, given the particular ethical and economic characteristics of WS services. It looks at typical problems of the WS sector from three different normative perspectives: equity, allocative efficiency, and internal efficiency. Based on this analysis, general policy implications are deduced. The analytical framework used is standard microeconomic theory.

The political–economic analysis in Chapter 3 explains how political governance and WS sector governance shape WS policies, regulation, and service delivery and, thus, access to and efficiency of services. Regarding the effects of political governance, it focuses on the aspects of democratic participation and checks and balances. The issue of different degrees of involvement of the private sector in service delivery (PSP versus purely public delivery models) is conceived as one important aspect of the institutional setting of the WS sector. Other important aspects of WS governance analysed are the institutional design of regulation, user participation, and the articulation of the actors responsible for policy making, regulation, and service delivery. The analytical framework used in this chapter builds on the work of the schools of new institutional economics, public choice and political economics.[15] It takes a perspective that looks in an integrated manner at the economic and political system of a society, acknowledging that the behaviour of actors is shaped by both economic and political incentives.

The **empirical part** of this study (Chapters 4 and 5) analyses the main and the complementary research questions previous mentioned, using both quantitative and qualitative empirical approaches.[16] Combining quantitative and qualitative approaches has the advantages (i) of getting a richer picture of the research subject, since the approaches elaborate on different aspects and (ii) of using one empirical approach to compensate for the supposed weaknesses or the blind spot of the other. For instance, qualitative approaches, as compared to quantitative approaches, have the disadvantage that the strength of the effect of one factor on another cannot be quantified and that the observed results, typically, cannot be generalised. However, qualitative approaches have the advantage that it is possible to dig deeper into causality mechanisms identified by quantitative research and to gain valuable information about the empirical plausibility of supposed causal relations. Or, to put it differently, qualitative case studies can contribute to the empirical microfoundation of causality relations derived from theory and from the statistical analysis of aggregated (macro) data.

Chapter 4 analyses the influence of political governance (democratic participation, checks and balances) on the coverage with WS services, using a multivariate regression model and cross-sectional data from 69 developing countries. The quality of political governance is measured by governance indicators conventionally used in econometric work. The chapter concentrates on the influence of political governance, because there is no comprehensive and reliable data available on WS governance (e.g. on the institutional characteristics of regulation, service delivery, or user participation). The data on coverage with WS services was taken from the database provided by the Joint Monitoring Programme of WHO and UNICEF. The model controls for conventional economic and demographic variables, as well as for the availability of freshwater resources. Based on the reasoning in Chapter 3, the main supposition analysed is that a higher level of democracy will have a positive influence on the coverage with WS services.

Chapter 5 investigates the case of Colombia. Colombia has quite a number of unique characteristics that justify performing a single in-depth case study to analyse the main and the complementary research questions of this study. The macro approach followed in Chapter 4 is suitable for analysing the influence of national political governance. Still, in many countries the responsibility for WS service provision lies within the realm of sub-national governments. Therefore, there is a need for investigating the role of local governance for WS service provision. Colombia is very well suited for this undertaking. First, thanks to political decentralisation, the country is marked by variation in local governance structures. Second, there is a diversity of delivery models in Colombia, including PSP and purely public delivery models. This allows one not only to analyse the relation between local governance and WS service performance on the sub-national level, but also to explore the effect of PSP on service performance and to assess the interaction of PSP and governance.

The chapter has two purposes. First, it applies the heuristic framework developed in the conceptual part of the study in order to describe and to assess the main elements that influence the provision of WS services in Colombia: the institutions and actors that are key for the policy making process, the main institutions and actors of the WS sector, and the principal WS policies.

Second, Chapter 5 analyses the influence of local governance and of PSP on the performance of WS service providers. The analysis is conducted in two steps. First, the effect of PSP on internal efficiency improvements and on coverage expansion is investigated by means of a multivariate regression analysis, using cross-sectional data from 30 Colombian providers. The data on ownership, internal efficiency and coverage has been provided by the two regulatory authorities *Comisión de Regulación de Agua Potable y Saneamiento Básico* (CRA) and *Superintendencia de Servicios Públicos* (SSPD). The main supposition analysed is that providers with PSP show a higher internal efficiency than their public counterparts. Second, the effect of local governance on provider performance is examined. This is done by a qualitative approach that compares the purposefully selected providers of the four provincial capitals of Manizales (public), Santa Marta (private), Tunja (private), and Villavicencio (public). The question analysed is whether local governance can dominate the expected effect of PSP on service performance and whether unexpected performance—such as a public provider with outstanding internal efficiency indicators (Manizales) or a private provider with poor internal efficiency indicators (Santa Marta)— can be explained by the quality of local governance. The main portion of information for the qualitative analysis has been collected by the author in interviews conducted in the four cities mentioned, and in Bogotá in June and July 2005.

Finally, Chapter 6 summarises the findings of the investigation and draws some overall conclusions. The key result of this study is the empirical evidence found on the influence of political governance on WS service performance. First, the cross-country regressions performed in Chapter 4 yield significant and robust statistical evidence that higher levels of democracy have a positive effect on coverage with WS services. This is an innovative result that, to the knowledge of the author, has not been reported in the econometric research literature so far. It supports the view that democratic governments, thanks to institutions such as free and fair elections, fundamental political rights, and alternative information, have greater incentives than autocratic governments to respond to the interests of the broad majority and, thus, to care more for the coverage of their citizens with WS services. Second, the qualitative comparison of the four Colombian cities finds some evidence that a higher quality of local governance (strong civil society and business organisations, better control of corruption, and lower levels of non-state armed groups' activities) has a positive effect on the internal efficiency of providers and on the coverage with WS services. This influence of the quality of local governance seems to be able to partially dominate the positive effect of PSP on the internal efficiency of Colombian providers, for which statistical evidence was found in the regression analyses performed in Chapter 5.

2 Normative and Problem-Oriented Framework for Assessing Water and Sanitation Policies

This chapter develops the basic principles for normatively assessing WS policies (the term *WS policies*, here, includes the design of WS sector institutions, e.g. concerning regulation). This is done by combining a descriptive perspective—which focuses on key supply, demand, and institutional characteristics of the WS sector and their consequences for the provision of WS services—and a normative perspective—which assesses the desirability of WS policies. A descriptive analysis is a necessary first step for a well-grounded normative analysis of WS policies, because assessing the desirability of WS policies implies (i) information about their effect on the given state of affairs (descriptive perspective), and (ii) value judgements about what shall be considered a problem and what a good solution (normative perspective).[1]

The argumentation presented in the following is based on a review of the relevant theoretical and empirical literature. The analytical framework used could be termed *standard microeconomic theory*, which is meant to comprise, basically, the school of neoclassical economics, as well as certain aspects of new institutional economics.[2] This chapter does not include a systematic and comprehensive analysis of the effect of governance on the provision of WS services. The concept of governance is introduced and discussed in Chapter 3.

This chapter is organised as follows. First, the main economic characteristics of the supply of and the demand for WS services are very briefly described (section 2.1). Afterwards, the key problems of the WS sector are discussed, and broad policy implications are deduced, looking from different normative perspectives that are relevant for the debate in development studies: Section 2.2 takes an equity perspective, section 2.3 takes an allocative efficiency perspective, and section 2.4 takes an internal efficiency perspective. Finally, section 2.5 draws some conclusions.

2.1. BASIC ECONOMIC SUPPLY AND DEMAND CHARACTERISTICS OF WS SERVICES

2.2.1. Supply

With respect to the technology used for supplying the final user with WS services, we can distinguish network solutions from on-site solutions. The focus of this study is set on urban areas for which networks are typically the most efficient,[3] as well as most adequate, solution from a public health and environmental perspective (some more details regarding adequacy of WS services are discussed in section 2.2).[4] This is why comments made in this section are limited to network supply technologies.

Supplying WS services via network technologies involves the following activities or production stages (Noll 2002, 44–45):

i. The physical process consists of capturing (and storing) surface water or groundwater, transporting it to the area of consumption, treating it in order to raise quality, transporting the water to the final user through a pipe system, collecting wastewater through a sewer system, and treating the wastewater before discharging it to the environment.[5] Neglecting the latter two steps can have serious consequences for the public health situation and the environment, depending on population density and local natural conditions (see section 2.3.4). Still, an important portion of the sewage in developing countries is not collected, and that portion of sewage that is collected is rarely treated (Winpenny 2003, 5).

ii. Besides the physical process, the commercial process has to be managed. This includes, above all, the purchase of services and materials and the sales of WS services including metering, billing, and collection. Figure 2.1 illustrates the production stages of network supply.

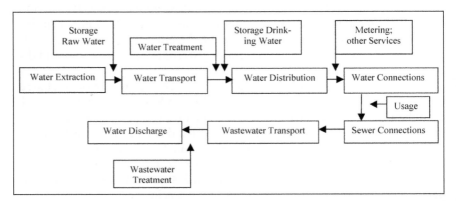

Figure 2.1 Network supply of WS services: Production stages. Source: Based on Sauer (2003, 16), adapted and complemented by the author.

Although the costs of WS service supply can show substantial variation due to differences in climate, location of freshwater sources, quality of
fresh water, topography, and spatial population patterns, the private costs[6]
of supply show some typical patterns that are due to the characteristics of
the supply technology previously described (Noll 2002, 43–45). Relatively
huge investments in capital assets (dams, canals, pipes, sewers) have to be
made, which imply relatively high fixed capital costs.[7] At the same time,
variable, costs are relatively low. One main component of the variable costs
is the energy required for pumping.[8] Systems that do not require pumping
(i.e., that are gravity fed) can show very low variable costs of supply. Therefore, the ratio of fixed-to-variable costs in the WS sector is high. According
to Komives et al. (2005, 30–35), fixed capital costs account up to 65%
(water) and up to 80% (sewerage) of total costs.[9] One implication of this
cost structure (and of the underlying supply technology) is that WS systems
often show decreasing average costs throughout a large range of production,
thanks to economies of scale (see subsection 2.3.3). Moreover, assets have
very long typical lives (water: 20–40 years; sewerage: 40–60 years), which
makes it possible to postpone maintenance and replacement investment
expenses—and consequently to "underfund" the WS provider—for quite a
long time. The negative effect of such a practice will become apparent only
gradually, as service levels decline (see subsections 2.4.1 and 2.4.2).

These characteristics of network supply of WS services have a series of
implications—for the optimal tariff structures, the desirability and feasibility of competition, the viability of private financing, and the amount of
financing needed in order to expand services—which are discussed to some
detail in sections 2.2 to 2.5.

2.1.2. Demand

The individual demand for WS services resembles the individual demand
for food which is price inelastic for a relatively small subsistence amount
and then becomes price elastic. Price elasticity of individual water demand
depends on the type of use and the implied necessary quality (contrary to
water for e.g. gardening, drinking water[10] has to be free of disease-inducing
micro-organisms and toxic elements). This is illustrated in the exemplary
individual demand curve in Figure 2.2, which shows a price inelastic area for
drinking use and a price elastic area for uses like laundry and gardening.

There is more empirical evidence on the demand for water services than
on the demand for sanitation services. Komives et al. (2005, 17–18) sum-
marise the findings regarding price and income elasticity of the demand for
piped water services. Estimated mean elasticities show the common sign for
superior goods (own price elasticity is negative, whereas income elasticity is
positive). Still, absolute values are well below 1, which means that demand
changes less than proportionally to price and income increases. Note that
the demand of industrial customers is more sensitive to price changes than
the demand of their residential counterparts.

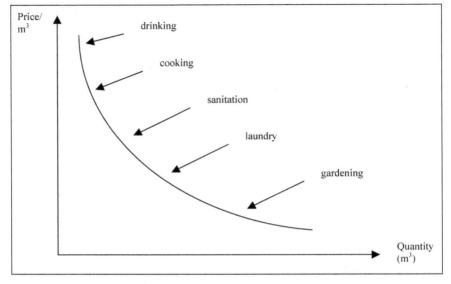

Figure 2.2   Exemplary individual water demand curve. Source: Based on Hansson (2004, 22), adapted by the author.

The tariff for water services (and its consequences for demand) is a matter of heated discussions in the political arena. Judgements on the optimal or just tariff depend on the normative position taken and on the problems focused on. These issues are discussed in more detail in the following sections, 2.2 to 2.5. In recent years, numerous empirical studies have been published that attempt to measure the individual willingness to pay[11] of households for good quality water services.[12] One important factor besides income that will, in general, affect the household's willingness to pay for piped water services is the availability of alternative sources of water supply, which, in its turn, depends on the natural conditions (quantity and quality of freshwater available). For instance, research from Sub-Saharan Africa indicates that households are willing to pay between 0.30 and 0.40 US Dollars per m³ for a service with an in-house connection (Komives et al. 2005, 39).

Average water consumption per household varies widely across countries, urban versus rural areas, income groups, type of connection (in-house, public taps, water vendors, etc.), water price, and water quality (Komives et al. 2005, appendix C.2); e.g. monthly average consumption of Latin American households connected to a pipe system in a sample of 16 cases ranges from 8.0 m³ (Colombia) to 40.8 m³ (Venezuela).[13] Households that rely on public taps consume considerably less than households with in-house or yard connections. For instance, in Kathmandu (Nepal), monthly average consumption in the former case amounts to 1.6 m³, whereas in the latter case it is 22.1 m³.[14]

The individual willingness to pay for sanitation is typically considered to be lower than for water, similar to the awareness among users for the benefits associated with sanitation services (McIntosh 2003, 72). This fits well with the fact that coverage rates are lower for sanitation than for water services (see subsection 2.2.2). Whittington et al. (1992) provide a careful study of the willingness to pay for improved[15] sanitation services in Ghana and find that willingness to pay is generally high enough to cover the costs of ventilated pit latrines, but not to cover the costs of sewer connections. One peculiarity of the demand for sanitation services is that individual demand for safe services is associated with positive external benefits for the neighbourhood, and that the full benefits of sanitation services are only likely to materialise if users have an adequate level of hygiene education. This aspect is touched upon in subsection 2.3.4.

After this brief descriptive overview of basic economic supply and demand characteristics of WS services, the following sections turn to assessing the key problems of the WS sector and to deducing broad policy implications looking from different normative positions.

2.2. KEY PROBLEMS FROM AN EQUITY PERSPECTIVE

2.2.1. Equity and its Relation to WS Services

Equity concerns is what has dominated the international and national political debates on WS policies and the coverage in newspapers and other mass media.[16] The concept of equity has different interpretations across nations, societies, and cultures.[17] A general definition that probably meets with rather broad approval is given by the World Bank (2005, 18–19). According to this definition—which draws on the theoretical work on justice of Rawls (1971), Dworkin (1981a; 1981b), Sen (1985), and Roemer (1998)—equity can be conceived in terms of two basic principles:

- Equal opportunity: "Predetermined circumstances—gender, race, place of birth, family origins—and the social group a person is born into should not help determine whether people succeed economically, socially, and politically" (World Bank 2005, 19).
- Avoidance of absolute deprivation: The livelihoods of the members of a society should be protected from falling below some absolute threshold of well-being[18] regardless whether the deprivation is due to bad luck or a person's own failings.

WS services are clearly relevant for achieving equity. Lacking access to adequate[19] WS services for personal and domestic use constitutes an absolute deprivation with respect to essential human needs (drinking, cooking, personal hygiene). At the same time, lacking access to these services is one important factor causing deprivations in other dimensions of well-being. It increases the risk of falling ill with the further consequences of decreasing productivity and economic possibilities of the household.[20] Productivity and economic possibilities do not only decrease due to the consequences of ill health, but also due to time and money spent in getting safe water, e.g. from a dug well two miles away or from an expensive source like water vendors. Therefore, besides constituting an absolute deprivation, lacking access to adequate WS services reduces the opportunities of a person with respect to several economic, social, and political dimensions of well-being.

The relevance of equity with respect to WS services is not confined to the debate in academia. Its political relevance is, e.g. manifest in international targets for development cooperation, in the international human rights charter and in many national legal frameworks. (i) Goal 7 (target 10) of the Millennium Development Goals (MDGs)–"[h]alve by 2015 the proportion of people without sustainable access to safe drinking water and basic sanitation" (Development Committee, International Monetary Fund, and World Bank 2004, xxii)—is an expression of the equity concerns of the international community with practical consequences for Official Development Assistance (ODA) flows from donor countries to developing countries. (ii) The General Comment No.15 of the International Covenant on Economic, Cultural and Social Rights states that "'[t]he human right to water entitles everyone to sufficient, affordable, physically accessible, safe and acceptable water for personal and domestic use'" (United Nations Economic and Social Council 2002; as cited by Budds and McGranahan 2003, 94). (iii) Finally, many national constitutions and sectoral laws contain some reference to the obligation of the state to take actions that assure an equitable access of its citizens to basic WS services (see Chapter 5 for the Colombian case).

2.2.2. Adequate WS Services and Coverage Situation in Developing Countries

Definition of Adequate WS Services

The exact definition of what shall be the characteristics of adequate and essential WS services anybody shall be able to use, irrespective of gender, race, wealth, social status, etc., differs across countries and societies, depending on the respective social values, economic means, and political institutions. The exemplification of adequate essential WS services that follows is based on the recommendations contained in the policy-oriented literature.[21] Any useful definition is likely to comprise the following dimensions:

    i. Safety—which means that the water has to be drinkable without health risks, and the sanitation service has to minimise the human contact with excreta.

    ii. Sufficiency—which means that 20 to 30 litres of water per person and day should be available.

iii. Regularity—which means that the availability of WS services should be close to 24 hours per day during the whole year.
iv. Physical accessibility and convenience of the service—which means that WS services should be available at the dwelling or close by (not requiring much time and effort) and, in the case of sanitation, in addition, should respect privacy and be suitable for the needs of women and children.
v. Affordability—which is typically conceived as a proportion of household income (common thresholds are 3% to 5%); it is argued that household expenditures for WS services shall not exceed this threshold because, otherwise, households could choose not to use adequate services or stop using them.[22]

In order to measure the share of population in a country that uses adequate and essential WS services as defined, WHO and UNICEF (2000, Annex A) have developed the concept of *improved WS services*. It is used, among other things, to monitor progress towards the MDGs. The definition of improved WS services—which is an attempt to operationalise the various dimensions listed for measurement—is basically based on two criteria:[23]

- the technology that is used by households, and
- an additional criterion: (i) water: "availability of at least 20 litres per person per day from a source within one kilometre of the user's dwelling;"[24] and (ii) sanitation: private or shared (not public) system that "hygienically separates human excreta from human contact" (WHO and UNICEF 2000, Annex A).

Table 2.1 shows the classification of common WS technologies by improved and unimproved (subsection 4.3.1 addresses to greater detail the methodology used by WHO and UNICEF to produce the worldwide coverage statistics).

Coverage Situation and Access Barriers in Developing Countries

According to estimates of the worldwide coverage situation by WHO and UNICEF (2006), in developing countries in 2004 about 1 billion people were not using improved water services and about 2.5 billion were not using improved sanitation services (see also Table A2.1 in the appendix). Coverage with improved services by the year 2004 does not only differ markedly between the group of developed countries (water: 99%; sanitation: 99%) and the group of developing countries (water: 80%; sanitation: 50%). Coverage rates also vary considerably within the group of developing countries. In Sub-Saharan Africa, only 56% of people enjoy improved water services and merely 37% improved sanitation services. By contrast, in Western Asia the respective figures amount to 91% (water) and 84% (sanitation). In addition, in developing countries, service levels are much lower in rural[25] areas (water: 70%; sanitation: 33%) than in urban areas (water: 92%; sanitation: 73%). Moreover, according to WHO and UNICEF

Table 2.1   Improved and Unimproved WS Technologies According to World Health Organization and United Nations Children's Fund.

	Improved	*Unimproved*[a]
Water	• Household connection (in-house or yard)	• Unprotected well or spring
	• Public standpipe	• Rivers or ponds
	• Borehole	• Vendor-provided water
	• Protected dug well or spring	• Bottled water
	• Rainwater collection	• Tanker truck water
Sanitation	• Connection to public sewer	• Public latrine
	• Connection to septic tank	• Open pit latrine
	• Pour-flush latrine	• Bucket latrine
	• Ventilated improved pit latrine	
	• Simple pit latrine	

Source: WHO and UNICEF (2000, Annex A).
[a]Water: Due to concerns about the quality or quantity of water supplied. Sanitation: Due to concerns about the privacy of the service or the hygienic separation of human excreta from human contact.

(2004, 20), the income-poor are more affected by inadequate services than the income-rich. Estimates indicate that the richest quintile of the income distribution is twice as likely (four times more likely) to use improved water services (sanitation services) than the poorest quintile. Finally, the coverage situation also depends on the local natural conditions, for instance, the availability of sufficient freshwater resources.

The high investment costs associated with WS network services work like an access barrier for the income-poor. In urban areas, the formal way to gain access to network services is to be owner or tenant of a dwelling or an official plot (authorised by the urban planning authority) for which, at its time of development, a water and sewer connection is constructed. In this case, the investment costs associated with the WS services (as well as with other public services, like electricity, etc.) are paid for by the company that develops the plot, and are ultimately borne by the owner when purchasing the plot or dwelling or by the tenant when paying the rent. The urban poor in developing countries typically lack the capital (the income) to purchase a developed plot (to rent an official dwelling), and thus settle on unofficial plots without improved WS services. Inappropriate urban planning and real estate registration procedures, as well as a lack of transparency in property markets often, compound the situation and further hamper access of the urban poor to adequate housing and improved WS services. Thus, the lack of access to improved WS services is linked to the problem of lacking access to formal property markets and adequate housing. Due to these access barriers, many households in developing countries use unimproved WS services; e.g. in Angola, 25.2% of the urban population relies on tanker trucks for water supply (WHO and UNICEF 2000, 78).

Consequences of Inadequate WS Services

If people do not have access to adequate WS services, one possible consequence is that they rely on unsafe services that considerably increase their risk to fall ill. Those most vulnerable to health hazards, above all children, are most likely to be affected by one of the several water-related diseases (diarrhoea, intestinal helminths, schistosomiasis, trypanosomiasis, among others) which are associated with considerable morbidity and mortality rates (Gleick 2002, 3). According to recent estimates, improved water (sanitation) services reduce diarrhoea morbidity on average by 25% (32%; WHO and UNICEF 2005, 13).

Another possible consequence is that people have to incur relatively high costs in terms of money (or time) for getting safe water from, e.g. water vendors (or public standpipes far away) or for investments in water reservoirs and water pumps at their home. Prices per litre charged by water vendors can be 5 times (Abidjan, Côte d'Ivoire) to 100 times (Nouakchott, Mauritania) higher than prices charged by public utilities[26] (Kessides 2004, 222). Therefore, those (mainly poor) households that have to rely on sources like tanker trucks and water vendors often spend a considerably higher share of income on WS services than those with access to adequate services.

Figure 2.3 shows estimates for residential expenditures on water services as income share by income quintile for Latin America, Eastern Europe, and South Asia. In Latin America and South Asia, the income share spent by the poorest quintile is more or less twice the income share spent by the richest quintile. The income share spent by the poorest quintile does not exceed

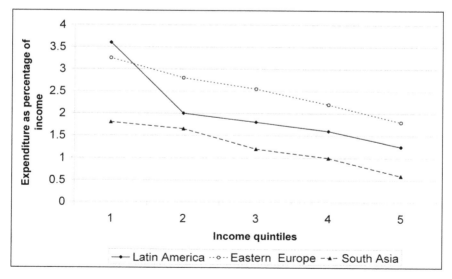

Figure 2.3 Residential water expenditure patterns by region. Source: Based on Komives et al. (2005, 42), adapted by the author.

the common threshold used to judge affordability (3% to 5% of income– as explained previously). However, the sample used for these calculations by Komives et al. (2005, appendix C.4) is biased towards expenditures for piped water services. If expenditures for non-piped services (water vendors and tanker trucks) were considered in a representative manner, it is expected that the income share spent by the poorest quintile would increase, whereas the income share spent by the richest quintile would not change significantly, as the latter typically rely on piped services.

Policy Implications

The challenge of these equity-related key problems for WS policy is to strive for a situation where anybody is able to use adequate essential WS services, irrespective of the economic situation, gender, race, etc. The WS target set in the MDGs points at that direction by aiming at halving the proportion of the population that does not use improved WS services by 2015.[27]

Table A2.1 in the appendix gives an overview of the projected increases in coverage necessary to meet this target in different world regions. It is estimated that in the developing regions, each year, 100.2 million people have to gain access to improved water services and 146.3 million to improved sanitation services to reach the objective (WHO and UNICEF 2006, 40).

The following broad policy issues emerge to this respect:

i. Expanding access to improved services means raising considerable financial means in order to finance the huge investments involved. According to estimates, an extra sum of about 10 billion US dollars[28] has to be invested annually if the MDGs shall be achieved, using the most basic standards of service and technology (Winpenny 2003, 3).

ii. Investments should be focused to benefit those who, at present, lack access to adequate WS services, i.e., should typically be concentrated in poor urban and in rural areas.

iii. Special emphasis should be given to removing access barriers for poor urban and rural households. This can be achieved by providing some sort of infrastructure expansion or connection subsidy in order to lower the burden of investment costs that have to be borne by the new users. Further measures in this context include removing legal and other obstacles related to land tenure, as well as raising awareness among future users for the benefits associated with improved services, especially with respect to sanitation.

iv. Apart from the aforementioned infrastructure expansion or connection subsidies, further subsidies should be targeted to low-income households if their current tariff expenditures for a basic service level, once connected, exceed a threshold that is considered affordable by society.

2.3. KEY PROBLEMS FROM AN ALLOCATIVE EFFICIENCY PERSPECTIVE

2.3.1. Allocative Efficiency, Internal Efficiency and Their Relation to Equity

Although section 2.3 deals with allocative efficiency, it is useful to introduce the concept of the internal efficiency of a single firm together with the concept of the allocative efficiency of the whole economy, because these concepts are related to each other.

The concept of internal efficiency is confined to a single firm, e.g. a WS service provider (Vickers and Yarrow 1988).[29] It serves to judge from the firm's individualistic perspective whether it makes the best use of its resources (production factors), assuming that the firm's objective is to maximise profits. A firm is internally efficient if it produces a given quantity and quality of output at minimum private costs.[30] An important determinant of internal *in*efficiency is managerial slack (the so-called X-*in*efficiency),[31] which, in turn, depends on the incentives managers are facing and on the ownership structure of the firm.[32] An in-depth discussion of the internal efficiency-related problems of WS service providers follows in section 2.4.

The concept of allocative efficiency, by contrast, applies to the whole economy. It is the classical criterion used in welfare economics to judge the desirability of a given state of affairs from the point of view of the society and to derive and justify welfare-enhancing policies (e.g. Atkinson and Stiglitz 1980, 333–65). It is a very encompassing concept, which builds on microeconomic theory. Allocative efficiency is used to make statements on how markets should be organised and which economic policies should be taken in order to maximise social welfare—which is conceived as an aggregate of individual utility[33]—and thus to make the best use of available scarce resources. There are two versions of the definition of allocative efficiency: (i) According to the Pareto criterion, a situation is allocatively efficient if consumers are provided with goods and services at the lowest possible social cost[34] and if the only way to make one person better off is to make another person worse off.[35] (ii) The Kaldor-Hicks criterion relaxes the second part of the Pareto criterion, as it allows for a compensation of the losers of a reallocation of resources by the winners (e.g. Zerbe, Bauman, and Finkle 2006).[36] An allocatively efficient situation presupposes both production efficiency (i.e., the economy produces along its production possibility frontier and it is not possible to expand the production of one good without reducing the production of another good) as well as exchange efficiency (i.e., individuals trade the goods produced consistent with their valuation; Rosen 1992, 42–51; Hemmer 2002, 62–69). Whether an economy reaches an allocatively efficient situation or not, relying on market transactions alone, depends on the allocative efficiency conditions explained below (subsection 2.3.2).

The relation between internal efficiency and allocative efficiency is as follows: Internal efficiency is a subconcept of allocative efficiency. An allocatively efficient situation of the economy implies that all firms are internally efficient and, thus, do not "waste" production factors. By contrast, a situation in which all firms are internally efficient does not automatically mean that the economy is in an allocatively efficient situation (i.e., internal efficiency is a necessary but not a sufficient condition for reaching allocative efficiency). For instance, a WS service provider may be internally efficient but sell services at a monopolistic price, which makes demand drop, and consequently means that less users than possible are supplied with services (for more details see subsections 2.3.2 and 2.3.3). When, in the following, the term *efficiency* is used without any attribute, it is meant to refer to the broad notion of allocative efficiency (which includes the internal efficiency of providers as one relevant aspect). Whenever it is referred to as the subconcept of internal efficiency alone, this is made explicit by using the attribute *internal*.

On the relation between allocative efficiency and equity, the following can be said: A situation that is allocatively efficient is not necessarily equitable according to the definition of equity given in section 2.2 (and vice versa).[37] This is so because allocative efficiency does not consider the *distribution* of utility (wealth, opportunities) within society. The allocative efficiency of an economy improves as long as the utility of anybody can be raised without reducing the utility of anybody else, irrespective to whom the utility accrues and irrespective to what the initial distribution of wealth between individuals was (put another way: assuming that the allocative efficiency conditions explained in the following hold, pure market transactions lead to different allocatively efficient situations, depending on what the initial distribution of wealth within society was); e.g. a situation in which some members of the society have considerably less opportunities than the rest because they do not enjoy adequate WS services can be allocatively efficient, but it is inequitable according to the definition given above.

In this study, both improvements in allocative efficiency and improvements in equity are considered valid arguments for justifying welfare-enhancing WS policies. Depending on the concrete empirical situation, pursuing these two social goals will imply either trade-offs or complementarities (see section 2.5).

2.3.2. Allocative Efficiency Conditions

It can be shown that, under certain restrictive conditions, a pure market economy theoretically achieves allocative efficiency.[38] According to Atkinson and Stiglitz (1980, 343) this statement (referred to usually as the first basic theorem of welfare economics) rests basically on three conditions:

   i. "[H]ouseholds and firms act perfectly competitively, taking prices as parametric,"
  ii. "there is a full set of markets, and"
 iii. "there is perfect information."

The first basic theorem of welfare economics implies that (allocative and internal) efficiency-related problems, which would call for specific policies to solve them, can arise only if one or more of these conditions do not hold in practice. Although the specific economic characteristics of WS systems in practice show substantial variation due to local differences in, e.g. location of freshwater sources, topography and spatial population patterns (Noll 2002, 43), it is clear that WS services are marked by several general features that contradict the previously stated conditions. This means that a pure market economy will not achieve an allocatively efficient situation in the WS sector.[39]

In what follows, the most prominent features of the WS service industry that are not in accordance with the allocative efficiency conditions are discussed.[40] The issues touched in the following two subsections are,

   i. with respect to the *lack of perfect competition*: the natural monopoly characteristics of the supply technology which largely preclude competition (2.3.3) and,
  ii. with respect to the *lack of a full set of markets*: the externalities associated with WS services—which can be conceived as a consequence of lacking property rights regarding natural water resources and, consequently, lacking raw water markets (2.3.4).[41]

The *lack of perfect information* is one underlying reason for the internal efficiency-related problems and is treated in section 2.4.[42]

2.3.3. Natural Monopoly Characteristics[43]

Urban water and sewer network services are usually cited in economic literature as being among the most relevant examples for natural monopolies (Joskow and Rose 1989, 1454; Shirley 2000, 148; Noll 2002, 46). According to the traditional and technology-oriented definition given by Kahn (1971, 2; as cited by Braeutigam 1989, 1292), a natural monopoly means "that the technology of certain industries or the character of the service is such that the customer can be served at least cost or greatest net benefit only by a single firm." In the single product case, a technology characterised by economies of scale (which translate into decreasing average costs) throughout the range of production given by the demand is a sufficient condition for this to hold[44] (see Figure 2.4). According to Noll (2002, 46) WS systems exhibit *engineering* economies of scale in some of their components (e.g.

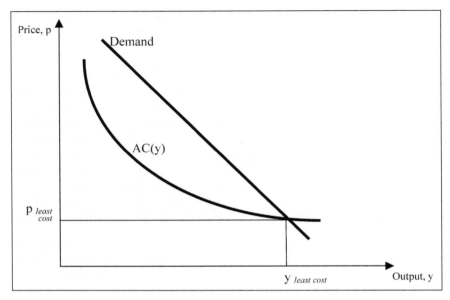

Figure 2.4   Decreasing average costs (AC) throughout the range of production given by demand. Source: Author.

pipes and canals) because investment costs per volumetric unit fall more than proportionally with an increase in capacity. Besides, literature points at economies of scope between water supply, sewerage and stormwater services (Shirley 2000, 153; Kessides 2004, 225). However, engineering economies of scale do not necessarily translate into *organisational* economies of scale (especially if effective competition is lacking) which are the ones relevant for judging the desirability of a monopoly.[45] For the empirical evidence on the existence of organisational economies of scale (in what follows the term *economies of scale* is used to refer to *organisational economies of scale*) in the WS service industry see e.g. Sauer (2005), Torres and Morrison Paul (2006).

If the production technology is marked by economies of scale throughout the relevant range of production,[46] competition is not desirable from an allocative efficiency point of view because the feasible least-cost price is higher if there are two or more firms serving the market than if there is only one. Non-desirability of competition presupposes that the natural monopolist produces at the least-cost optimum and does not charge a monopolistic mark-up (or at least that allocative efficiency losses in the natural monopoly situation are lower than those in the alternative situation with more than one firm serving the market).

If the production technology, in addition to economies of scale, shows substantial sunk costs,[47] competition in the market is not feasible. Sunk costs are highly relevant for the WS service industry, because long-lived assets like buried water and sewer pipe systems or aqueducts for water transportation are specific investments with a limited alternative economic use. Competition in the market is, in this case, restricted because the sunk costs associated with market entry can serve as an effective barrier that protects the incumbent firm from potential competitors.[48] The conventional view in literature is that feasible (and desirable) competition in the WS industry is limited to capture and storage of raw water in systems that rely on multiple sources, as well as to the contracting out of certain activities like construction, maintenance, metering, and billing.

Policy Implications

Effective competition in the core activities of the WS industry is under plausible and empirically relevant conditions hardly feasible and typically not desirable. In order to minimise losses in allocative efficiency, WS policies have to provide incentives for the service provider to take advantage of the economies of scale (and thus to produce at the least-cost point) and at the same time counteract the negative effects of monopolistic power (by compensating for the lack of competition). These characteristics call for an economic regulation of the WS industry with the two main available sets of instruments being

    i. competitive bidding procedures (referred to in research literature as *Demsetz competition*)[49] for allocating franchise contracts that comprise the right to serve a certain area as a monopolist;
   ii. price and quality regulation of an established service provider to avoid the abuse of market power in terms of charging monopolistic prices or delivering bad quality services.

2.3.4. Externalities

Private Costs, External Costs and Social Costs

According to Noll (2002, 44), the total social costs of providing WS services can be decomposed into the following elements:[50]

    Private costs

| + | *intratemporal external costs* | = | *direct social costs* |
| + | *intertemporal external costs* | = | *total social costs* |

The distinction between private costs and external costs is very important within the framework of welfare economics (for an illustration of the intratemporal and intertemporal external costs associated with WS services, see Box 2.1). External costs arise if the assumption of a full set of markets

---

Box 2.1   Externalities Associated with WS Services

Intratemporal Externalities

There are several intratemporal externalities (i.e., externalities that occur immediately or in the present) associated with the production and usage of WS services:

- *External costs of water production* arise if, at prices reflecting the private costs of water supply, the associated water abstraction from its source causes negative effects on competing (downstream) uses by fishery, agriculture, the energy industry, the ecosystem, other urban water supply systems, etc. due to a reduction of the water flow.

- *External costs of water spillage or inadequate drainage:* If prices reflecting the private costs of water supply are very low, it may be perfectly rational from an individual point of view not to repair leaky pipes or taps, but to constantly release water into the environment, even when it is not used. However, if there is no drainage (sewer) system or if natural soil conditions are disadvantageous, such a practice leads to the formation of standing puddles that serve as a breeding ground for disease-carrying insects and disease-causing micro-organisms implying health hazards for the neighbourhood.

- *External costs of pollution:* The usage of water for domestic (or other) purposes typically implies a deterioration of water quality because different polluting substances (including excreta from sanitation) are added to the water. From an economic point of view, the release of wastewater into the environment causes costs on downstream uses that are very similar to those mentioned previously regarding water abstraction. Moreover, it imposes costs in terms of health hazards or costly treatment for domestic downstream users.

- *External costs and benefits of sanitation:* (i) Sewer-based sanitation technologies directly imply water pollution if wastewater is not treated (as mentioned previously). Non-sewer-based sanitation technologies like, e.g. latrines do not directly imply water pollution, but can lead to pollution of ground water via infiltration if soil conditions, installations, or maintenance are inadequate, implying external costs of pollution (as discussed previously). (ii) Inadequate sanitation installations or practices (unsafe separation of excreta from human contact) do not only constitute health hazards for the individual household in question but, in addition, increase the risk of contagion for neighbours. A household faced with the private costs of sanitation may, therefore, choose an inadequate sanitation technology (underconsume sanitation services) because it does not take into account the benefits of a superior (more expensive) sanitation technology that accrue to his neighbours.

Intertemporal External Costs

Intertemporal external costs occur in the future thanks to an activity carried out in the present. They arise if a water source is used (polluted) in an unsustainable manner, i.e., if water consumption (pollution) of all current

(continued)

> *Box 2.1 (continued)*
>
> uses—including the ecosystem—at prices reflecting private costs plus intratemporal external costs (ie., direct social costs) exceeds the refreshment (regeneration) rate of the source. Intertemporal external costs take the form of higher future intratemporal external costs (as mentioned previously) and higher future private costs of water production.
>
> Source: Based on Noll (2002)

does not hold and are the result of an "activity of one person affecting the welfare of another in a way that is outside the market" (Rosen 1992, 66).[51] Private costs, by contrast, are those costs that accrue to households and firms via their transactions at market prices within the given set of markets. From the perspective of the welfare of a society, it is not the private costs of WS services that should determine their price, and thus their allocation, but the sum of private and external costs (total social costs).

The implication for WS policy is that private, as well as external, cost components have to be considered when ascertaining optimal water tariffs, abstraction permits, sanitation standards, etc. Otherwise, allocative efficiency cannot be achieved, because service providers and users will consider only their private costs (and benefits) when deciding on WS service supply and demand, but not the external costs associated with these services.

Optimal Tariff Policy if External Costs Equal Zero

The least complex scenario is one in which intratemporal and intertemporal external costs equal zero. This is not likely to happen very often in practice. It is an approximation to reality for the situations in which the sum of current water uses (wastewater releases) is very low compared to the refreshment (regeneration) rate of a source and in which there are no significant competing uses within a hydrological system. In these cases, the problem is reduced to the question of the optimal tariff for the private costs of WS service supply. This would not be an issue for public policy if markets for WS services were fully competitive. But given their natural monopoly characteristics, it is a highly relevant question for economic regulation. The high ratio of fixed- to variable costs that is typical for network systems has implications for the optimal water and sewerage tariff.[52] The optimal tariff conventionally recommended in literature is a two-part tariff, with the first part being a fixed charge and the second part a variable usage price equalling the private marginal cost of supply—that typically is very low compared to private average costs (Noll 2002, 47–48).[53] A variable usage price implies metering.[54]

In principle, there are no practical problems in quantifying the private costs of water and sewerage services (they are recorded in the books of the utility, provided that the utility keeps its book in accordance with the facts).[55] As a rule of thumb, it can be said that, in low-income countries, the average private costs of urban water services (operating, maintenance, and capital costs) range between 0.40 and 1.00 US dollar/m^3 (Media Analytics Ltd. 2004, 9). Actual average water tariffs frequently lie below this private cost covering level (see also subsection 2.4.2), which means that services are used for purposes for which the private benefits for users are less than the private costs of supply, implying a wasteful use of the resources of the economy.

Policy Implications for Situations with Positive External Costs

Things get more complex in the empirically more relevant situations in which there are positive intratemporal and intertemporal external costs. The challenge for environmental policy and regulation is to provide the necessary incentives and instruments so that all actors involved internalise these costs when choosing their water usage, and thus put the resource to its socially most valuable uses. These issues are extensively treated in the specialised literature on environmental and natural resource economics.[56] As the environmental problems associated with WS services are not in the focus of this study, here, just some few remarks are made:

- The relevant geographical area for environment-oriented WS policy is not given by a single urban WS system, but by the boundaries of the hydrological system the settlement belongs to, typically a river basin.
- There are four types of instruments available for environment-oriented WS policy: (i) price-related instruments: taxes or fees, subsidies, price regulation, etc.; (ii) quantity-related instruments: maximum limits for water abstraction, minimum flow requirements for water bodies, maximum limits for the discharge of pollutants etc.; (iii) the definition of tradable water rights and the creation of an institutionalised water market that all users of a river basin have access to; and (iv) mandatory technological standards, e.g. for wastewater treatment.
- As compared to the private costs of WS services, there are considerable practical problems[57] in assessing intratemporal and intertemporal external costs due to the information requirements on (i) water flows within the boundaries of the hydrological system, (ii) the natural regeneration capacity of the water bodies, (iii) the quantification of competing uses, (iv) the valuation of costs associated with environmental degradation, and (v) due to lacking markets for future water uses.

Real-world tariff structures in developing (and industrialised) countries differ remarkably from what economic literature recommends (Renzetti 2000; Kessides 2004, 236–40; Komives et al. 2005, 19–27). This is due to the fact that tariff design in practice has to take into account various normative goals (equity, internal efficiency), not only allocative efficiency, and that the governance factors (see Chapter 3) that shape the making of tariff policies in practice introduce rationalities that differ from the normative goals discussed here.

2.4. KEY PROBLEMS FROM AN INTERNAL EFFICIENCY PERSPECTIVE

Internal efficiency has been defined in subsection 2.3.1. Internal efficiency is a necessary, but not a sufficient, condition for reaching allocative efficiency. This means that in situations in which the conditions of the first basic theorem of welfare economics do not hold, achieving internal efficiency in firms does not automatically imply achieving allocative efficiency in the economy. We cannot say that a situation (A) in which firms are internally efficient but welfare losses occur due to monopolistic price setting and external costs, is generally preferable to a situation (B) in which firms are not internally efficient but less welfare losses due to monopolistic price setting and external costs arise.

Still, achieving internal efficiency is a necessary first step for achieving allocative efficiency. In what follows, three aspects that condition the internal efficiency of WS service providers are highlighted:

- Quasi-rents,
- Financial sustainability, and
- Private versus public ownership.

2.4.1. Quasi-Rents

Sunk costs have been treated in subsection 2.3.3 because they can work as a market entry barrier, substantially limiting competition in WS service markets. Here, a further aspect of sunk costs discussed by Noll (2002, 48–50) and Spiller and Savedoff (1999) is touched: quasi-rents. Unlike monopoly rents, quasi-rents do not arise from market power, and they do not harm allocative efficiency. Quasi-rents arise if the ratio of fixed, sunk costs (SC) to variable costs (VC) is high and if the service provider earns a tariff covering the full costs of service (T). Then, the difference between tariff receipts and variable costs are quasi-rents (QR):

$$SC + VC = T; \quad T—VC = QR \rightarrow QR = SC \qquad (E2.1)$$

Quasi-rents do not need to be collected to induce continued supply in the short run, because technical workability can be secured by collecting just an amount equal to the variable costs (see also section 2.4.2). Given the extremely durable nature of capital assets, the "short run" can last more than a decade. However, if quasi-rents are not collected, investors do not recover their capital, with the consequence that the service company will lose access to the private capital market due to the debt default. And, if quasi-rents are not collected, the company does not dispose of any of its own reserves that can be used to pay for future replacements of capital assets (see also Table 2.2 for an illustration of cash flow requirements).

Quasi-rents are prone to be captured by public officials and politicians either by rechannelling the receipts to other uses or by imposing tariff reductions—typically before elections—for their political benefit. The availability of quasi-rents in the WS sector leads to the problem that, for politicians, it is hard to credibly commit to not capturing them.[58] This may have negative implications for the financial sustainability of WS providers, as well as the feasibility and sustainability of private investments (discussed in the following).

2.4.2. Financial Sustainability

In competitive markets, financial sustainability of firms is not an issue for efficiency-oriented public policy. In competitive markets, financial sustainability of firms is a function of a firm's competitiveness: If a firm lacks competitiveness (and thus creditworthiness), it becomes financially unsustainable and has to exit the market. This is no problem for consumers, because demand is satisfied by the competitors remaining in the market or by new firms that enter the market.

However, in the context of WS sector reform in developing countries, the issue of financial sustainability of service providers has received quite some attention. This is explained by the special characteristics of WS services previously discussed, which suggest the adoption of equity- and efficiency-enhancing WS policies by governments. These policies, in practice, often condition financial sustainability of the service provider (e.g. by regulating tariffs, prescribing public ownership, ruling out disconnection from the service, etc.). Financial sustainability, in its turn, can be regarded a necessary (but not sufficient) condition for achieving internal efficiency and has, thus, to be taken into consideration when designing WS policies.

There is no unanimously accepted definition of financial sustainability in the context of WS services.[59] In a very general way, it can be said that the situation of a service provider is financially sustainable if it generates the cash flow necessary to pay for its expenses. However, this definition is not useful for the purpose of this study, as financial sustainability on its own is no goal for public policy. A more useful definition is to say that *desirable* financial sustainability is given if a service provider generates the cash flow necessary to produce a given output (quantity and quality) at a minimum private cost (i.e., we define financial sustainability conditional on internal efficiency). With respect to the necessary cash flow requirements for achieving financial sustainability it seems useful to distinguish three dimensions:

Cash flow requirements in order to:

i. maintain the technical workability of the system: (a) short run (capital assets need *not* to be replaced), and (b) long run (capital assets need to be replaced);
ii. amortise the financing of the initial capital assets: (a) grant, and (b) debt (or other market-based financing);
iii. gain or sustain independence from public financing sources (gain or sustain access to the private capital market): (a) no building up of equity capital, and (b) building up of equity capital.

From Table 2.2, it can be seen that cash flow requirements—and, therefore, the necessary tariff levels—vary depending on these three dimensions. The term *sustainability* always implies a long-term perspective, which is why the relevant aspect of dimension I here is the long run, in which the replacement of capital assets has to be faced. Unlike grant financing, debt financing implies additional cash flow requirements in order to cover debt repayment and payment of interest (dimension II). With respect to dimension III, the WS service company achieves a higher degree of financial autonomy if it accumulates (or preserves) reserves in the long run, i.e., if it is economically profitable. This holds irrespective of whether the initial capital assets have been financed by grants or debt. If the company does not accumulate (or preserve) some reserves in the long run, its financial sustainability—and thus the technical workability of the system—depends completely on whether it is able to integrally finance necessary replacements of capital assets by new grants, new debt, or new equity capital. However, a company that is not economically profitable will hardly be able to get private capital and will thus, de facto, depend on grants.

The conventional position in literature is that in order to achieve financial sustainability, the cash flow should be generated through tariff receipts (alternatively, the cash flow could be generated through government transfers; government transfers are, however, judged less reliable than tariff receipts). This is, in principle, perfectly compatible with the goal of allocative efficiency but might conflict with the equity goal in case of low-income households (the trade-offs between the equity and the efficiency goals are illustrated in Table A2.2).

In practice, average tariffs are, in many cases, too low to meet even the minimum requirement for financial sustainability that is to cover operating costs.[60] According to estimates based on data drawn from water utilities serving 132 major cities worldwide (OECD, 47; South Asia: 24; Latin America and the Caribbean: 23; East Asia and Pacific: 19; Middle East and Northern Africa: 12; Non-OECD Europe and Central Asia: 6), average tariffs appear to be too low to cover basic operating costs in 39% of cases (OECD: 6%; Latin America and the Caribbean: 13%; East Asia and Pacific: 53%; Middle East and Northern Africa: 58%; Non-OECD Europe and Central Asia: 100%; South Asia: 100%; Komives et al. 2005, 21).

Table 2.2　Dimensions of Financial Sustainability: The Cash Flow has to Cover...

I) Technical Workability	II) Financing of Initial Capital Assets			
	a) Grant		b) Debt	
	IIIa) No Building up of Equity Capital	IIIb) Building up of Equity Capital	IIIa) No building up of Equity Capital	IIIb) Building up of Equity Capital
a) Short run	...operating costs	...operating costs	...operating costs	...operating costs
b) Long run	...operating costs	...operating costs ...reserves	...operating costs ...debt repayment ...interest	...operating costs ...debt repayment ...interest ...reserves
	Replacement of capital assets has to be integrally financed by new grants, new debt or new equity capital	Replacement of capital assets can be (partially) financed by accumulated equity capital; equity capital makes access to private capital market easier	Replacement of capital assets has to be integrally financed by new grants, new debt or new equity capital	Replacement of capital assets can be (partially) financed by accumulated equity capital; equity capital makes access to private capital market easier
Tariff level that covers cash flow requirements	Operating costs	Operating costs + Reserves	Operating costs + Debt repayment + Interest	Operating costs + Debt repayment + Interest + Reserves

Source: Author

2.4.3. Private Versus Public Ownership of the Provider

This subsection turns to an issue that has received much attention in theoretical and empirical research in recent years, and that has been associated with a marked controversy between supporters and opponents:[61] the question whether private WS service providers achieve a higher internal efficiency than public ones. In order to work out the main arguments of this debate, here just the two exemplary cases of fully privately-owned and fully state-owned providers are considered. Subsection 3.2.3.3 treats, in more detail, the whole spectrum of public and PSP delivery models that exist in the WS industry, when discussing the institutional design of service delivery from a governance perspective.

The mainstream view in academic literature is that the most effective force spurring the internal efficiency of firms (and the allocative efficiency of an economy) is competition in product and factor markets, thanks to the associated incentive and information effects (e.g. Vickers and Yarrow 1988, 67–69; Shirley and Walsh 2000, 5–6).[62] As has been exposed, there is only little scope for competition in WS service markets, due to their natural monopoly characteristics. Given this situation, the incentives stemming from ownership may play a prominent role. The question is whether private owners are generally more effective in providing internal efficiency-enhancing incentives—for instance, by monitoring the firm's management—than public owners (it is emphasised here that internal efficiency-enhancing incentives are not suited to prevent the service provider from appropriating monopolistic rents, and are thus not a substitute for economic regulation).

Theoretical Arguments for a Superior Internal Efficiency of Private Firms

There are quite convincing theoretical arguments for the position that privately-owned firms will generally show a superior internal efficiency (Shirley and Walsh 2000).[63] In the absence of competition in the product market, managerial slack is likely to occur in both privately and state-owned firms. However, state-owned firms show three general handicaps with respect to internal efficiency as compared to their privately owned counterparts:

- In a world of asymmetric information, internal efficiency depends on the monitoring of the management by owners. Private owners have a strong incentive to monitor the management, as improvements in internal efficiency will translate into higher returns. In the case of public firms, ownership is often highly diffuse (in the extreme case all citizens are owners) and ownership shares may not have any value or cannot be sold,[64] which implies extremely low-powered incentives for public owners to monitor the management with respect to the returns to capital. Moreover, state-owned firms face no credible bankruptcy threat, and thus managers do not have to fear the associated loss in reputation. This lowers the incentives for the management to spur internal efficiency.

- Public officials and politicians acting as representatives of the public owners are likely to induce managers of public firms to follow other goals than the provision of WS services at low costs (e.g. maximisation of employment or construction activities, tariff reductions below cost recovery levels, special treatment of certain neighbourhoods). If monitoring by owners and regulatory authorities is weak, the monopolistic and quasi-rents available in the WS market are very attractive sources to finance such activities. However, such a practice is harmful for internal efficiency.
- Public firms may be constrained by legal conditions in achieving internal efficiency. Administrative and public service law may limit flexibility of the management, e.g. with respect to accommodate the labour force by prescribing public service pay scales or by making dismissals very difficult and costly (Kessides 2004, 12–13).

One assumption underlying this argumentation is that private ownership insulates the management effectively from negative political governance factors. However, it is emphasised here that negative political governance effects will generally not be confined to state-owned providers, but will also affect the internal efficiency of private firms. One example is the incentives stemming from the availability of quasi-rents. If public officials cannot credibly commit to abstain from capturing quasi-rents, then it is likely that private investors will engage in one of the following strategies to compensate for the risk of "expropriation:" (i) underinvestment in capital assets; (ii) siphon off returns to capital above the market rate in order to compensate for the high risk (which implies charging "too high" tariffs or incurring "too low" costs); or (iii) bribery of public officials or intense lobbying activities in order to prevent "expropriation" of quasi-rents. All these strategies imply losses in efficiency. Section 3.2 returns to this issue and provides a thorough discussion of the influence of governance on the provision of WS services.

Empirical Evidence

The empirical evidence concerning the expected superior internal efficiency of private firms in the WS sector is inconclusive.[65] Reviews of the econometric and statistical literature are provided, among others, by Clarke, Kosec, and Wallsten (2004, 4–7), Jouravlev (2000, 5), Renzetti and Dupont (2004, 12–16), Wolff and Hallstein (2005, 97), Estache and Rossi (2002, 139), Kirkpatrick, Parker, and Zhang (2004, 7–8; the latter two articles, in addition, present results from own empirical analyses on the internal efficiency of WS service providers). Results from this body of literature show no clear tendency: Although some studies find a significant superiority of private firms, others yield the opposite result, and yet others do not find any significant differences between private and public utilities. Several studies point at the importance of regulation and governance for the internal efficiency of providers.[66] Besides the econometric and statistical work, there have been published numerous case studies,[67] typically comparing performance before and after privatisation. Clarke, Kosec, and Wallsten (2004, 7–11) provide a review of this body of literature and conclude that—except from some notable failures—most case studies find that coverage, productivity, and service quality improved after privatisation. These reforms were associated with price increases. Lobina (2005) instead, based on his review of the case study literature, reaches a critical conclusion concerning the performance of WS service providers after privatisation.

Conclusions and Policy Implications

Financial sustainability of WS service providers is a necessary (but not a sufficient) condition for achieving internal efficiency. One threat to the financial sustainability of service providers is that public officials can take away the quasi-rents that are associated with the production of WS services. Private ownership of service providers makes the direct access of public officials to the provider's resources more difficult and can, thus, up to a certain point prevent the "expropriation" of quasi-rents (private ownership has further positive expected effects on internal efficiency like the closer monitoring of the management through owners). However, even with private ownership, public officials can "expropriate" quasi-rents by indirect means, e.g. through tariff policy. This suggests that the effect of private ownership on internal efficiency will be strongly influenced by political governance. The expected effects of governance on widespread access to and on the (internal) efficiency of WS services will be thoroughly discussed in the following chapter. Here, just some preliminary policy implications are mentioned:

i. Economic regulation seems not only desirable to avoid the abuse of market power (see subsection 2.3.3). If the regulation succeeds in substituting the lacking competitive forces, it can also contribute to spur internal efficiency by reducing managerial slack.
ii. The monitoring by owners provides important incentives for managers to achieve profitability and, thus, internal efficiency. As, in state-owned firms, these incentives are typically low-powered, they should be strengthened, either by privatisation or by other means, like corporatisation under public ownership (see also subsection 3.2.3.3).
iii. The management should be insulated from direct political interference in investment and staffing decisions.
iv. The application of private-sector (labour) law to state-owned service providers gives managers more flexibility to pursue internal efficiency.

v. Financial sustainability is a necessary condition for achieving internal efficiency. The level of cash flow that has to be generated (and thus the tariff level) in order to achieve financial sustainability depends, among other things, on the type of capital financing (grants versus market-based financing). The financial sustainability of providers that do not manage to accumulate some reserves thanks to their cash-flow depends completely on public grants or guarantees.

2.5. CONCLUSIONS

Chapter 2 has developed a general framework for judging the desirability of WS policies on a rather aggregate level. This has been done by reviewing the theoretical and empirical literature and by combining two perspectives:

i. A descriptive perspective that has focused on key characteristics of supply (e.g. cost characteristics, interaction with the environment), demand (e.g. basic needs aspect, interaction with individual and public health), and market institutions (e.g. the feasibility of competition, absence of a full set of markets, ownership of service providers) as well as on their consequences for the behaviour of actors and the state of affairs in the WS sector in general.
ii. A normative perspective that has judged the desirability of the state of affairs (e.g. use of adequate WS services), policies (e.g. WS tariff levels), market institutions (monopolies, ownership) and related problems in developing countries, taking an equity, an allocative efficiency, and an internal efficiency perspective.

Through the combination of these two perspectives, key problems, underlying reasons, and broad policy implications have been identified which are systematised and summarised in Table A2.2 (appendix). In addition, the table contains statements regarding plausible trade-offs and complementarities between equity and allocative and internal efficiency, associated with the respective policy interventions. Although some of the policy interventions imply trade-offs between these goals (e.g. raising WS tariffs in order to internalise external costs will typically mean that some low-income households will stop using adequate WS services, assuming that tariffs rise above their willingness to pay) several other policy interventions are likely to entail complementarities (e.g. introducing regulation of WS services will typically improve allocative efficiency by abolishing monopolistic rents and, at the same time, improve equity, because with lower tariffs and higher-quality services, a greater share of households will be able to afford adequate WS services).

It is not claimed that the normative perspectives, key problems, underlying reasons, policy implications, and trade-offs or complementarities listed are relevant for any WS sector in any country. The relevance of these factors for any particular case in consideration is an empirical question that has to be answered through empirical research. Also, it is not claimed that Table A2.2 is a complete list. The table is rather a general system that relates key problems, policy implications, and trade-offs or complementarities based on theoretical reasoning and stylised empirical facts.

3 Political-Economic Framework for Analysing the Relation Between Governance and the Provision of Water and Sanitation Services

Together with the preceding chapter, this Chapter lays the analytical groundwork for the empirical analysis that follows (Chapters 4 and 5). It sets the framework for investigating the relation between governance and the provision of WS services. The normative and problem-oriented analysis carried out in Chapter 2 has yielded a list of typical problems affecting the WS sector, underlying reasons, and broad policy implications. This analysis has largely abstracted from the effects of political governance and WS governance on the provision of WS services. There is a (i) theoretical argument and a (ii) practical argument, which both strongly suggest including governance into the analytical framework:

i. Given the great responsibility of the state to enact and implement the equity- and efficiency-enhancing WS policies deduced in the preceding chapter, and given the complexity of the related measures and institutional arrangements, it is necessary to take a closer look at *the state* and to choose a framework that explicitly takes into account those governance factors that systematically influence the process of collective decision making and implementation within the state. Or, to put it differently, it is necessary to analyse under which conditions the WS policies deduced in Chapter 2 are likely to being implemented. Governance factors may well be the underlying reasons for a low coverage with WS services (e.g. certain regions may lack political representation in the government with the consequence that they do not receive public funds in order to finance WS infrastructure). And governance factors are likely to affect the implementation of desirable policies (e.g. necessary tariff increases to improve allocative efficiency may not be authorised by the regulator because politicians concerned with their re-election put pressure on the regulator).

ii. In practice, public actors (national ministries, local governments, regulatory agencies, state-owned enterprises, etc.) play a vital role in the WS sectors all over the world. This is not only true for the roles of WS policy-making and regulation that are quintessential responsibilities of the state and, therefore, are shaped by governance factors the same way as in any other policy area. This is also true for financing and service delivery. According to estimations for developing countries, in the mid-1990s 75% to 85% of the financing for the WS sector came from public sources (65% to 70% from public domestic sources and 10% to 15% from international donors) and, at present, just about 3% of the population is served by providers that are fully or partially private owned (Winpenny 2003, 6–7). Even for Latin America, the continent where PSP in WS services has spread fastest during the last 15 years, it is estimated that the share of urban population served by fully or partially private-owned providers amounts to just 15% (Foster 2005, 1).

These two arguments illustrate the particular importance of governance factors for the WS sector. An approach that does not explicitly account for the political incentives of public actors is, therefore, of limited empirical relevance for analysing the allocation of resources in the WS sector and the performance of WS services.

Consequently, this chapter presents a political-economic framework in order to systematically investigate the influence of governance on the provision of WS services. This framework makes it possible to model the state as being composed of various actors[1] that act within a setting of political institutions that shape their actions (see section 3.1). This political-economic framework differs from neoclassical microeconomic theory that treats the state and the political system as a black box. In neoclassical microeconomics, if from the normative and problem-oriented analysis it is concluded that state interventions are desirable, typically a benevolent government is assumed that implements equity- or allocative efficiency-enhancing policies in a selfless manner, without opposition and for the benefit of society as a whole. These are, without doubt, unrealistic assumptions.

The framework developed in the following tries to link two bodies of literature that commonly are treated separately in research. (i) The literature that investigates the role of fundamental political institutions—such as political rights, electoral systems, or checks and balances—on policy making in general.[2] (ii) The literature that analyses the effects of the sectoral governance characteristics, particularly of regulatory authorities, on infrastructure policies and on the performance of infrastructure services.[3] Furthermore, the chapter places the issue of PSP into the broader context of WS governance.

The remainder of this chapter is organised as follows. Section 3.1 defines the basic concepts of the political-economic framework used. Section 3.2 enters into a detailed analysis of the influence of governance on the provision of WS services. First, the three WS sector roles of policy making, regulation, and service delivery are briefly defined (3.2.1). Afterward, the effects of political governance factors (3.2.2) and of WS governance factors (3.2.3) on these roles are discussed to some detail. Finally, section 3.3 draws some conclusions.

3.1. POLITICAL-ECONOMIC FRAMEWORK: DEFINITIONS

In order to model the behaviour of actors, whose actions are shaped by both political and economic contexts and incentives, this study uses a theoretical framework that builds on the schools of new institutional economics, public choice, and political economics.[4] In what follows, the most important concepts and definitions of this framework are treated.

3.1.1. Political Economy

Political economy is a broad term covering a great variety of approaches from social sciences and meaning different things to different people.[5] From the late 18th through the 19th century, the term was used to describe what political philosophers, social theorists, and economists did (Offe 1996, 676).[6] The classical period of political economy starts with the writers of the Scottish Enlightenment and ends with Karl Marx. In the course of the 20th century, the expression became somehow "old-fashioned" (Atkinson 1996, 702), thanks to the differentiation of the social sciences (economics, political science, sociology), and the term *economics* began to be commonly used to refer to what economists do. With the differentiation of economics and political science, economic and political aspects of society are typically analysed separately. During the 20th century, the term *political economy* was often used to refer to Marxist analysis. Since the 1960s authors from the Chicago school started to use the expression (Groenewegen 1991), typically with the attribute *new*. Later, the expression spread to the schools of new institutional economics, public choice, and political economics, which build the basis of the framework chosen here.

In this study, *political economy* is used to describe a theoretical approach that, above all, looks at the economic and the political system of a society in an integrated manner. Individual actions, and thus social phenomena, are shaped by both economic incentives (the decision of a household to connect to a network will depend—among other things—on the connection costs, the tariff of the WS service and the subsidies received) and political incentives (the decision of a public official to subsidise WS services will depend—among other things—on whether this policy measure will improve his chance for re-election or strengthen his political power). "[P]olitical economy emphasizes both 'economic' behaviour in the political process and 'political behaviour' in the marketplace" (Alt and Alesina 1996, 645–46).

3.1.2. Institutions

Institutions are a crucial element of the approach chosen. According to Scharpf (1997, 38) we can define institutions[7] as "systems of rules that structure the courses of actions that a set of actors may choose. In this definition we would, however, include not only formal legal rules that are sanctioned by the court system and the machinery of the state but also social norms that actors will generally respect and whose violation will be sanctioned by loss of reputation, social disapproval, withdrawal of cooperation and rewards, or even ostracism." Institutions are thus characterised by (i) a set of (formal or informal) rules and (ii) (formal or informal) sanctioning mechanisms that will determine their effect on human actions.

Institutions structure human actions in two ways.[8] First, institutions directly affect the choices of actors by influencing the expected cost–benefit relations (payoffs) that result from actions, e.g. the formal rule that tapping into a service provider's pipe system without permission is forbidden by law may prevent urban dwellers from making illegal connections and receiving water for free if they judge the expected benefits (clean water for free) lower than the expected costs (the payment of a fine when the illegal connection is discovered). However, this judgement will depend on the effectiveness of the sanctioning mechanism for illegal connections. Informal institutions, like, e.g. the norm that water is God-given and thus free, may affect the effectiveness of formal sanctioning mechanisms. Another way of how institutions affect expected payoffs from interactions is by systematically increasing (decreasing) the bargaining power of certain actor groups (e.g. prohibiting by law the formation of trade unions will limit the bargaining power of workers to employers).

Second, institutions indirectly influence the actions of actors by structuring their perceptions and reducing the complexity of reality. In this way, institutions reduce the number of cognisable choices and affect expectations and judgements on payoffs that result from certain actions. This does not imply a departure from the assumptions of rational and self-interested actors that choose their actions based on an individual optimisation calculus (and, instead, an adherence to a sociological model of human behaviour that asserts that there is a deterministic relation between rules or norms and individual action[9]). An important assumption, however, is that actors are *boundedly* rational.[10]

So far it has been stressed that institutions have an influence on human actions. This is the relevant aspect of the relation between institutions and human actions if the institutional setting is held fixed and we are looking at the behaviour of actors. This is also the predominant perspective taken in this study. However, it has to be kept in mind that institutions change over time and that new institutions are created. Formal institutions (e.g. a decentralisation law for the WS sector) are changed or created through the policy-making process which, in its turn, is governed by higher-order institutions like the electoral system or administrative law. The following subsection discusses in greater detail the subject of the policy-making process and its outcomes.

3.1.3. Public Decision Making and Policy Making: Actors, Interactions and Institutions

The conceptualisation of the making of policies, which is described in what follows, is based on Scharpf's (1997) actor-centred institutionalism. According to this view, public decisions and policies are not the product of a unitary actor ("the state") but result from the strategic interaction of various actors with different preferences and understandings of policy problems, within a given institutional setting (see Figure 3.1).

Actors can be individual or composite. Examples for composite actors are coalitions, clubs, movements, associations, or hierarchical organisations (examples for the latter are political parties, enterprises, or state agencies).[11] Actors are characterised by specific capabilities, perceptions and preferences:

- The term *capabilities* describes all those action resources that an actor controls directly and, hence, enable him to influence policies (or other publicly-relevant actions) that are produced in a given interaction. Capabilities include personal properties (intelligence, experience, etc.), physical and financial resources (financial capital, land, military power, etc.), the access to information and technologies, and so on. Together with the institutional setting (i.e., the general rules of the "game") and the specific actor constellation (i.e., the number and the characteristics of the other "players"), the capabilities will determine the relative power of an actor.
- Perceptions and preferences together determine the action orientation of an actor, i.e., the strength of his motivation to engage in an interaction with other actors in order to influence a certain outcome (e.g. the drafting of a WS sector reform law or the decision of a regulatory agency concerning tariff increases). Action orientation

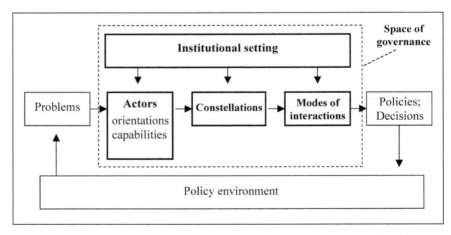

Figure 3.1   Governance and the making of policies. Source: Based on Scharpf (1997, 44), adapted and complemented by the author.

is activated by an underlying policy problem that is perceived as desirable or undesirable with respect to the actor's preferences and triggers off activities pro or contra this issue. Actors maximise their expected utility given their capabilities, the institutional setting, and the actor constellation.

The outcome of policy interactions can be explained by specifying the actor constellation and the mode of interaction. The relevant actor constellation is given by the actors involved in the production of particular empirically observable policies that are to be explained. The modes of interaction are shaped by the specific rules that govern a given interaction (or by the absence of such rules). Scharpf (1997, 46–49) distinguishes four general modes of interaction: (i) unilateral action, (ii) negotiated agreement, (iii) majority vote, and (iv) hierarchical direction.

Finally, the manifold influences of institutions in the process of public decision making and policy making is once again highlighted. Institutions structure the perceptions of actors and, thus, their action orientation, influence the number and characteristics of actors involved (e.g. the amendment of a WS law may need to be approved by both the upper and the lower legislative chamber) and shape the mode of interaction (e.g. prescribing a majority of two thirds of the votes).

3.1.4. Governance

The term *governance* (and its normatively connoted twin term, *good governance*) has been widely used for some years in development studies. There is no generally accepted definition of governance, and authors and development agencies often focus on different aspects when using it.[12] However, with respect to the general meaning, there is a consensus that governance is essentially about collective decision making and implementation, i.e., about the principles according to which a collective (a company,[13] a local community, or a nation) makes and sanctions decisions that concern the members of the collective. In this sense, governance describes the way a collective is steered or steers itself. A brief definition of governance along these lines is given by the Commission on Global Governance, as cited in Weiss (2000, 796): Governance is "the sum of the many ways individuals and [.] [organisations], public and private, manage their common affairs" (citation adapted by the author). With the actor-centred institutionalism approach introduced previously, we have a theoretical model at hand that describes fairly precisely the main elements of this process of managing the common affairs or—which is essentially the same—of public decisions taking and policy making: institutions, actors, constellations, and modes of interactions (see the "space of governance" in Figure 3.1).

This study distinguishes two aspects of governance that differ from each other in relation to the level of generality: (i) political governance and (ii) WS governance.

i. Political governance refers to those elements that describe the way a nation is governed in *general* terms and that, therefore, affect the way policy making and public decision making is organised in *general* terms. Fundamental elements to this respect are (i) the rules by which those actors in government power acquire their public office (e.g. by means of majority vote in free and competitive democratic elections versus by means of negotiation among small elites and repression of basic political rights), (ii) the organisation of government (e.g. separate legislate, executive and judicial branches versus concentration of government branches), and (iii) the delegation of power from the public officials to the bureaucracy and the various government agencies (Cox and McCubbins 2001, 21–22). In this study, the focus is set on the first two elements and their effects on the provision of WS services (see subsection 3.2.2).

ii. WS governance refers to those elements that are more specific to the provision of WS services. Literature usually distinguishes three roles that have to be accomplished in order to provide WS services: (a) policy making, (b) regulation, and (c) service delivery (for more details see subsection 3.2.1). The institutions that shape the way how and by which kind of actors each of these roles is accomplished and the institutions that determine how these three roles are articulated with each other are the main ingredients of WS governance. Important questions to this respect are, e.g. whether the three roles are institutionally separated or accomplished by one single (composite) actor, whether citizens or users participate in these activities and whether the regulators and service providers are autonomous in their decisions (see subsection 3.2.3).

3.2. THE RELATION BETWEEN GOVERNANCE AND THE PROVISION OF WS SERVICES

Figure 3.2 describes in a very condensed manner the postulated relation between political governance, WS governance and WS services which will be discussed to some detail in this section. Before this governance analysis is started, it is reminded that governance factors are not the only factors that can "deviate" WS policy making from the "equity cum allocative efficiency avenue". The economic characteristics discussed in Chapter 2—like the absence of competition in the market and the availability of (quasi-)rents—create strong incentives for actors to take advantage of this situation to their individual benefit but to the detriment of equity and allocative efficiency. Governance factors work together with these economic factors. In the best case governance characteristics can "correct" these incentives and in the worst case they can compound the situation.

This problem is addressed by Noll (2002, 61–62) who, after an analysis of the allocative efficiency-related problems of the WS service industry, concluded:

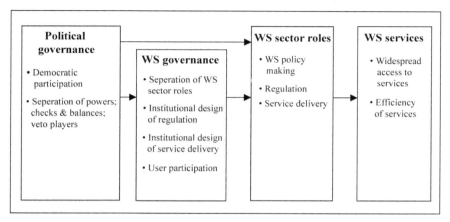

Figure 3.2   Relation between governance and WS services. Source: Author.

The optimal design of urban water delivery systems (including their governance institutions) is deceptively complicated. [. . .] [The] features of water utilities inevitably lead to the conclusions that extensive government intervention in the industry is inevitable, and likely to take forms that are at variance with the conventional prescriptions from the research literature. Moreover, government interventions are especially likely to be distorted by distributive politics because of both measurement problems (and hence the difficulty of resolving controversies through evidentiary inquiries) and the competition for the enormous rents that are available from the system in an environment in which many of the social costs of inefficient policies that redistribute rents are likely to be delayed and difficult to observe.

In what follows, first, the three WS sector roles are briefly defined (3.2.1). Afterwards, the effects of political governance factors (3.2.2) and of WS governance factors (3.2.3) on these roles–and consequently on the equitability and efficiency of service provision–are discussed to some detail.

3.2.1. WS Sector Roles: Policy Making, Regulation and Service Delivery

The practice- and policy-oriented literature usually distinguishes three roles that have to be accomplished in an economy in order to provide WS services for citizenry (e.g. Foster 1996, 2–5; Rouse 2007, 3–4):

- WS policy making,
- Regulation, and
- Service delivery.

Although policy making and regulation are tasks of the state (see Chapter 2 for a justification on normative and problem-oriented grounds) and will thus be strongly influenced by the political governance factors discussed in subsection 3.2.2, service delivery can be delegated to the private sector with the consequence that, in this case, it will be more influenced by market and private sector incentives.[14]

The scope of service delivery is, in principle, well defined. It includes the whole physical and commercial process of supplying final users with WS services (see subsection 2.1.1), as well as the financing of these activities (see subsection 2.4.2). There are contractual arrangements that further subdivide service delivery into ownership of assets, investment, and operations and that assign the responsibility for these activities to different public or private actors, giving rise to several ways of PSP (for more details see subsection 3.2.3.3).

The distinction between policy making and regulation is not clear-cut. Economic literature typically does not distinguish between policy making and regulation. The term regulation is used to describe the whole process of state interventions in markets, typically with respect to market entry and prices (e.g. Joskow and Rose 1989, 1450). The practice- and policy-oriented literature on infrastructure regulation characterises policy-making, often, as the process of *setting* policies and regulation as the process of *implementing* policies (Brown 2003, 1; Foster 2005, 8–9). Another way of drawing the line of distinction, which is preferred here, is to look at the scope of the policy issue in question, at the level of detail of the norm, at the level of specific expertise implied, and at the intensity of monitoring or the promptness of reaction required by the issue:[15]

- Policy-making typically deals with fundamental issues (like the principles of tariff policy, the definition and assignment of certain responsibilities to certain actors, the decision to award a concession to a private firm). Norms rarely enter into many technical details. Typically, the public actors that are formally responsible for policy-making (legislative actors: national or local parliaments; executive actors: president, ministers, governors, mayors) have the authority for deciding on a broad scope of policy issues.
- The scope of regulation and the authority of the actors responsible is typically much more limited (e.g. setting the precise rules for tariff definition and monitoring the provider's compliance with these rules). Norms often enter into greater detail and typically require specific technical, economic, and legal expertise. Regulation often has to do with implementing the outcomes of the policy-making process (norms, decisions), but usually also involves genuine decisions or setting of norms on a lower hierarchical level (e.g. the definition of standards for service quality). Moreover, the process of regulation typically includes monitoring activities in order to control the compliance of

regulated actors with legal norms. The quality of drinking water is a good example for an issue that requires a constant monitoring.

3.2.2. The Effects of Political Governance Factors

With respect to the political governance factors that influence WS sector roles, this study focuses on political institutions (e.g. electoral systems, political and civil rights, systems of separation of powers, and checks and balances). Following Cox and McCubbins (2001) and others, it is argued that political institutions have systematic effects on policy-making. The focus here will be on two aspects that are relevant for WS policy making:

First, in subsection 3.2.2.1, those aspects of political institutions will be discussed that have an effect on whether the policies implemented are likely to be more public regarding or more private regarding.[16] Usually, the literature identifies public-regarding policies with general welfare improvements (provision of public goods, improvements in allocative efficiency) and private-regarding policies with redistributive measures and the creation of rents that benefit narrow special interests (e.g. Cox and McCubbins 2001, 47–48). The definition chosen in this study is the following: As has been argued in subsection 2.3.1, both equity and allocative efficiency can be considered valid normative goals for justifying welfare-enhancing WS policies. Therefore, both equity- and allocative efficiency-enhancing WS policies are considered public regarding in this study. With respect to the desirable WS policies deduced in Chapter 2 (Table A2.2), it is possible to state the following. Those WS policies that are either equity- *or* allocative efficiency-enhancing *and* that do not involve trade-offs can be clearly considered as public regarding. Those WS policies that diminish both equity *and* allocative efficiency can be clearly considered as private regarding. The remaining WS policies imply trade-offs between the normative goals and cannot clearly be divided into public or private regarding without considering further criteria.

After, in subsection 3.2.2.2, those aspects of political institutions are discussed that have an effect on whether governments are more or less able to credibly commit to maintaining policies implemented in the past.[17]

3.2.2.1. Public-Regardedness of Policy: The Role of Democracy and of Veto Players

The Role of the Fundamental Institutions of Power
Delegation: Democracy Versus Autocracy

The way public officials acquire government power is important for the question whether policies will be likely to be more public regarding or more private regarding. The way power is delegated from citizens to governments determines to whom public officials are accountable, which, in its turn, has an effect on the responsiveness of governments to the interests of citizenry. From a bird's eye perspective, two opposed regime types can be distinguished: democracies and autocracies.[18] According to the widely used definition of Dahl (1989, 221) the constituent attributes of democracies ("polyarchies") are:

> (i) elected officials; (ii) free and fair elections; (iii) inclusive suffrage; (iv) the right to run for office; (v) freedom of expression; (vi) alternative information; (vii) associational autonomy.

Free and competitive elections (attributes i to iv), together with fundamental political rights and alternative information (attributes v to vii) give rise to vertical accountability of governments to a broad majority and permit citizens to voice their demands on public officials (O'Donnell 1998, 112–13). Democratically elected public officials, for their own interest, are likely to take into account these demands because (i) thanks to the freedom of expression and the availability of alternative information, citizens are capable of judging whether policies are in accordance with their interests and with the policies announced by candidates before the election date; and (ii) thanks to periodically held free and competitive elections, citizens can sanction governments at the next election date by giving their vote to another candidate or party.[19]

In autocracies, by contrast, one or several of the aforementioned attributes are not satisfied. Autocratic regimes typically base their power on repression and on the support of relatively small groups (like the military and the business elite). Their vertical accountability is thus limited to the narrow interests of these small groups, and they cannot be sanctioned by citizenry as long as the repressive system works. It is true that also autocratic regimes, for their own interest, have an incentive to provide the public goods and policies necessary to promote economic development (i.e., to enact public-regarding policies) because the larger the economic output is, the greater is the share that governments can redistribute to themselves via, e.g. taxation. However, other things being equal, a democratic majority government will choose a policy mix of public goods and taxation that is associated with a greater welfare because it has a more encompassing interest in the productivity of the society than an autocratic government. This is due to the fact that the broad majority it represents depends directly on the market earnings of the economy, which are reduced by excessive taxation. A democratic government will, therefore, redistribute less to itself than an autocrat (Olson 1993, 570).[20]

This is not to claim that democratic governments always pursue public-regarding policies. As will be discussed in the following, democracies can show institutional characteristics that may hamper public-regardedness of policy-making.[21] Nor is this to claim that, in democracies, the different social groups and actors representing them have similar

capabilities that would enable them to voice their preferences in the policy-making process with a similar strength: e.g. poor citizens with low
educational achievements and a low level of organisation will have more
difficulties to voice their preferences than wealthy, well educated, and
well organised citizens.[22]

But this is to claim that, as compared to autocratic governments, democratic governments have incentives to design their policies in response to
the interests of relatively bigger parts of the society (have a greater vertical
accountability) and thus, other things being equal, are more likely to implement public-regarding (water and sanitation) policies.

The Role of Separation of Powers and Checks and Balances

The characteristics of the separation of powers (separation of government
branches: legislative, executive, and judicial branches; and federalism: separate spheres of action for national and subnational governments) shape the
way mutual control among public actors is exerted, and hence the system
of checks and balances (O'Donnell 1998). The mainstream view in the literature is that a system of checks and balances enhances public-regardedness of policy-making because horizontal accountability of governments is
strengthened. This argument is elaborated first (*enhancement of horizontal
accountability and public-regardedness*).[23]

However, some analysts (e.g. Cox and McCubbins 2001) have argued
that an excessive separation of powers, which manifests in a high number of veto players,[24] enhances private-regardedness of policy-making.[25]
This argument is elaborated second (*the number of veto players and
private-regardedness*).

Enhancement of Horizontal Accountability and Public-regardedness

The separation of government power and the related establishment of a
system of checks and balances is an important element of the institutional
design of democratic governments. According to many scholars, it is seen
as a means to enhance the accountability of public officials to a broad citizenry, and thus to strengthen public-regardedness of policy-making. The
underlying question is: Why should public officials be accountable to citizens once they are elected or appointed? Periodical elections may prove to
be an incentive that is too weak to keep officials accountable to the public
between election dates. Furthermore, a free media lacks means to sanction
abuses of power, omissions of duties, or embezzlement of public funds that
it may bring to the public.

According to O'Donnell (1998, 113–117) these potential weaknesses
can be overcome by institutional arrangements that enhance the horizontal
accountability[26] of governments and that include essentially the following
two elements:

    i. A system of checks and balances, i.e., the factual mutual oversight among independent state agencies and the sanctioning of actions that infringe the laws (state agencies include the executive, legislative, and judicial government branches, as well as oversight or regulatory agencies, accounting offices, etc.)

    ii. A system of rule of law, i.e., the existence of a constitution and of laws that set the rights and duties of state agencies, their boundaries and overlaps.

Typically, a network of mutually controlling authorities is necessary to render horizontal accountability effective, with the courts having an especially important function to uphold the rule of law.

The Number of Veto Players and Private-regardedness

The concept of veto players is related to the issue of separation of powers (Cox and McCubbins 2001).[27] A veto player is an (individual or composite) actor that holds an effective veto over policy change. This entails two aspects: (i) The actor has de facto power to veto political decisions. For example, in presidential systems, the president typically can veto policies proposed by the parliament. (ii) There is diversity of purposes among actors holding vetoes. The importance of this latter aspect is illustrated by the following example. In a presidential system, one single party may control both the majority of the parliament and the presidential office (e.g. Mexico before the late 1990s). In such a situation, although formally seen there are two[28] vetoes, there is only one effective veto player: the party. This is due to the fact that the two formal veto players share the same purpose and, thus, will not veto any policies proposed by the other.

    In general, it can be said that, at the constitutional level, the effective number of vetoes is established by

    i. "the institutional separation of powers; and"

    ii. "the separation of purpose, which depends both on the electoral code used to 'filter' societal interests into seats in the national assembly (and other offices) and on the diversity of preference in society" (Cox and McCubbins 2001, 26).

It can be argued that democracies, which show constitutional rules that underscore the separation of powers and at the same time are characterised by electoral systems that favour a separation of purposes among members of parliament (which, together, implies a relatively high number of effective vetoes), are likely to produce more private-regarding policies than democracies that do not show this combination of institutional characteristics (Cox and McCubbins 2001, 47–52). The more veto players are involved in the policy-making process,

    i. the likelier it is that actors use their veto power to channel geographi-
cally targetable public expenditures or rents (e.g. monopoly rights) to
their constituencies, and

    ii. the likelier it is that a veto player representing a constituency that
loses with the policy change will demand side payments for this
constituency.

Veto players will engage the more in such activities, the more the electoral
system favours candidate-centeredness (instead of party-centeredness),
and thus separation of purposes. Legislators in candidate-centred electoral
systems need targetable expenditures and rents in order to win elections
because—contrary to larger parties in party-centred electoral systems—
they cannot credibly claim credits for the provision of broad public goods,
but only for narrowly targeted benefits.

It can be concluded that the expected effect of the separation of powers
on the public-regardedness of WS policy making is ambiguous. On the one
hand, it can be argued that the separation of powers—if combined with a
system of rule of law and mutual oversight—makes public officials more
accountable to the public, and thus favours the formulation and implementation of policies that respond to the interests of a broad citizenry. On the
other hand, it can be argued that an "excessive" separation of powers—if
combined with an electoral system and societal characteristics that favour
a separation of purpose among public officials (e.g. candidate-centred electoral systems)—gives rise to a relatively great number of effective vetoes
and a tendency towards private-regarding policies that benefit above all
narrow special interests.

3.2.2.2. Ability to Commit to a Given Policy: The Role of Veto Players

Like other infrastructure, WS services require substantial investments in
long-lived assets (see subsection 2.1.1). The materialisation of such investments depends not only on the characteristics of the property-rights institutions but also on the reliability and credibility of the policy environment
(Levy and Spiller 1996; Spiller and Savedoff 1999; Henisz 2002). As the
production of WS services entails considerable sunk costs (see subsection
2.4.1), the reliability and credibility of WS policies is critical for the WS
service industry. The quasi-rents linked to sunk costs are prone to be captured by public officials (e.g. by discretionary changing regulatory or subsidy policy) with the consequence that investors will refrain from investing
in WS services unless politicians are able to credibly commit to a given
WS policy.[29] Although this argument is clearest when considering private
investment, Henisz (2002, 362) argued that it can partially be extended to
public investment. So long as public sector managers pursue subgoals, like
maximising discretionary income streams, their investment decisions will
be affected by the credibility of the policy environment.

The question is thus: How can governments credibly commit to a given WS policy? Typical solutions discussed in the literature on regulation are the delegation of decisions to an independent regulatory body and the adoption of written policy rules (e.g. the tariff formula) which are fixed in contracts or laws.[30] These kind of institutional arrangements are discussed in the subsection on WS governance (see 3.2.3.2).

Here, the closely related issue on the relation between political institutions and the ability of governments to credibly commit to a given policy is briefly treated. According to several analysts, this ability hinges on the characteristics of the separation of powers and the number of effective vetoes (Levy and Spiller 1996; Cox and McCubbins 2001; Henisz 2002; Keefer and Stasavage 2003). Policy measures meant to improve WS governance, like the creation of an independent regulatory body, may lack credibility, and thus effectiveness, if they are easily reversed by the government. With an increase in effective vetoes, however, transaction costs for policy change rise as more actors have to be involved in the policy making process. Because more interest groups are provided with effective veto power, it becomes increasingly difficult to structure negotiations and to ensure that every actor receives enough value to accept the deal. Consequently, policy change becomes increasingly costly, and thus less likely, and the maintenance of a given policy gains credibility in spite of the existing incentives for politicians and public officials to discretionarily change it. Levy and Spiller (1996) put special emphasis on the role of one specific kind of veto player: the courts. An independent and strong judiciary, whose decisions are enforceable, appears to be a necessary condition for making credible commitments, because it can protect investors from discretionary administrative expropriation.

With respect to the effect on WS services, it can be summarised that, other things being equal, an increase in the number of effective vetoes makes government commitment to a given WS policy more credible and, thus, enhances investments in WS assets. The greater credibility and policy stability related with multiple veto players may, however, come at the expense of inflexibility and indecisiveness. The same way multiple veto players curb administrative and legislative discretion, they may hinder introducing sensible policies in the first place, as well as adapting to technological, environmental, or social change.

3.2.3. The Effects of WS Governance Factors

Similar to the procedure in the preceding subsection, here, the focus is on institutions, in order to work out the systematic effects of WS governance on WS service provision. The core institutions structuring the WS sector are those that articulate the actors responsible for policy-making, regulation, and services delivery (3.2.3.1), and those that shape the governance of regulators (3.2.3.2) and of service providers (3.2.3.3). In order to work out their systematic effects on policies and decision-making within the WS sector, this section tries to maintain the same perspective as that used previously, i.e., to scrutinise their influence on public-regardedness (allocative efficiency- and equity-orientation) and on the ability to commit to a given policy.

3.2.3.1. Horizontal and Vertical Articulation of Roles and Actors

This subsection builds on the definitions of the WS sector roles presented in subsection 3.2.1. Horizontal articulation, here, means the characteristics of the relations amongst the main actors responsible for the "supply side" of the three roles, i.e., of the relations between public officials, regulators, and service providers. By contrast, vertical articulation describes the relation of each of these supply-side actors with the demand-side actors, i.e., the relations public officials–citizens, regulators–users and service providers–users.

Figure 3.3 depicts a specific configuration of the horizontal articulation, to be precise, one in which each role is carried out by a different set of (composite) actors. In theory, as well as in practice, there are configurations in which one type of public actor takes two, or even all three, of the roles, e.g. the ministry of public services through its staff might be responsible for policy making, tariff and quality regulation, as well as for producing and delivering WS services to the users. The fact that WS services are often decentralised complicates the articulation of roles and actors because, in addition, the territorial dimension has to be considered. The issue of decentralisation is not discussed in further detail here (Chapter 5—the case study on Colombia—treats this subject to more detail).

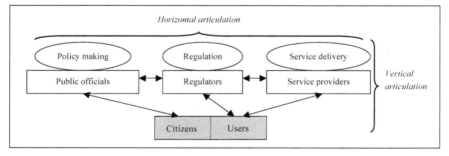

Figure 3.3 Horizontal and vertical articulation of roles and actors. Source: Author.

Horizontal Articulation and the Principle of
Institutional Separation of Roles

During the past decade, the design of the horizontal articulation has received much attention in the literature on WS sector and infrastructure reform (e.g. Foster 1996; Stern and Holder 1999; World Bank 2004). There is a considerable consensus among analysts that the three roles should be accomplished by different actors, i.e., that there should be a separation of roles in order to increase accountability of actors as well as effectiveness and problem-orientation. There is no consensus whether this separation of roles, in the case of service delivery, necessarily requires privatisation, which is the strongest form of institutional separation (see discussion below in subsection 3.2.3.3).

From a governance perspective, the effects of the separation of roles—which always presupposes a legal reform of the WS sector—are very similar to those of the separation of powers discussed previously, in the context of political governance:

i. It is expected that, thanks to a separation of roles, the horizontal accountability (and thus the public-regardedness) of the actors responsible increases, because the clear assignment of roles to actors and the definition of institutional boundaries between actors render their actions and the scope of their responsibilities more visible. It limits the power of politicians to decide on issues assigned to the responsibility of regulators or service providers (like, e.g. the technology to be used for wastewater treatment). By assigning the responsibility for deciding on the (possibly conflictive) principles of WS policy to public officials, the separation of roles can pave the way for more problem-oriented action of regulators and service providers within the scope of their responsibilities.

ii. The separation of roles between policy making, regulation, and service delivery can turn the commitment to a given WS policy or WS sector framework more credible. Those responsibilities delegated to the regulator cannot easily be changed by public officials because changes would require legislative action—which typically entails considerable transaction costs. Moreover, the separation of roles makes it easier for regulators and service providers to take a long-term perspective—which is appropriate given the durability of assets and given the fact that many policies and measures require a long time to bear results. Such a desirable long-term perspective contrasts to the short-term orientation by the next election date, which is common among politicians (Ugaz 2003, 88).

A further effect of the institutional separation of roles is that regulators and service providers are more likely to become professional and specialised organisations—provided that, in addition, the corresponding monetary and further incentives are in place (e.g. appropriate salary and reputation). Without an institutional separation of roles, it is likelier that politicians use their influence to hire staff that has ties to their political party or clientelistic network, i.e., that staff is hired on political grounds, instead of on technical and professional grounds.

However, as Levy and Spiller (1996) underline, these expected effects of WS sector institutions will depend on the surrounding environment of political institutions. If there is no independent judiciary, no transparent information and no tradition of rule of law, the legal separation of roles in the WS sector may be ineffective, and encroachment[31] a common issue. And if there are no effective veto players in a polity, creating a separate regulator may add no credibility to a given WS sector framework, because the regulator can very easily be passed over by the government.

Vertical Articulation and the Principle of User Participation

The vertical relation between citizens and public officials via elections has already been addressed in the context of political governance where the importance of the fundamental institutions of democracy was highlighted (see subsection 3.2.2.1). This paragraph deals with the relations of users with regulators and users with service providers. In the relevant literature, this issue is discussed under the headings of user, public or consumer participation (cf. Goetz and Gaventa 2001; Rouse 2007, 79–99; Ugaz 2003).

User participation is a means for enhancing the vertical accountability of regulators and service providers, and thus for increasing their responsiveness to the user's interests.[32] This short route of accountability (users–service providers; users–regulators) complements the long route of accountability that links users and service providers (users and regulators) in a "roundabout way" via the elected public officials.[33] This complementation entails two potential benefits:

i. At the election date, citizens vote for candidates that represent very broad policy packages with no or only limited reference to specific WS policies. The participation in regulation and service delivery is a means for users to voice their specific demands regarding WS services in an immediate way and on a timely basis.
ii. Political institutions can show characteristics that detract policy making from public-regardedness (see subsection 3.2.2.1). User participation can be a means to enhance public-regardedness in the provision of WS services and to hold public officials accountable between election dates (Goetz and Gaventa 2001, 3).

Whether participation is an effective way to enhance the responsiveness of regulators and service providers to the interests of users depends on the institutions that govern these vertical relations (e.g. are users represented in the regulatory commission or in the service provider's board of directors?) and on the capabilities of the actors involved (e.g. does the representative of the users have the educational background and enough information to gasp the issues decided upon in the regulatory commission or the board of directors?). Limited capabilities (organisational, material, educational) can be an important limitation for poor user groups to engage effectively in participation (e.g. Goetz and Gaventa 2001, 6, 10). In addition, contrary to, e.g. industrial and commercial WS service users, domestic WS service users are a very big, disperse, and heterogeneous group, characteristics that make the organisation of common interests more difficult.

Goetz and Gaventa (2001, 8–9) distinguish three degrees of intensity in participation with an increasing level of user influence on decision making and, thus, an increasing level of responsiveness of officials and managers to user interests:[34]

i. *Consultation* means opening arenas for dialogue and information sharing and can take the form of one-off consultations or on-going dialogue.
ii. *Representation* involves an institutionalisation of the regular access for user groups to regulatory decision making or utility management decision making.
iii. *Influence* is given if users achieve a tangible impact on regulation and management decisions.

Again, the effects of the WS sector institutions that structure user participation will depend on the surrounding environment of political governance. To this respect, the characteristics of civil society participation in other policy areas or in local government, the capabilities of civil society organisations, as well as the conditions of transparency and the existence of independent courts, seem especially relevant. If there is no tradition of civil society participation and civil society organisations are weak, if there is a lack of transparent information and if there is no independent judiciary, the influence of user participation is likely to be insignificant.

In what follows, some further details of the institutional design of regulators (3.2.3.2) and of service providers (3.2.3.3) are discussed.

3.2.3.2. Institutional Design of Regulation

The governance of regulation has received quite some attention in the policy-oriented literature during the last decade (e.g. Levy and Spiller 1996; Sappington 1996; Smith 1997; Stern and Holder 1999; Ugaz 2003; Rouse 2007). Many analysts focus on the dimension of horizontal articulation and on the problems that result from a lack of independence of regulation. These problems are:

- Low credibility of the commitment to a given regulatory policy, which implies a high uncertainty and, thus, (i) low or costly[35] private capital investments, or conversely (ii) a great need for government financed capital investments;

- Use of regulation by politicians and public officials to pursue short-term and particularistic benefits to the detriment of long-term efficiency- and equity-orientation ("state capture"); and
- Use of regulation by service providers to earn monopolistic rents and other benefits to the detriment of efficiency- and equity-orientation ("industry capture").

Regulation is often described as being the task of balancing the interests of users, service providers, and governments (e.g. Foster 2005, 10). A major challenge is to design institutions that enhance the *independence* of regulators—in order to prevent the problems previously listed—but that at the same time hold them *accountable* to the public—in order to prevent regulators themselves pursuing a particularistic agenda.

Independence and Accountability

Usually, two broad models of institutionalising the regulatory function are distinguished (Bakovic, Tenenbaum, and Woolf 2003; Joskow 2007, 1265–72):

- The French tradition of regulation by contract, which means that the regulatory instruments and procedures are fixed in an explicit concession contract between a national or local government and a private service provider; and
- The Anglo-American tradition of an independent regulatory body created by law that usually possesses a good degree of discretion with respect to the instruments and procedures to regulate service providers.

In the pure version of the regulation by contract—the French case—the responsibility to regulate is not delegated to a separate actor, but stays with the executive actor that is responsible for granting the concession and typically also for WS policy making (for more details concerning the French case, cf. Bakovic, Tenenbaum, and Woolf 2003, 17). However, the process of regulating is, in a certain manner, "separated" from the policy-making process because the instruments (e.g. formula for defining and adapting the tariff), procedures (e.g. concerning the information regulated firms have to provide), appeals procedures, and penalty clauses are fixed in a written contract that cannot be changed by any party, unless the terms are renegotiated or the contract is violated.

The Anglo-American model of an "independent" regulatory body has been in the focus of the literature on regulatory reform. It has been implemented in various transition and developing countries (Stern and Holder 1999, 37; Foster 2005, 8–18). Table 3.1 lists important institutional design

Table 3.1 Factors Influencing Independence and Accountability of Regulatory Bodies

Objective	Institutional Design Features	Comments
Independence	**Institutional separation:**	
	• Distinct legal mandate, free of ministerial control	• Degree of independence depends on the legal instrument: constitution (high), law (medium), decree (low) • Degree of discretion depends on the level of detail of the mandate, e.g. with respect to price regulation: general criteria like "efficient" and "just" (low level of detail), specific tariff formula (high level of detail)
	• Appointment for fixed terms; clearly specify causes for removal	• Prevents arbitrary removal
	• Involve executive and legislative branch in appointment process	• Prevents the risk of state capture
	• Staggering terms so that they do not coincide with election cycle	• Prevents the risk of state capture
	• Autonomous source of finance, e.g. levy on the WS industry turnover	• Prevents the risk of state capture (by ruling out the threat of cutting the budget)
	• Make regulators responsible for various utility sectors (e.g. WS, electricity, telecommunications)	• Prevents the risk of industry capture

Resources:	
• Prescribe professional criteria for appointment	• Regulation is a complex task that requires economic, engineering and legal expertise
• Provide the agency with reliable and sufficient funding	• Enables the regulatory body to hire well-trained staff
• Avoid high proportion of inspectors with a background in WS industry	• Prevents the risk of industry capture
• Exempt the agency from civil service salary rules	• Salaries fixed by civil service rules may be too low to attract well-qualified staff
Accountability	
• Establish mechanisms for appellative review of the agency's decisions for users/ regulated firms	• Effectiveness depends on the judiciary's independence and capabilities
• Provide for scrutiny/ overview of the agency's budget	• Prevents embezzlement of funds/ corruption
• Rigorous transparency of decision making processes and publication of decisions and justifications	• Prevents industry and state capture as well as corruption; enhances participation

Source: Own compilation based on Smith (1997, 11–12), complemented by the author

features that influence independence and accountability. Independence means that the regulatory body is autonomous in fulfilling its legal mandate. Independence is not only enhanced by the institutional separation from governments and service providers, but also by the degree of human (and financial) resources devoted to the regulatory body: "technical expertise can be a source of resistance to improper influences, and organizational autonomy helps in fostering (and applying) technical expertise" (Smith 1997, 11).

Although most analysts focus on the independence from governments, independence from regulated service providers is also a relevant issue. The borderline between desirable co-operation with the regulator and capture by the WS service industry may be difficult to draw in practice (co-operation is necessary and desirable to foster exchange of information and to save on expensive supervision and monitoring). Ugaz (2003, 90–91) emphasised that the same conditions that foster co-operation promote capture of the regulator. Moreover, the author draws the attention to the disequilibrium in bargaining power that exists when a developing country's regulator with limited (technical, financial, human) capabilities has to regulate companies owned or operated by one of the powerful multinational corporations that dominate the worldwide private WS service industry.[36] Such a disequilibrium in bargaining power entails a high risk of regulatory capture by the WS service industry. However, this risk is not confined to the interaction of the regulator with private companies. Stern and Holder (1999, 36) point out that, in developing countries, state-owned utilities often dominate the ministries that have the responsibility to regulate the utilities but little power and capabilities to do so.

Independence is not a goal in itself, but instrumental for achieving public-regardedness of regulatory policy. This is why institutional design features to strengthen the accountability of regulatory bodies are so important. Appellative review, budgetary control, transparent regulatory processes, and the obligation to publish regulatory decisions enable the public to hold the regulator accountable (for more details on user participation, see the following).

Commitment Power

Although both the Anglo-American and the French models seem to work acceptably well in their countries of origin, it is not clear whether they will perform similarly when introduced to another country with a different environment of political institutions and with different levels of WS service coverage and efficiency achievements. In practice, regulatory reforms in developing countries have encountered difficulties in achieving the objectives of independence and accountability (Stern and Holder 1999; Bakovic, Tenenbaum, and Woolf 2003; Foster 2005).[37]

One practical problem the literature has insisted in is the inability of many governments to credibly commit to a given regulatory policy. This has involved negative consequences for the amount of (private) investments in the WS industries. Stern and Holder (1999, 38) emphasise that, even if a newly created regulatory agency succeeds in building up a reputation of making independent decisions, it stays vulnerable to government intervention. One regulatory decision that is perceived as being driven by political considerations can suffice to undermine credibility. Bakovic, Tenenbaum, and Woolf (2003) argue that one part of the problem is the regulatory discretion which the Anglo-American model entails. If—due to general weaknesses of the political institutions—independence and accountability are weak, the regulator's discretion is an avenue for politicians to intervene in regulation. Therefore, the authors recommend complementing the model of an independent regulator with the model of regulation by contract (as discussed previously) in order to restrict the regulator's discretion.[38] However, the commitment power of such a combined model still depends on the government's expected respect for contracts with private parties and on the judiciary's independence and treatment of private property rights. One possibility to overcome doubts with respect to these points is to include international arbitration into concession contracts.

Interaction With Users and User Participation

User participation in regulation may seem like a contradiction to the principle of independence of regulation.[39] However, this contradiction clears up if we bear in mind that one important purpose of regulation is to balance the interests of service providers, governments, and users in order to achieve equitable and efficient WS services. In this context, the participation of users should be conceived as being relative to the participation of other actors, like public officials and service providers. These latter actors have closer ties to the regulator, and potentially more means to voice their interests. Ideally, by making the bargaining power between these actor groups more equal, user participation complements the principles of independence and accountability, and enhances public-regardedness of regulation (Ugaz 2003, 91–95).

   Whether participation in regulation should take the form of consultation or the form of representation (see subsection 3.2.3.1) depends on the remaining institutional features. Here, it is argued that—as long as the institutions for pursuing independence and accountability work acceptably well—participation by consultation is probably preferable. User participation by representation means that representatives of the users (together with representatives of the service providers and the government) become members of a regulatory commission. This entails some potential drawbacks: The regulatory commission may become indecisive with regard to conflictive issues (provided that the commission members have veto power), it may take, predominantly, a short-term perspective concentrating on day-to-day WS politics, and its technical expertise may suffer. However, if the institutional features suggest that the regulatory body is likely to be captured by politicians' or service providers' interests, then user participation by representation is probably preferable. The potential drawbacks previously mentioned might be a tolerable "price" for balancing the bargaining power in the regulatory process by voicing more strongly the interests of the users.

Apart from the issue of balancing bargaining power, user participation is an important source of information for regulators. Regulation is an activity marked by a pronounced information asymmetry between the regulator (who is less informed) and the regulated firms concerning the costs and quality of WS services (e.g. Joskow 2007, 1285–86). The information basis of the regulatory body improves, if—in addition to the information delivered by service providers—it receives information from the users. This information provided by users is essential for the regulator to monitor the compliance of service providers with tariff rules, service standards, user's rights, etc., and to sanction infringements (see also subsection 3.2.3.3).

The effectiveness of user participation depends—in addition to the rules and procedures regarding consultation and representation in regulation—on the existence of user advocacy organisations. Although industrial and commercial users are typically relatively well organised (e.g. by the local chambers of commerce), the group of domestic users is much bigger, more disperse, and more heterogeneous, and thus more difficult to organise. In general, user participation in regulation is not very well developed in developing countries. In Latin America—a region were regulatory reforms are relatively advanced and widespread—public hearings, which are a form of consultation in regulatory decision making, are rather the exception, than the rule. Moreover, there have been only few attempts to build up user advocacy organisations (Foster 2005, 15–18). The complex economic, engineering, and legal nature of regulation suggests that strong user advocacy organisations with well-trained staff are key for effective user participation.

3.2.3.3. Institutional Design of Service Delivery

The institutional reform of service delivery, namely privatisation of service providers, is the topic that has dominated the debate on WS service industry reform during the last 15 years, and has been associated with a marked controversy between supporters and opponents.[40] This subsection builds on subsection 2.4.3, which already has entered into this question and—among other things—has reviewed the empirical evidence regarding the performance of private providers as compared to state-owned providers with respect to internal efficiency—which is inconclusive.

Institutional Design Features and Independence from Public Officials

Subsection 2.4.3 has identified three governance problems of state-owned providers with potential negative impacts on internal efficiency:[41]

- Public officials can easily intervene in management on a day-to-day basis and demand to pursue objectives like maximising employment or construction activities or keeping tariffs below a financially sustainable level;
- The incentives of the public owners (and its representatives) to monitor the management with respect to returns to capital are low-powered; and
- Public and administrative law constrains the choices of the management to achieve internal efficiency, e.g. with respect to payment of the staff and accommodation of the labour force.

As is discussed in what follows, these problems depend on whether the service provider is private or state-owned, but also on additional institutional features like the corporate form of the service provider and the question of whether public law or private-sector law applies.

Table 3.2 gives an overview of the whole spectrum of delivery models that exist in the WS service industry, from fully public over PSP to fully private delivery models. Privatisation is the strictest form of institutionally separating service delivery from the processes of policy making and regulation. In its extreme form, privatisation means divestiture, i.e., the complete transfer of ownership to private actors and the transformation of the entity into a private corporation that operates under private-sector company law. Privatisation withdraws direct access to the service provider's (financial, technical, and human) resources from the sphere of political governance (i.e., from public officials and bureaucrats) and shifts it to the sphere of private governance (i.e., to private investors). Private investors—due to their profit motive and the bankruptcy risk they bear—have strong incentives to monitor the management with respect to internal efficiency achievements. The management is not only monitored by the owners who provide the equity capital but also by lenders that provide the borrowed capital. Provided that the private corporation receives no subsidies, investment financing has to be raised completely on the private capital market. In practice, full divestiture of formerly state-owned providers is the big exception in the WS industry (Kirkpatrick, Parker, and Zhang 2004, 6).

At the other extreme of the spectrum, there is the model of WS service delivery by a government department. Access to the service provider's resources lies completely within the sphere of political governance. The formal institutions that govern WS service management are budget and administrative law and the monitoring occurs via the usual procedures of public accountability—like expenditure audits and legislative reviews—which just provide low-powered incentives with respect to internal efficiency. The formal independence of the management from public officials is very low. The minister of, e.g. public services may be both the chief officer responsible for WS policy-making and the chief officer responsible for WS service delivery. Investments have to be integrally financed through transfers from the public budget.

Table 3.2   Characteristics of Public and Private Sector Participation Delivery Models

Contractual Arrangement/ Corporate Form	Ownership of Assets	Responsibility for Investment (Typical Source of Finance)	Responsibility for Operations	Source of Revenue	Typical Contract Duration	Type of Delivery Model
Government department or agency	Public	Public (public budget)	Public	User tariffs, budget transfers	Indefinite	Public
State corporation	Public	Public (government guaranteed loans)	Public	User tariffs	Indefinite	Public
Service contract	Public	Public (public budget)	Partially private	Service fee	1–2 years	PSP
Management contract	Public	Public (public budget)	Private	Management fee	3–5 years	PSP
Lease/Affermage	Public	Rehabilitation: Private capital market; Expansion: Public (public budget)	Private	User tariffs	8–15 years	PSP
Concession	Public	Private (capital market)	Private	User tariffs	25–30 years	PSP
BOT-type (new assets)	Private then public	Private (capital market)	Private then public	User tariffs	20–30 years	PSP
Private corporation/ Shared ownership	Private and public	Private (capital market; government guaranteed loans)	Joint	User tariffs	Indefinite	PSP
Private corporation/ Divestiture	Private	Private (capital market)	Private	User tariffs	Indefinite	Private

Source: Own compilation based on Shirley (2000, 150); Budds and McGranahan (2003, 89–90); Foster (1996, 12)

Between these two extremes, there is a spectrum of intermediate PSP models that result from a contractual subdivision of ownership of assets, investment, and operations. Public operations can, e.g. be complemented by privately financed investments in new assets via build–operate–transfer (BOT) contracts or private operations can be combined with public investment finance via management or lease contracts. According to Kirkpatrick, Parker, and Zhang (2004, 6) the most common form of PSP in the WS service industry has been the concession, where public ownership of assets is combined with private investments and private operations. Between 1990 and 2002, concessions accounted for 40% of the number of worldwide WS projects with PSP and for 64% of the total amount invested (data form the World Bank's PPI Project Database).

Private ownership of assets, private investment financing, and private operations are institutional design features that are expected to provide strong-powered incentives with respect to the internal efficiency problems listed previously. Irwin and Yamamoto (2004) discuss further institutional design features to address the problems of state-owned providers, apart from privatisation and PSP.[42] These design features point at commercialisation and corporatisation while maintaining state ownership. Important points are the following:

- Application of private-sector company law, which ensures that the company has a legal identity separate from the government and which gives more flexibility to the management;
- Special law that regulates the relation between the government and the company and that prescribes, e.g. that companies have to operate as profitably as possible;
- Regular public reporting of the financial and technical performance of the service provider;
- Subject the company to monitoring by lenders by raising borrowed capital on the private capital market; and
- Alleviate the government's conflict of interest as owner and policy maker by splitting the responsibility among ministries (e.g. ownership: ministry of finance; policy making: ministry of public services).

It is emphasised that the effects of the institutional design features previously discussed will be influenced by the characteristics of political governance. Foster (1996, 4–5) wrote to this respect:

A key question is how far along the spectrum from private to public provision it is necessary to go before an effective depoliticization of management is achieved. The answer is likely to depend on the nature of the political system in each country.

This view is shared by the author of this study. In a political system marked by effective systems of checks and balances and by a strong respect for the rule of law, it may suffice to just require by law that public service providers are to operate profitably and to publish their performance regularly in order to succeed in avoiding negative interferences from public officials in the management. Then again, in a political system marked by weak checks and balances, as well as by a disrespect of the rule of law, far reaching PSP may not improve the independence of the management because public officials may use the threat to "expropriate" quasi-rents in order to bargain favours, or the management may offer bribes to prevent interference or to obtain a special treatment by the regulator.

Interaction with Regulation

The institutional design of service providers, in particular ownership, corporate form, and the degree of commercialisation, will influence the effectiveness of regulation (Stern and Holder 1999, 36–37; Foster 2005, 2–8). For regulation to be effective, regulatory governance and regulatory instruments have to be coherent with the institutional design of service providers and vice versa.

In a country where services are provided by government departments, regulatory instruments that build on economic incentives (i.e., on the provider's profit motive) cannot work. Colombia (see section 5.4 for a thorough discussion) is an illustrative example in this context. Due to his concerns with financial sustainability and allocative efficiency, the regulator demanded from all service providers to raise their tariffs to the cost-covering levels ascertained in audited cost studies. However, several public providers refused to do so putting forward equity arguments. A monopolist refusing an invitation by the regulator to raise tariffs may seem an oddity at the first glance, but it is easily explained by the governance features of fully public service providers. In a fully public WS service industry without notable commercialisation and corporatisation of service providers, the most appropriate way of regulating is probably hierarchical regulation by the means of command and reporting foreseen in public and administrative law. However, given the governance problems of public service delivery previously mentioned, internal efficiency achievements are likely to be low in such a system.

Conversely, in a country with a high degree of commercialisation, corporatisation, or even privatisation of the WS service industry, hierarchical regulation by the means of command and reporting is not appropriate. Instead, regulatory instruments that build on economic incentives can be used that—given the fundamental problem of asymmetric information between the regulator and the regulated firms—are considered to be superior to hierarchical regulation, which presupposes complete information. An example for such instruments is the price cap regulation that provides an incentive for managers to drive down costs, even in the absence of competition.[43] So, in a certain way, private or highly commercialised providers are more easily regulated than public providers, because the regulator can use instruments that make it financially attractive for the provider to act in the interests of users (Foster 2005, 5).

Interaction with Users and User Participation

With respect to the interaction of users with service providers, it is reminded here, that the mode of interaction in competitive markets—which gives a considerable client power to users because they can easily switch the provider ("exit"-option)—shows important limitations in the WS service industry. This is why, in order to increase the responsiveness of providers to their interests, users have to rely more heavily on the "voice"-option via participation.[44] In addition, the provider's responsiveness to the user's interests will depend on the legal institutions that govern the user's consumer rights.

Just like user participation in regulation, user participation in service delivery depends on the existence of user advocacy organisations. Participation in service delivery can take a variety of forms. Participation via *consultation* is crucial for the exchange of information between users and the service provider, e.g. concerning the preferences of households for different technical and financial options related to new connections,[45] concerning user concerns about service and water quality, or concerning user education on maintenance of individual water tanks or on water saving. The strongest form of user participation via *representation* is given if the service provider is organised as a cooperative where households are, at the same time, owners—and thus choose the management—and users. In state-owned or private companies, representation can be achieved by making a representative of the users a member of the board of directors of the company. In the case of private companies, this would require a special law, as—in accordance with private sector logic—the board of directors of private companies is usually composed of the representatives of the owners who, in general, will be reluctant to accept a director that does not represent owner interests.

The complaints and sanctioning procedures regarding the provider's infringements of the user's consumer rights are a further crucial element of the interaction among both. Examples for such infringements are undue charges, service interruptions, and bad quality service. The procedure to bring a charge at the ordinary courts has the drawbacks to be relatively lengthy, cumbersome, costly, and not easily accessible for poor user groups. This is why, often, special complaints and sanctioning procedures are created in which the regulatory agency typically acts as an arbitrator of first instance (Foster 2005, 16–17). Still, even access to these special procedures may be difficult for households that live far away from the next complaints office or that lack the necessary education.

Finally, from the point of view of the provider, sanctioning of infractions of the user's responsibilities, namely the obligation to pay for the service, is a crucial aspect. The effectiveness of sanctioning will shape the willingness of the provider to invest in the expansion and improvement of the system (this is at least true for private or commercialised providers).

3.3. CONCLUSIONS

This section summarises the discussion of this chapter (see also Figure A3.1 in the Appendix, which graphically describes the principal relations between political governance, WS governance, WS sector roles, and WS services treated in this chapter):

A first thing to note is that governance factors work via the WS sector roles (policy making, regulation, and service delivery) on WS services. Governance factors influence important aspects of these roles like the public-regardedness and the credibility of policy making and regulation, the professionalism and problem-orientation of regulators and service providers, investment in WS assets and the responsiveness of regulation and service delivery to user interests. These aspects of the WS sector roles in turn influence access to and efficiency of WS services, e.g. if policy making and regulation in a certain country is marked by private-regardedness and a low credibility, it is unlikely that the kind of equity- and efficiency enhancing policies and regulations deduced in Chapter 2 will be implemented and, consequently, access to and efficiency of services will be low (as compared to a country marked by public-regardedness and high credibility of policy making and regulation).

Second, other things being equal, more democratic governments have greater incentives to implement public-regarding WS policies than autocratic governments.

Third, the effect of the separation of powers on WS services is not fully unambiguous. Although, in combination with a strong respect for the rule of law, the separation of powers enhances public-regardedness and credibility of policy making (by strengthening the horizontal accountability of the government and the commitment power to given policies), an "excessive" separation of powers in combination with an electoral system that underscores separation of purpose among elected officials (and thus produces multiple veto players) may drive private-regardedness of policy making.

Fourth, the institutional independence of regulators and service providers from politicians enhances the problem-orientation and professionalism of these actors. Concerning service providers, there is a whole spectrum of delivery models in the WS service industry that entail different degrees of institutional independence. Independence is lowest if services are delivered by a government department and highest if services are delivered by a completely private corporation.

Fifth, the independence of regulators and of service providers is no goal in itself, but is instrumental for achieving widespread access to efficient services. User participation is essential to hold regulators and service providers accountable to the broad public and to render them responsive to the interests of the users.

Sixth, it is emphasised that WS governance factors and political governance factors are interrelated and together influence WS policy making, regulation, and service delivery, e.g. in a polity that is marked by a separation of powers with a system of mutual oversight among state agencies, as well as by a strong respect for the rule of law, it should be easier to establish a regulatory body that is at the same time independent and accountable than in a polity that shows a high concentration of government power and a disrespect for the rule of law. And in a democracy, where fundamental political rights and civil liberties are respected, user participation is more likely to succeed in making regulators and service providers responsive to user interests than in an autocracy.

Finally, it shall be pointed out that the given political and WS sector institutions can limit the effective regulatory policy choices that are available (Levy and Spiller 1996; Sappington 1996). As discussed, there are various regulatory instruments suited to curb the abuse of monopolistic power, but not all regulatory instruments are compatible with any given institutional environment. Regulatory instruments aiming at maximising efficiency (e.g. price caps) require discretion for the regulator. However, in an institutional environment marked by a concentration of government power and the absence of checks and balances, it is likely that the regulator's useful discretion will be confounded with (or displaced by) opportunistic government behaviour. In such cases, given the characteristics of the institutional environment, it might be preferable to choose a second-best regulatory instrument (e.g. cost-of-service-regulation), provided that this second-best policy is more credible—and, thus, possibly more effective.

4 Political Governance and Access to Water and Sanitation Services
A Cross-Country Regression Analysis

This first empirical chapter analyses the relation between political governance and access to WS services for a sample of 69 developing countries, using multiple regression analysis. It builds on the postulated relations between political governance factors, WS governance factors, WS sector roles and WS services that have been discussed in detail in Chapter 3. This first step of the empirical investigation takes a marked bird's eye perspective. It does not attempt to model the whole complexity of the relations between governance and the provision of WS services as analysed in the preceding chapter. It rather concentrates on analysing the influence of political governance on access to WS services without explicitly modelling the influence of WS governance and WS sector roles (see Figure 4.1).

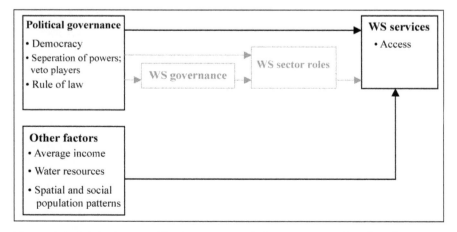

Figure 4.1 Main factors affecting access to WS services considered in the econometric analysis. Source: Author.

There are several reasons that justify such a procedure:

i. Supposedly, fundamental political institutions, like free and competitive elections and separation of powers, have an important influence
on the access to WS services. They not only directly influence public-
regardedness of policy making and, thus, access to WS services; they
also work via WS governance factors, e.g. on investments in WS assets
and on professionalism and public-regardedness of regulation, which,
in their turn, influence access to WS services (Figure A3.1). Given this
supposed pattern of influence and given the need to reduce complexity
in order to keep the econometric model tractable, it makes sense to
concentrate on the influence of fundamental political institutions.

ii. Data restrictions play an important role for econometric analyses. For
political institutions and coverage with WS services there is acceptably reliable and comparable data available for a great number of
countries. This is not the case for WS governance factors, WS sector
roles and the efficiency of WS services.

iii. The second step of the empirical investigation—the case study on
Colombia in Chapter 5—takes into account a higher degree of complexity by explicitly considering WS governance and WS sector roles.
Moreover, in order to assess WS policies and regulations, it applies
the framework developed in Chapter 2. Hence, the investigation in
Chapter 5 complements certain aspects that are ignored here, this way
enriching the empirical picture of the relation between governance
and the provision of WS services.

In order to analyse the influence of political governance, the econometric model controls for other plausible variables affecting access to WS
services (see Figure 4.1). As is discussed in section 4.2.4, factors like the
average income of the country, the abundance of freshwater resources,
and spatial and social population patterns are expected to have an effect
on the demand for and the supply of WS services, and, thus, on access to
these services.

The remainder of this chapter is organised as follows. Section 4.1 reviews
the relevant econometric literature on the subject. Section 4.2 discusses the
expected effects of political governance and describes the key variables and
the data. Afterwards, the econometric model and the regression estimates
are presented and discussed in detail (section 4.3). Finally, some concluding
remarks are made (section 4.4).

4.1. REVIEW OF THE RELEVANT ECONOMETRIC LITERATURE

The relevant econometric work for this study comes from three bodies of
literature:

- Studies concerned with the relation between governance and economic growth;
- Studies concerned with the effects of governance and PSP on the performance of utility services; and
- Studies concerned with the relation between access to WS services on the one hand and socio-economic and environmental factors on the other hand.

4.1.1. Governance and Economic Growth

Even though this strand of research does not enter into the subject of WS or other utility services, it is briefly reviewed in order to get familiar with the operationalisation of governance issues for regression analyses and with the use of commonly applied governance indicators. Since the mid-1990s, the number of articles using econometric procedures to investigate the relation between institutional or governance factors on the one hand and GDP per capita levels or growth rates on the other hand has increased considerably. Parallel to this trend, scholars have developed a growing number of indicators to measure, in a quantitative and comparable way, the quality of different aspects of governance, or they have improved the scope and reliability of already existing indicators. This, in its turn, has further spurred the spreading of econometric work on this topic and has contributed to the enlargement of the corresponding body of literature.[1]

The evidence that some aspects of political and economic governance (security of property rights, rule of law, control of corruption) matter for economic growth is strong. Keefer and Knack (1997) perform a cross-country regression for a sample of 97 developing and industrialised countries. The dependent variable is the average GDP per capita growth rate between 1960 and 1989. Controlling for the initial GDP per capita gap between countries, human capital, labour force growth and price changes, they test the effect of several governance indicators:[2] (i) the aggregate country risk index[3] and (ii) the corresponding sub-index for rule of law (both from the International Country Risk Guide provided by the PRS Group); (iii) the aggregate business risk index[4] and (iv) the corresponding sub-index for contract enforceability (both provided by the Business Environmental Risk Intelligence); (v) the index for constraints on executive action provided by the Polity Project.[5] The authors find significant and robust impacts on the growth rate for the indexes (i) to (iv) with the expected sign (i.e., the stronger rule of law, the lower country and business risks, and the better contract enforceability, the higher economic growth). The evidence that more constraints on executive action spur growth is less strong—although the direction of the effect is as expected. These results confirm findings from earlier work (Knack and Keefer 1995; Mauro 1995) concerning the role of property rights, rule of law, and corruption.[6]

The evidence on the relation between the level of democracy and economic growth is inconclusive and more controversial. In an influential paper on this topic, Barro (1996) analyses the effect of democracy on growth rates for a panel of 100 countries covering the period from 1960 to 1990. In order to operationalise the level of democracy, the author uses the political rights index published by Freedom House.[7] He controls for the initial level of real GDP per capita, rule of law (from the International Country Risk Guide), the level of market distortion (black-market premium on foreign exchange), investment ratio, government consumption, and human capital. Barro finds no significant linear relation between the level of democracy and growth once the control variables are entered into the model. However, the author discovers a curvilinear relation between these two variables: the highest growth rates are observed for partly free countries, the lowest for both not free and free countries. Moreover, he presents some evidence that suggests that economic growth and increasing standards of living exert a positive effect on democracy rather than vice versa.

Two more recent studies (Plümper 2001; Faust 2006) report a significant and positive impact of democracy on economic development. Both studies use democracy indicators published by the Polity Project. Plümper analyses the effect of increasing levels of democracy on GDP per capita growth rates for a sample of 50 *autocratic countries*,[8] covering the period 1976–1997. The author controls for the initial GDP per capita level, the investment ratio, foreign direct investment, government consumption and the share of services in GDP and performs both a cross sectional regression with OLS estimation and a pooled panel data regression with fixed effects. He finds a robust and significant positive effect of the democracy variable. Faust investigates the effect of democracy on total factor productivity for a sample of 81 developing and OECD-countries, controlling for initial GDP per capita levels, openness for trade, the growth of factor accumulation, the growth of labour force, schooling, ethnic fractionalisation, and total population. The author performs a cross sectional regression with OLS estimation and finds a positive and significant effect of democracy on total factor productivity.

Butkiewicz and Yanikkaya (2004) explore the reasons for the inconclusive evidence regarding the effect of democratic institutions on economic development. They find that results are sensitive to sample selection and estimation techniques.

4.1.2. The Effects of Governance and PSP on Utility Services

Only a minor group of this body of literature—which is reviewed first—is primarily concerned with the effect of political governance on access to utility services. The majority of the studies focus on the effects of PSP and competition on utility services—controlling for some political and regulatory governance aspects. As the econometric evidence concerning the effects of PSP on the performance of utility services has already been reviewed in sub-section 2.4.3, the following review is limited to those papers that explicitly include variables on political or regulatory governance when investigating the effects of PSP.

Political Governance and Access to Utility Services

This is a quite recent strand of research—as far as the econometric work is concerned—with relatively few publications. The regression analysis presented in this chapter intends to contribute to this body of research literature.

Horrall (2002) explores the effects of institutional, political, and cultural factors on access to basic telephony for a sample of 37 African countries, using pooled panel data and a fixed-effects regression model. In order to measure the influence of the institutional quality, the author uses the country risk index provided by the PRS Group. She reports a positive and significant effect on the dependent variable. Unexpectedly, the level of democracy or political rights (measured alternatively by the democracy index published by the Polity Project, as well as by the index of political rights published by Freedom House) has a negative impact on the access rate in the model tested.[9] The study finds positive effects of GDP per capita and the degree of urbanisation on access rates. This is confirmed by the econometric work on access to WS services (see the following discussion).

Henisz and Zelner (2001) analyse the effect of veto players on changes in the telephone access rates for a sample of 147 industrialised and developing countries (period 1975–94) using pooled panel data and a fixed-effects model. The sample includes public and private service providers. In order to measure the influence of veto players, the authors use the index developed by Henisz (2002).[10] They control for the existing levels of telephone access, per capita income (annual levels and growth rates), and real investment in telephone assets. Two results are highlighted here:

i. The veto player index has a significant positive effect on the change rate of telephone access. The authors explain this result with the positive effect of veto points on government commitment and thus on investment activity.[11]

ii. Initial levels of penetration are significantly and negatively correlated with the change rate of telephone access, i.e., there is a catch-up effect: Access grows faster in countries with low initial penetration levels than in countries with high initial penetration levels.

The Effects of PSP and Governance on WS and Other Utility Services

The evidence of this body of literature concerning the effects of governance aspects on utility services is inconclusive. Whereas some studies find significant impacts of political and, especially, regulatory governance on utility services, others do not.

Estache and Kouassi (2002) and Kirkpatrick, Parker, and Zhang (2004) investigate the internal efficiency of African WS service providers and the relation of internal efficiency to PSP. Both use data on the company level (21 companies covering the period 1995–97 in the first case, and 110 companies covering the year 2000 in the second case) in order to estimate efficiency scores. Estache and Kouassi (2002) apply a stochastic and parametric production frontier approach for estimating efficiency scores, followed by a censored tobit regression model in order to analyse the effects of PSP, corruption and "governance"[12] on internal efficiency. They report significant negative (positive) effects of corruption (governance, PSP). Kirkpatrick, Parker, and Zhang (2004) use both a non-parametric data envelope analysis (DEA) and a stochastic and parametric cost frontier approach in order to estimate efficiency scores. In their cost frontier analysis—apart from the usual data on outputs, inputs and input prices—the authors include the economic freedom of the world index provided by the Fraser Institute[13] in order to account for "governance,"[14] as well as two dummy variables reflecting the existence or lack of (i) PSP and (ii) regulation in the water sector. None of the three variables shows a significant effect on the costs of WS service providers.

For the telecom sector, Wallsten (2001) analyses the effects of competition, PSP, and independent regulation on different performance measures using panel data on the country level (30 African and Latin American countries covering the period 1984–97). Among other standard control variables that were already touched in this review, the author controls for the risk of expropriation of private investments.[15] The relevant results for the discussion here are that PSP, by itself, is not associated with many benefits, whereas PSP combined with an independent regulator is positively correlated with performance measures. Besides, a high risk of expropriation has a negative impact on most performance measures. Zhang and Kirkpatrick (2002) analyse the same topic for the electricity sector based on panel data from 51 developing countries covering the period 1985–2000. They reach a very similar conclusion concerning the effect of PSP by itself versus the combined effect of PSP and an independent regulator.

Cubbin and Stern (2006) model the subject of regulatory governance to much more detail than the before mentioned articles in order to asses its impact on electricity generation capacity as well as on the internal efficiency of providers.[16] The authors use panel data from 28 developing countries covering the period 1980–2001. They build a regulatory governance index with the four elements: (i) electricity regulatory law in place versus not in place; (ii) autonomous versus ministry regulator; (iii) regulator's funding from licence fees versus from government budget; and (iv) staff paid by market pay scales versus by civil service pay scales. Besides controlling for standard macroeconomic variables, PSP, and competition, they test the effect of political governance using the rule of law index and the control of corruption index provided by Kaufmann, Kraay, and Mastruzzi (2004). The authors find a robust and significant positive effect of the regulatory governance index on generation capacity. This effect increases with the experience of the regulatory agency (years of existence). They also find some—although weaker—evidence that (i) internal efficiency (capacity utilisation) improves with regulatory governance and that (ii) the better the rule of law, the stronger the regulatory effect.

4.1.3. Access to WS Services and its Relation to Socio-Economic and Environmental Factors

The body of literature reviewed here, is relevant for this investigation, as it deals with the relation between other important variables than governance—control variables from the perspective of this study—and access to WS services. An important body of literature analyses the effects of physical infrastructure (WS, electricity, transport, and telecommunication) on economic output or growth and uses the coverage rate with WS services as an independent variable.[17] From the cross-country studies performed in this context, we know that there is a strong correlation between per capita income and access to WS services (World Bank 1994, 14–17; Estache, Speciale, and Veredas 2005, 6–7).

Mainardi (2003) explores the relationship between macroeconomic and environmental conditions, access to WS services and availability of water resources for a sample of developing countries and countries in transition using regression and principal components analysis. As far as the regression analysis is concerned, he finds a significant influence of wealth (measured by both per capita income and poverty incidence), as well as of spatial population patterns (population density) and population dynamics (growth of urban population) on coverage rates. Moreover, the results from the principal components analysis suggest that there is a trade-off between access to improved water supply service on the one hand and availability of internal renewable water resources[18] on the other hand (Mainardi 2003, 46–49).

4.2. EXPECTED EFFECTS OF POLITICAL GOVERNANCE, DESCRIPTION OF KEY VARIABLES AND SAMPLE

Building on the discussion of the expected effects of political governance (Chapter 3) and on the preceding literature review, this section does the first step in operationalising the research question of this chapter for econometric analysis. First, the main suppositions to be analysed are stated (sub-section 4.2.1), afterwards the key variables and the respective data sources are described (sub-sections 4.2.2 to 4.2.4), and finally the sample selection is explained (sub-section 4.2.5). The second step—the econometric model—is discussed in section 4.3.

4.2.1. Expected Effects of Political Governance

Chapter 3 has argued that political institutions have systematic effects on WS policy making, regulation, and service provision, and thus on coverage with WS services. The argumentation has highlighted two important sets of political institutions (for a thorough discussion, see sub-section 3.2.2):

i. *The institutions that govern the power delegation from citizens to public officials (the level of democracy):* Other things being equal, the expected effect of a higher level of democracy on coverage with WS services is positive (*supposition 1*). The way power is delegated influences to whom governments are accountable and to whose interests governments respond. Due to institutional characteristics, governments in democratic regimes have systematic incentives to respond to broader interests than autocratic governments, i.e., they are characterised by a greater public-regardedness. It is, thus, expected that democratic governments care more for the coverage of their citizens with WS services than autocratic governments.

ii. *The institutions that govern the separation of powers, as well as the number of constitutional veto players:* The effect of this set of institutions on coverage with WS services is expected to be ambiguous, depending on further governance characteristics:

a. Together with a system of *rule of law*, a higher number of constitutional veto players is expected to have a positive influence on coverage with WS services (i) by strengthening the horizontal accountability of governments and thus the responsiveness to broad interests and (ii) by increasing the credibility of government policies and, therefore, investments in long-lived WS assets (*supposition 2a*).

b. Together with electoral systems and societal structures that favour a *separation of purpose* among elected officials, a higher number of constitutional veto players is expected to increase private-regardedness of policy making and, thus, counteract widespread access to WS services (*supposition 2b*).

In order to analyse the effects of these fundamental political institutions on the coverage with WS services, three classes of variables are included in the regression model (for the model specification see section 4.3.1):

- *Variables on coverage with water and sanitation services*: COV02: dependent variables; COV90: control variables for the historical coverage level;
- *Variables on political governance*: GOV_j: independent variables of interest;
- *Control variables*: CON_j: further independent variables.

As is explained in some detail in the following, the following fundamental relation between these variables is proposed:

$$COV02 \rightarrow F(COV90, GOV_j, CON_j) \tag{E4.1}$$

In what follows, the key variables used in the regressions are described. The full documentation of all variables and data sources is given in Table A4.1 in the appendix.

4.2.2. Coverage Variables (COV)

Following WHO and UNICEF (2000, Annex A) national coverage with water supply services (WATTOT) is defined as the percentage of the population that uses improved water services (see discussion in sub-section 2.2.2). Correspondingly, national coverage with sanitation services (SANTOT) is the percentage of the population that uses improved sanitation services. WATTOT and SANTOT can take values between 0 and 100. The information is taken from the database of the Joint Monitoring Programme for Water Supply and Sanitation of WHO and UNICEF,[19] which is the only up-to-date source of systematic and comparable data on the status of WS service coverage for a large number of countries.

Assessing the share of the population of a given country that has access to improved WS services poses diverse methodological problems.[20] The criteria used by WHO and UNICEF in order to judge whether a household is considered to be covered with improved services are summarised in Table 2.1. Coverage rates published by the Joint Monitoring Programme are estimates based on the revised information contained in two main types of data collection instruments: expert assessment questionnaires and household surveys. One problem that arises is that household surveys often use different indicators and (sampling) methodologies, posing, e.g. difficulties to account for some informal supply solutions (Komives, Whittington, and Wu 2003, 78–79).[21] Moreover, for several countries the information available does not suffice to estimate the coverage rate for 1990, and consequently the database includes cases with missing data. The descriptive summary statistics of the coverage variables (WATTOT; SANTOT) for the sample analysed is given in Table A4.2.

4.2.3. Political Governance Variables (GOV_j)

In order to analyse the main suppositions (1), (2a), (2b) stated in sub-section 4.2.1, it would be desirable to dispose of four different variables that measure separately (i) the level of democracy, (ii) the number of constitutional veto players, (iii) the level of rule of law, and (iv) the degree of separation of purpose among public officials. In what follows, five "candidates" for measuring the governance aspects (i), (ii), and (iii) are discussed. The variable ETHNIC—that can be interpreted as a proxy for measuring the separation of purpose—is discussed in sub-section 4.2.4, together with the remaining control variables.

The five governance indexes that have been considered in this study—POLITY, POLRIGHTS, POLCON, CHECKS, RULAW—are described in detail in Box 4.1. These variables are commonly used in econometric work

Box 4.1 Description of Political Governance Variables

POLITY

The values of this variable are taken from the original indicator "POL-ITY" of the database on regime characteristics provided by the Polity IV project (Jaggers and Gurr 1995; Marshall and Jaggers 2000). The database contains codes for the political authority characteristics of a large number of states in the world from 1800 to date. The data is widely used for empirical research and has been applied in econometric work in order to measure the level of democracy (see literature cited in section 4.1). The values of POLITY range from −10 to 10, with −10 being the value for the most autocratic and 10 the value for the most democratic regime. Coding is done by a small group of researchers following a uniform standard. The level of democracy (autocracy) is determined by aggregating following sub-indicators: competitiveness of political participation, regulation of political participation, openness and competitiveness of the executive recruitment, and constraints on the chief executive. The emphasis of POLITY is on measuring the level of democracy as defined in sub-section 3.2.2.1, although it also contains elements linked to the separation of powers and veto players (constraints on the chief executive).

POLRIGHTS

The values of POLRIGHTS are taken from the original indicator "political rights" published annually by Freedom House (various years). This indicator is widely used in empirical research on governance issues and is commonly interpreted as a measure of democracy (Knack 2002, 5). The values of POLRIGHTS range from 1 to 7, with higher scores indicating greater political rights (the values of the original indicator have been transformed—see Table A4.1). The coding of "political rights" is done by survey teams made out of experts that base their judgement not primarily on legislation (formal institutions) but rather on perceptions of "real-world situations caused by state and nongovernmental factors" (Freedom House 2002, 722). In order to do so, survey teams rely on different sources of information including news reports, nongovernmental organisation publications, academic analyses, and professional contacts. POLRIGHTS is intended to measure the level of democracy as defined in sub-section 3.2.2.1. It focuses on the characteristics of the electoral process, associational autonomy and freedom from repression (Freedom House 2002, 744).

POLCON

The values of this variable are taken from the original indicator "POL-CONIII" published by Henisz (2002). It is specifically designed to measure constraints on the executive via veto players by estimating the feasibility of policy change. The variable can take values from 0 to 1, with higher values indicating more constraints on the executive. It is an application of the veto

(continued)

Box 4.1   (continued)

player concept (see sub-section 3.2.2.1) to the construction of an indicator. Original values are calculated based on three types of information on veto points and distributions of preferences of actors within a political system: (i) First the number of independent branches of government with veto power are identified; (ii) in addition, the extent of alignment across branches of government is taken into account using information on the party composition of government branches; (iii) finally, the heterogeneity of preferences within each legislative branch is considered. Data sources are the Polity Database (as discussed previously), The Political Handbook of the World, and The Stateman's Yearbook, among others. Examples for the application of this variable in econometric work are Henisz and Zelner (2001; 2004).

CHECKS

The values of this variable are taken from the original indicator "CHECKS" of the Database of Political Institutions (Beck et al. 2001; Keefer and Stasavage 2003; Keefer 2005). The data is compiled and coded by the Development Research Group of the World Bank. Important sources of information are The Europa Yearbook and The Political Handbook of the World (Knack 2002, 16). The concept underlying the construction of this indicator is similar to the one of POLCON. CHECKS counts "(. . .) the number of veto players in a political system, adjusting for whether these veto players are independent of each other (. . .)" (Beck et al. 2001, 170). The variable takes values from 1 to 18 (higher values correspond to more veto points). Countries where legislatures are not competitively elected are coded 1 as it is assumed that only the executive holds a veto.

RULAW

The values of RULAW are taken from the original index "rule of law" published by Kaufmann, Kraay, and Mastruzzi (2004) and provided by the World Bank Institute through its Governance and Anti-Corruption Database. "Rule of law" is an aggregate index constructed from various single indicators that, in turn, are based on surveys of business, households, public officials, and experts based on their perception of different dimensions of the rule of law in a certain country like the incidence of crime, the effectiveness and predictability of the judiciary, and the respect for private property rights. The index is intended to measure "the extent to which agents have confidence in and abide by the rules of society" (Kaufmann, Kraay, and Mastruzzi 2004, 4). In recent years, this indicator has been frequently used in econometric work (e.g. Kaufmann and Kraay 2002). The variable takes values from −2.5 to +2.5. Higher values correspond to greater rule of law.

in order to account for political governance aspects (see, also, the literature review in section 4.1).

- POLITY and POLRIGHTS are both commonly used as measures for the level of democracy. They focus on the freedom, competitiveness, and fairness of electoral procedures, on the right to run for office, on associational autonomy and on the freedom of expression. However, they partially consider broader issues that are linked to veto players or separation of powers like the constraints on the chief executive (in the case of POLITY).
- POLCON and CHECKS have been both developed for measuring the number of veto players in a political system. However, some issues linked to the level of democracy are also contained in these indicators, e.g. CHECKS is set on its lowest value if the legislature is not competitively elected.
- RULAW is intended to measure the extent to which public and private actors have confidence in and respect the rules of society, i.e., the level of rule of law.

Despite the widespread use of these kind of indexes in the literature, there is an ongoing debate in political science about the appropriateness of applying them in empirical work. The critics in this debate put forward (i) that there is no consistent conceptualisation of democracy in the methodological literature and (ii) raise concerns regarding the validity of measurement, among other criticism.[22] However, with regard to the first issue, according to Müller and Pickel (2007), there appears to be a consensus in the research community that democracy can be defined building on a few fundamental dimensions, like (i) political competition/contestation, (ii) participation, and (iii) horizontal control/checks and balances. The aforementioned indexes try to capture these dimensions. Regarding the second issue, Bollen and Paxton (2000) quantitatively test the internal validity of democracy indexes and find convergent results. Although the author of the present study is aware that there are still methodological challenges to be overcome in order to further improve the validity of these indexes, he judges that their use in the econometric regressions presented below is justified.[23]

The values of the five governance variables have been calculated by taking the averages of the available annual observations between 1990 and 2002 from the original governance indicators described in Box 4.1. The exception is RULAW which has been calculated by taking the average of the available observations between 1996 and 2002, since data prior to 1996 is not available (see also Table A4.1). All variables are ordinally scaled.

The summary statistics of the five governance variables are given in Table A4.2. It can be seen that three of the variables show some missing values for the 69 developing countries included in the sample (see sub-section 4.2.5 for a description of the sample). From the two variables that measure the level of democracy, POLITY shows four missing values, whereas POLRIGHTS shows no missing value. From the two variables that measure the number of veto players, CHECKS presents three missing values whereas POLCON shows just one missing value. RULAW presents no missing value. In the regressions performed in the following those variables are preferred that show less missing values, i.e., POLRIGHTS (to account for the level of democracy), POLCON (to account for the number of veto players) and RULAW (to account for the level of rule of law), in order to not "waste" degrees of freedom.[24]

The matrix of the pairwise Spearman rank correlation coefficients of POLRIGHTS, POLCON, and RULAW is shown in Table 4.1. It becomes evident that POLRIGHTS and POLCON are highly correlated (the coefficient is 0.7758). The rank correlation between RULAW and the remaining two variables is considerably less pronounced (0.4565 in the case of POLRIGHTS and 0.4375 in the case of POLCON). The high correlation between POLRIGHTS and POLCON indicates either

- that the two variables do not succeed to measure accurately the two distinct political governance aspects of interest (level of democracy on the one hand and number of veto players on the other hand) due to measurement problems, or
- that the two variables do accurately measure the two political governance aspects of interest and that there is a strong systematic and positive relation between the level of democracy and the number of veto players in a country.

Both explanations are plausible. Sub-section 4.3.2.1 returns to the issue of the high rank correlation between POLRIGHTS and POLCON when discussing the regression results.

4.2.4. Control Variables (CON$_j$)

The main control variables (per capita income, spatial population patterns, availability of water resources, ethno-linguistic fractionalisation, and historical levels of coverage) have been chosen based upon a review of the relevant literature (as discussed previously), the plausibility of being related to coverage with WS services and the results of various test regressions.

Table 4.1   Pair-wise Spearman Rank Correlation Selected Political Governance Variables

Variable	POLRIGHTS	POLCON	RULAW
POLRIGHTS	1.0000		
POLCON	0.7758	1.0000	
RULAW	0.4565	0.4375	1.0000

The idea is to capture the main factors affecting the demand for and supply with these services apart from political governance. The values of the main control variables described in what follows have been calculated by taking the averages over the period 1990 to 2002.[25]

GDP per capita (GDPCAP) is used as a proxy for purchasing power that will influence the demand for services (prices for WS services are not included into the model, because there is no internationally comparable information available for a great number of countries). Spatial population patterns (population density: POPDENS; share of the urban population: POPURB) and the availability of internal renewable fresh water resources per capita (WATRESCAP) are used as proxies for the cost of providing services. A low availability of water resources per capita will, *ceteris paribus*, tend to increase the cost of providing water (and sewer-based sanitation) services because water will have to be transported over long distances or need costly treatment; and a relative concentration of the population (in urban areas) will, *ceteris paribus*, tend to make it easier to take advantage of economies of scale and of agglomeration and, thus, reduce unit costs.[26]

In recent years, empirical evidence has been growing that ethno-linguistic fractionalisation negatively affects economic growth, institutional quality, and public goods provision (Alesina et al. 2003). The variable ETHNIC[27] is used to control for such effects. Moreover, in this study ETHNIC is used as proxy to account for a high degree of separation of purpose as discussed in sub-section 3.2.2.1. The argument is that a high ethno-linguistic heterogeneity is typically related with a high heterogeneity of political preferences among citizens which, other things being equal, translates into a high degree of separation of purpose among elected officials.

Finally, the coverage levels by the year 1990 (WATTOT90 and SANTOT90) are used to control for historical factors that have affected coverage prior to the period of investigation, as well as to account for unobserved factors (see sub-section 4.2.2 for a description of these variables). The summary statistics of the key control variables is given in Table A4.2 in the appendix.

4.2.5. Sample

The main purpose of this study is to analyse the effects of governance on the provision of WS services in *developing countries*, i.e., in countries with coverage levels lying considerably below 100%. Accordingly, all those countries were included in the sample for which coverage with water supply (WATTOT90) and sanitation services (SANTOT90) by the year 1990 shows values below 95%.[28] For this country group, expanding coverage in order to meet the MDGs is a big challenge and efforts by governments and development agencies to accomplish this task need to be especially strong. The supposition is that political governance factors will make a difference in mastering this challenge. The 69 countries contained in the sample are listed in Table A4.3 in the appendix.

The exact sample selection process was as follows. The starting point was the set of countries contained in the Joint Monitoring Programme (WHO, UNICEF) database, which did not show missing data for either WATTOT90,02 or SANTOT90,02 (108 cases). Countries with a population below 500,000 (average of the years 1990 and 2002) were dropped (remaining 91 cases).[29] Papua New Guinea presented implausible coverage values and was, therefore, dropped.[30] Finally, all countries that presented values above 94% for WATTOT90 or SANTOT90 were excluded from the sample, as well as those countries that showed missing data for the main independent variables discussed earlier (remaining the 69 cases listed in Table A4.3).

4.3. REGRESSION ANALYSIS

4.3.1. Econometric Model

According to Ahlfeld, Hemmer, and Lorenz (2005, 3–4) the econometric model used in this study can be classified as an informal regression model because it is not derived from a formal mathematic model on the provision of WS services but rather on informal, although theoretically based, reasoning.[31] The general form of the multivariate linear regression model that describes the proposed relation between the dependent variable and the independent variables is expressed in the following equation (E4.2):

$$COV02_i = \beta_0 + \beta_j\ COV90_i + \beta_j\ GOV_{j,\,i} + \beta_j\ CON_{j,\,i} + U_i \qquad \text{(E4.2)}$$
$$(i = 1,\ldots m;\ j = 1,\ldots n)$$

The dependent variable COV02[32] stands for WATTOT02 or SANTOT02 (the model is estimated separately for the case of water and the case of sanitation; see the following). COV90 stands for WATTOT90 or SANTOT90, GOV_j is the vector of political governance variables, CON_j is the vector of all remaining control variables and U is an error term that contains all factors affecting COV02 other than the independent variables. i is the cross-sectional subscript for the country case. β_0 is the intercept and β_j are the slope parameters that are estimated in the regression analysis. Because it is a cross-sectional analysis, for each variable and country only one observation over time is entered into the model (the average value for 1990 to 2002, as discussed previously). The exception is COV, which appears measured at two points in time: as dependent variable (COV02) for the year 2002 and as control variable (COV90) for the year 1990. Using COV measured by 2002 on the left-hand-side of E4.2 has an important advantage: simultaneity[33] can be largely precluded. By logic, the coverage level measured in 2002 can hardly be jointly determined with the variables on the right-hand-side which are averages for a prior period (1990 to 2002).

One important argument for including COV90 on the right-hand-side of E4.2 is to control for "history" (which will explain much of COV02) in order to isolate the effects of the variables of interest (GOV_j) on the dependent variable, as well as to capture inertial effects. COV90 has the characteristic of capturing all economic, political, social, cultural, demographic, and geographic factors having affected coverage prior to 1990. It is, therefore, also suited for accounting for unobserved factors that are not explicitly included in the model but that may have an effect on COV02 and, thus, cause an omitted variable bias.[34] Another desired aspect is that the model can be interpreted as explaining coverage *expansion* because COV02 is estimated given the values of COV90.

As far as the functional form of the relation COV02 → F(COV90) is concerned, both a linear relation with constant returns of COV90 on COV02, as well as a non-linear relation with diminishing returns have been tested.[35] We would expect diminishing returns as being the appropriate functional form because countries with relatively low initial coverage levels in 1990 are more likely to expand coverage by X percentage points between 1990 and 2002 than countries with relatively high initial coverage levels.[36] It turns out that, for the sample analysed in the case of water, actually diminishing returns is what best fits the data. This is modelled by using the natural logarithm of WATTOT90: WATTOT02 → F(WATTOT90LN)[37]. However, in the case of sanitation the linear relation SANTOT02 → F(SANTOT90) is what seems to best fit the data (see Figures A4.1 and A4.2 in the appendix).

The other independent variables (GOV_j, CON_j) enter the model in level form except for GDPCAP, POPDENS, and WATRESCAP: These three variables are plugged in in logarithmic form (GDPCAPLN, POPDENSLN, WATRESCAPLN).[38]

4.3.2. Results and Discussion[39]

The models discussed below are initially estimated using ordinary least squares (OLS). In several specifications (especially when regressing WATTOT02) there is evidence for heteroscedasticity in the error terms.[40] In these cases estimation procedures with (White-) heteroscedasticity-robust standard errors (HRSE) are performed. Moreover, outlier analysis suggests that in several model specifications estimation results may be sensitive to single influential data points. Therefore, a maximum likelihood-like estimation with iteratively reweighted least squares[41] (*robust regression* = RR) which down-weighs the influence of outliers is used to check the sensitivity of the results.

Results are discussed in four steps. First, the baseline regressions for the water case are presented (4.3.2.1), followed by the baseline regressions for the sanitation case (4.3.2.2). Afterward, the introduction of further institutional factors into the model is discussed (4.3.2.3). Finally, it is checked if the results are altered when controlling for region-specific effects (4.3.2.4).

4.3.2.1. Political Governance and Coverage With Water Supply Services

Results of the Baseline Regressions

Table 4.2 reports the results of the baseline regressions of WATTOT02. The main suppositions (1), (2a), (2b) have been checked by the following procedure. First, the effect of POLRIGHTS, together with a core set of control variables, has been tested (model W1). This has been repeated using POLCON instead of POLRIGHTS (model W2). Afterward, RULAW has been added to model W2 (model W3) and alternatively ETHNIC (model W4).

The results of models W1 and W2 are very similar. POLRIGHTS and POLCON present statistically significant positive effects[42] (W1a, W2: $p <$ 0.05; W1b: $p < 0.1$) just as WATTOT90LN ($p < 0.01$). The effects of the remaining core control variables (GDPCAPLN, POPDENSLN, WATRES-CAPLN) are not statistically significant. These results appear not to be sensitive to potentially influential outliers because estimations with RR (models W1b, W2b) largely confirm those with HRSE (models W1a, W2a). The $\bar{R}^2$ (adjusted R^2) is 0.857 with WATTOT90LN explaining the greatest part of the variance.[43]

Adding RULAW or ETHNIC to model W2 does not markedly alter results.[44] The effect of RULAW is not statistically significant (W3). ETHNIC shows a statistically significant ($p < 0.1$) negative effect when slope parameters are estimated with HRSE (W4a). However, when estimating with RR, the effect is not significant at conventional levels (W4b), indicating that it is sensitive to influential data points. Because suppositions (2a) and (2b) state that the effect of veto players is expected to depend on the level of rule of law and on the level of separation of purpose, models W3 and W4 have been re-estimated, including an interaction term (POLCON*RULAW respective POLCON*ETHNIC) that accounts for a dependent relation between two explanatory variables (see sub-section 4.3.2.2 for a discussion of interaction terms). However, results remained largely the same, not yielding any evidence for an interaction of POLCON either with RULAW or with ETHNIC.

As expected, the signs of the slope parameters of WATTOT90LN, GDPCAPLN, and GOV$_j$ (POLRIGHTS, POLCON, RULAW[45]) are positive, and the sign of the slope parameter of ETHNIC (which measures ethno-linguistic fractionalisation) is negative. Whereas the interpretation of the slope parameters in case of the cardinal variables WATTOT90LN and GDPCAPLN is immediately meaningful (e.g. the slope parameter of 40.934 in model W1a means that a 1% change in WATTOT90—say from 70.0 to 70.7—leads to an increase of approximately 0.4 units of WATTOT02—say from 80.6 to 81.0), in case of the ordinal variables (GOV$_j$, ETHNIC) it is not.[46] In the latter cases interpretation of the slope parameters is limited to the direction (positive or negative) and the statistical significance of the effect.

Table 4.2 Results of Regression Estimates (Baseline Models): Dependent Variable WATTOT02

Independent Variables	Coefficients and t-Statistics [†]							
	Model W1a[#]	Model W1b[##]	Model W2a[#]	Model W2b[##]	Model W3a[#]	Model W3b[##]	Model W4a[#]	Model W4b[##]
WATTOT90LN	40.934 (10.26)***	40.611 (11.56)***	42.195 (10.51)***	42.42 (12.13)***	42.253 (10.46)***	42.426 (12.00)***	42.431 (10.35)***	43.344 (11.80)***
GDPCAPLN	1.632 (0.97)	2.46 (1.65)	1.115 (0.64)	1.703 (1.12)	0.955 (0.46)	1.917 (1.13)	0.179 (0.10)	1.038 (0.64)
POPDENSLN	0.132 (0.23)	0.289 (0.45)	−0.175 (−0.29)	−0.069 (−0.11)	−0.151 (−0.25)	−0.094 (−0.14)	−0.613 (−0.94)	−0.423 (−0.59)
WATRESCAPLN	−0.032 (−0.07)	−0.076 (−0.14)	−0.083 (−0.18)	−0.043 (−0.08)	−0.021 (−0.04)	−0.109 (−0.18)	−0.058 (−0.13)	−0.027 (−0.05)
ETHNIC							−4.665 (−1.77)*	−4.653 (−1.17)
RULAW					0.420 (0.23)	−0.473 (−0.25)		
POLRIGHTS	1.11 (2.41)**	1.044 (1.97)*						
POLCON			12.884 (2.57)**	11.324 (2.23)**	12.361 (2.54)**	11.806 (2.10)**	12.918 (2.62)**	10.782 (2.13)**
INTERCEPT	−110.952 (−8.19)***	−116.319 (−11.49)***	−109.709 (−7.61)***	−115.835 (−11.14)***	−108.97 (−6.67)***	−117.219 (−10.67)***	−99.351 (−5.90)***	−110.789 (−8.32)***
N	69	69	68	68	68	68	67	67
$\bar{R}^2$	0.857		0.860		0.857		0.863	
F	52.80***	90.19***	49.08***	88.95***	48.08***	73.34***	44.07***	77.94***

[†]*t*-statistics in brackets. ***$p < 0.01$; **$p < 0.05$; *$p < 0.1$.
[#]Heteroscedasticity-robust standard errors (HRSE); [##]Robust regression (RR; command rreg in STATA).

The signs of the slope parameters of POPDENSLN (models W2, W3, W4) and WATRESCAPLN are not as expected: other things being equal, a higher population density and more water resources per capita lead to a lower coverage with water services in 2002.[47] However, the effects are far from being statistically significant. As with POPURB (share of urban population in total population), there is an alternative measure of the spatial population pattern available, models W1 to W4 have been re-estimated using POPURB instead of POPDENSLN. Nevertheless, results remained very similar.

As has been said (section 4.3.1), simultaneity can largely be ruled out thanks to the model specification chosen. However, it is still possible that the effect of POLRIGHTS (or POLCON) on WATTOT02 is due to a third variable that jointly determines both POLRIGHTS (or POLCON) and WATTOT02: economic growth. This was tested by adding the average growth rate (1990 to 2002) of GDP per capita to the model. The effect of the GDP per capita growth rate proved to be statistically not significant whereas the effect of POLRIGHTS (POLCON) remained largely the same (results not reported). The same holds for the case of sanitation, which is analysed in the following.

Reconsidering the Interpretation of the Political Governance Variables

As has been discussed, the effects of POLRIGHTS and POLCON are significantly positive when entered solely into the model (the same is true for POLITY and CHECKS—results not reported). When, however, POLRIGHTS and POLCON are plugged in pairs into the model, the effects on WATTOT02 are not significant any more for any of them. The signs of the slope parameters remain, nonetheless, positive, and the test for joint influence of POLRIGHTS and POLCON is significant ($p < 0.05$ when estimating with HRSE; $p < 0.1$ when estimating with RR). The same pattern holds for the case of sanitation services.

This phenomenon can be explained by the high correlation between POLRIGHTS and POLCON (see sub-section 4.2.3), which means that the two variables are not suited to capture two distinct effects when used in the same model. In other words, we are asking questions that seem to be too subtle for the available data to answer with precision (Wooldridge 2006, 102–104). From a theoretical point of view, it is useful to distinguish between the effect of democratic participation via free elections and the effect of the separation of powers or the number of veto players (see Chapter 3). However, when considering the available data, this distinction makes no sense: The available variables POLRIGHTS and POLCON (as well as POLITY and CHECKS) seem to measure more or less the same. Therefore, these variables should be considered as four alternative measures of one single concept that could be termed *"democratic participation cum separation of powers."*

4.3.2.2. *Political Governance and Coverage With Sanitation Services*

Results of the Baseline Regressions

From Table 4.3, it becomes evident that the baseline regressions of SAN-TOT02 yield results that are very similar to the water case as far as the historical coverage level (SANTOT90), political governance (POLRIGHTS, POLCON, RULAW), and ETHNIC are concerned. In all four models (S1 to S4) SANTOT90 has a highly significant ($p < 0.01$) positive effect on SANTOT02 (a change of one percentage point of SANTOT90 leads to an increase of approximately 0.8 percentage points of SANTOT02). The slope parameters of POLRIGHTS and POLCON are positive and statistically significant at $p < 0.05$. The effects of RULAW (positive) and ETHNIC (negative) are not statistically significant. The $\bar{R}^2$ is 0.905.[48]

As for the other independent variables, there are some differences. First of all, all slope parameters show the expected sign. Moreover, GDPCA-PLN has a higher influence on the dependent variable as compared to the water case but the effect is still small in economic terms (e.g. in model S1a a change of GDP per capita by 1% is related with an increase of SANTOT02 by approximately 0.036 percentage points). The statistical significance of this effect varies between the models (the extrema are model S1a: $p < 0.05$; and model S4: not significant at conventional levels). POPDENSLN shows a statistically significant positive effect (except for model S4b), whereas the effect of WATRESCAPLN (positive) is not significant at conventional levels. The relatively strong positive effect of the population density on SAN-TOT02 is somewhat surprising, especially as compared to the water case where the effect was slightly negative (but not significant). We will briefly return to this point in sub-section 4.3.2.4, when discussing the results of the regressions with regional dummy variables.

Interaction of Political Governance and GDP

In addition to the regressions previously discussed, an interaction effect between POLRIGHTS and GDPCAPLN has been tested. The hypothesis underlying this test is that the effect of *democratic participation cum separation of powers* on coverage may not be independent from the GDP per capita of a given country—as has been assumed in E4.2—but vary conditional on GDP per capita. An increase in democratic accountability in a low-income country may have a greater effect on coverage than in a middle-income country: Non-accountable governments in poor countries are likely to make a bad use of scarce financial resources with respect to the provision of WS services. An improvement in accountability may, thus, make a big difference for a poor country. This effect may become less strong the more financial resources per capita are available in an economy because, even if governments make a bad use of resources, on average there will be more

Table 4.3 Results of Regression Estimates (Baseline Models): Dependent Variable SANTOT02

Independent Variables	Coefficients and t-Statistics †							
	Model S1a	Model S1b##	Model S2a	Model S2b##	Model S3a	Model S3b##	Model S4a	Model S4b##
SANTOT90	0.825 (14.76)***	0.831 (14.14)***	0.814 (14.57)***	0.816 (13.92)***	0.814 (14.42)***	0.815 (13.76)***	0.819 (14.53)***	0.826 (14.21)***
GDPCAPLN	3.586 (2.11)**	3.333 (1.86)*	3.593 (2.13)**	3.488 (1.97)*	3.448 (1.89)*	3.356 (1.75)*	2.899 (1.54)	2.280 (1.17)
POPDENSLN	1.894 (2.81)***	2.017 (2.85)***	1.665 (2.43)**	1.725 (2.40)**	1.698 (2.40)**	1.758 (2.36)**	1.343 (1.71)*	1.262 (1.56)
WATRES-CAPLN	0.314 (0.53)	0.227 (0.37)	0.238 (0.40)	0.183 (0.29)	0.306 (0.45)	0.247 (0.35)	0.406 (0.66)	0.333 (0.53)
ETHNIC							−4.426 (−0.98)	−6.847 (−1.47)
RULAW					0.473 (0.22)	0.434 (0.19)		
POLRIGHTS	1.420 (2.34)**	1.546 (2.42)**						
POLCON			13.870 (2.39)**	14.526 (2.39)**	13.274 (2.06)**	13.926 (2.06)**	14.333 (2.45)**	15.766 (2.62)**
INTERCEPT	−26.374 (−2.17)**	−24.996 (−1.96)*	−22.528 (−1.80)*	−21.756 (−1.66)	−21.686 (−1.65)	−20.999 (−1.52)	−15.250 (−0.98)	−8.934 (−0.55)
N	69	69	68	68	68	68	67	67
$\bar{R}^2$	0.905		0.902		0.901		0.902	
F	130.81***	118.74***	124.84***	113.63***	102.45***	92.89***	101.76***	96.30***

†t-statistics in brackets. ***$p < 0.01$; **$p < 0.05$; *$p < 0.1$.
##Robust regression (RR) (command rreg in STATA).

resources left that can be invested in WS. This effect can be modelled by including an interaction term $(GOV_j*GDPCAPLN)$ into the equation:

$$COV02_i = \beta_0 + \beta_1 COV90_i + \beta_2 GOV_{j,i} + \beta_3 GDPCAPLN_i + \beta_4 GOV_{j,i}*GDPCAPLN_i + U_i \qquad (E4.3)$$
$$(i = 1,\ldots m; j = 1,\ldots n)$$

In E4.3, the total effect of GOV_j on COV02 is: $\beta_2 + \beta_4 GDPCAPLN$ (for convenience the vector CON_j of the additional control variables is omitted in E4.3).

Adding the interaction term to the baseline models previously discussed yields some interesting results for the case of sanitation (results are reported just for POLRIGHTS[49]).

The total effect of *democratic participation cum separation of powers* is significant at $p < 0.01$ (test of joint influence of POLRIGHTS and POLRIGHTS*GDPCAPLN). The slope parameter of the interaction term is negative, which means that the positive effect of POLRIGHTS on SANTOT02 is more pronounced the lower GDP per capita. The total effect of POLRIGHTS on SANTOT02 $(\beta_2 + \beta_4 GDPCAPLN)$ has been calculated by evaluating E4.3 at three interesting values of GDPCAPLN: the lower quartile, the mean, and the upper quartile.[50] It is greatest for the lower quartile of GDPCAPLN (3.552) and smallest for the upper quartile of GDPCAPLN (0.148).[51]

As for the water case, adding an interaction term to the baseline models yields no statistically significant robust results.

Preliminary Conclusions

The preliminary conclusions from the baseline models discussed so far are:

- The suppositions formulated in sub-section 4.2.1 are too subtle for the available data. The political governance variables of major interest (POLRIGHTS, POLITY, POLCON, CHECKS) are not suited to separate the effects of democratic participation on the one hand and separation of powers (veto players) on the other hand. They are best interpreted as alternative measures for one single concept *democratic participation cum separation of powers*.
- The results support, on a statistically significant level, the supposition that stronger *democratic participation cum separation of powers* is positively related with water and sanitation service coverage expansion.
- For coverage with sanitation services, the results support on a statistically significant level the supposition that this relation is strongest when GDP per capita in a given country is low and becomes weaker with increasing GDP per capita.
- There is no evidence that the effect of *democratic participation cum separation of powers* depends on the level of rule of law or on the separation of purpose among elected officials (the latter being measured by approximation by the degree of ethno-linguistic fractionalisation).

4.3.2.3. Controlling for Corruption, Security of Private Property Rights and PSP

From the econometric literature on economic growth (see literature review in 4.1) there is quite strong evidence that the security of private property rights and the control of corruption have positive effects on growth rates. These institutional factors may, therefore, also affect the expansion of coverage with WS services. As explained, the variable RULAW, which partially measures security of private property rights, yielded no statistically significant results. In order to further check for the influence of corruption and security of private property rights, the variables CORRUPT[52] and PROPRIGHTS[53] are added to the models (the estimation results discussed in the following are not reported here).[54]

Plugging CORRUPT—which measures the degree of control of corruption—into the model, together with the core set of control variables, yields no statistically significant effect for CORRUPT. Combining CORRUPT with POLRIGHTS and the core set of control variables does not alter, markedly, the results of the baseline regressions. The influence of POLRIGHTS remains positive at the conventional levels of significance.[55]

One problem linked to the variable PROPRIGHTS is that, because of missing values for 13 countries contained in the sample, the degrees of freedom drop to a level that can be considered as critical. Therefore, the control variable WATRESCAPLN, which has not shown significant effects so far, is dropped from the model when testing PROPRIGHTS. The results of the reduced model and the reduced sample are comparable to the baseline regressions. Again, the slope parameters of POLRIGHTS stay positive at conventional levels of significance.[56] However, in the water case, this effect is sensitive to influential data points. The effects of PROPRIGHTS are far from being statistically significant.

In addition, the effect of PSP in the WS sector was tested, which proved to be insignificant in any chosen specification. It was analysed both the influence of the total volume (1990 to 2002) of investments with PSP in the WS sector as well as the influence of per capita investments.[57] One problem is that the available data on PSP in the WS sector from the PPI Database provided by the World Bank and PPIAF presents many missing values (47) for the countries contained in the sample. Therefore, this finding should not be overinterpreted.

4.3.2.4. Controlling for Region-Specific Effects

In order to further check the sensitivity of the results, regional dummy variables[58] that capture region-specific effects have been introduced into the models (the estimations are not reported here).[59] In the case of sanitation, the results are very clear. The two variables that show statistically significant and robust effects are SUBSAFRICA (Sub-Sahara Africa: negative) and EASTSEASIA (Eastern and Southeast Asia: positive). Regional dummies were plugged into the baseline models first solely, and then by pairs. In all cases, the two regional dummies mentioned show significant effects. The influence of the four political governance variables measuring *democratic participation cum separation of powers* (POLRIGHTS, POL-CON, POLITY, CHECKS) remains positive on a statistically significant level. The positive effect of POPDENSLN, which was significant in the baseline models (S1 to S4; see table 4.3), loses significance after introducing regional dummy variables.

The fact that the influence of the two regional dummy variables is significant suggests that, although the baseline models control for economic, geographic, and demographic factors, they do not seem to capture important further influences that work in the specific regional contexts of Sub-Sahara Africa and Eastern and Southeast Asia. One possible explanation for the positive (EASTSEASIA) and negative (SUBSAFRICA) regional effects could be economic growth dynamics (average annual change of GDP per capita) that has differed markedly between these two regions during the period 1990–2002 (4.13% for Eastern and Southeast Asia versus 0.15% for Sub-Sahara Africa; regional averages for those countries included in the sample).[60] However, substituting GDPCAPLN for the average annual growth rate of GDP per capita does not change the results obtained in a substantial manner (regional dummy variables stay significant).

Plugging regional dummies into the baseline models for water services does not yield conclusive results.

4.4. CONCLUSIONS

This chapter has analysed the effect of political governance (focusing on democratic participation and separation of powers) on the coverage with (i) water and (ii) sanitation services, using a multivariate regression model and cross-sectional data from 69 developing countries. To the best knowledge of the author, this question has not been treated in econometric research literature so far. The following findings are highlighted:

- Results from the regressions show that there is a significant and surprisingly robust positive effect of higher levels of *democratic participation cum separation of powers* on coverage with both water and sanitation services.
- By contrast, results do not support the same for higher levels of rule of law.
- For the case of sanitation services, there is statistically significant evidence that the positive effect of democratic participation and separation of powers is strongest for countries with low GDP per capita, and becomes weaker the higher GDP per capita of a given country.

- No evidence was found that the effect of democratic participation and separation of powers depends on the (i) level of rule of law or on the (ii) degree of separation of purpose among officials (as measured by approximation by the degree of ethno-linguistic fractionalisation).
- The results do not change substantially when regional dummy variables are included in the regression in order to account for region-specific effects.
- The effect of PSP proved to be not statistically significant. However, this result could be biased, because the available data on PSP in the WS sectors of developing countries is rather incomplete.

The chapter concludes with two short remarks concerning the interpretation of the results. As the sample is restricted to developing countries with a coverage of less than 95% in 1990 (with both water supply and sanitation), so is the scope of the results, i.e., the results do not necessarily apply to industrialised countries with a higher WS service coverage. Moreover, although the data has been checked for plausibility, measurement errors can not be precluded. In case the data should be plagued with measurement errors, estimations reported in this chapter are likely to be distorted.

5 The Role of Governance and Private Sector Participation for the Provision of Water and Sanitation Services
Case Study on Colombia

This second empirical chapter gives up the bird's eye perspective of the preceding chapter and plunges deeper into the complexity of the real world. It does so by investigating the role of governance and PSP for the provision of WS services in Colombia. The chapter has two complementary purposes:

i. To apply the framework developed in Chapters 2 and 3 to Colombia in order to describe and assess the key elements of political governance (section 5.2), WS governance (section 5.3) and WS policies (section 5.4)—this way laying the foundations for the second purpose;
ii. To explore the sources of sub-national variation in WS service provider performance by focusing on two different explanatory factors: PSP and local governance.
   a. Section 5.5 analyses whether the variation in provider performance can be explained by the variation in the delivery model (PSP versus purely public). It performs a quantitative analysis based on a data set comprising 30 Colombian providers.
   b. Section 5.6 analyses whether provider performance is influenced by the quality of local governance. It performs an in-depth qualitative comparison of the four cities of Manizales, Santa Marta, Tunja, and Villavicencio.

By exploring both, the influence of local governance and of PSP on the performance of WS services, I expect the reader to learn more about the relation between these two factors and about how they affect the different dimensions of service performance.

Before starting with the main investigation, the following introduction to Chapter 5 explains the motivation for choosing Colombia as subject of investigation (5.1.1). Moreover, in order to set the context for the subsequent analysis, it gives a brief overview of the overall WS service situation in Colombia (5.1.2). Finally, it describes the further procedure of this chapter, as well as the methodology followed (5.1.3).

5.1. INTRODUCTION

5.1.1. Motivation for Performing a Case Study on Colombia

This case study on Colombia is an important complement to the cross-country regression in Chapter 4 for several reasons.

First, cross-country regressions rely on aggregate national data and the results are, therefore, applicable to the national level only. Thanks to the evidence obtained in Chapter 4, we know that countries with higher national levels of democracy show a higher average coverage with WS services than countries with lower national levels of democracy. This is highly valuable information that underscores the importance of democracy for human development. However, the results do not necessarily apply to the sub-national level. It cannot be taken for granted that the sub-national variation in service performance of a given country can be explained by differences in the quality of sub-national political governance. Empirical evidence about the determinants of sub-national variation in service performance is crucial for WS policy, if coverage gaps and low quality services in certain regions are to be overcome. In order to analyse this question, it is necessary to perform country studies.

Second, due to data restrictions, the influence of WS governance on service performance could not be investigated in Chapter 4, and the analysis had to concentrate on access to services, neglecting the aspect of efficiency. The heuristic framework developed in Chapters 2 and 3 postulates that access to and (allocative and internal) efficiency of services depend on a whole set of factors, including the quality of political governance, of WS governance, and of WS roles (see Figure 3.2). A country study offers the possibility to dig deeper into these postulated causality mechanisms and to gain information about their empirical plausibility.

Third, the complementary research question of this study—the influence of PSP on service performance—could not be addressed in a wholly satisfactorily manner in Chapter 4, because the available data on PSP in the WS sectors of developing countries is rather incomplete. Therefore, it is necessary to select a country for the case study that offers PSP, as well as purely public delivery models, in order to be able to analyse the influence of PSP on service performance and to assess its interaction with governance features.

Colombia is very well suited as the subject of a case study for the first and the third reason given. The country is characterised by a political and administrative decentralisation. Citizens elect their local governments, which are responsible, among other things, for the provision of WS services. This decentralised structure enhances differences in local governance that could explain the sub-national variation in service performance. Moreover, thanks to the wave of PSP in infrastructure that began to spread over Latin America since around 1990, and that also reached Colombia in the early 1990s, PSP in the WS service industry is in a relatively advanced stage in Colombia, as compared to many other developing countries.[1] Within a unified regulatory and legal framework, one can find a diversity of delivery models in Colombian cities, including PSP and purely public delivery models. This makes it possible to consider both the delivery model and the quality of local governance when attempting to explain the variation in the performance of Colombian WS service providers.

5.1.2. Overview of the Overall WS Service Situation in Colombia

5.1.2.1. Coverage With WS Services

Table 5.1 presents total, urban, and rural coverage levels for Colombia. It can be seen that total coverage has been considerably expanded from 79.7% (water)[2] and 73.2% (sanitation) respectively in 1993 to 90% (water) and 82% (sanitation) respectively in 2003. Another thing that becomes evident from the table is that coverage levels in rural areas in 2003 are still well below those in urban areas. The coverage gap between rural and urban areas in the case of water services has been reduced, as compared to 1993. By contrast, in the case of sanitation services it has slightly widened, not least thanks to the huge increase in coverage with urban sewerage services

Table 5.1   Colombia–Coverage With Water and Sanitation Services 1993–2003

Type of Service	1993 (Share of Population Served)	2003 (Share of Population Served)	New Beneficiaries 1993–2003 (Million Habit.)	Increase in Population Served
Urban				
Piped water	94.6%	97.4%	6.7	2.8%
Sewerage	81.8%	90.2%	7.7	8.4%
Rural				
Piped water and other improved technologies*	41.1%	66.0%	3.4	24.9%
Sewerage and on-site technologies	50.8%	57.9%	1.3	7.1%
Total				
Piped water and other improved technologies	79.7%**	90.0%	10.1	10.3%
Sewerage and on-site technologies	73.2%	82.0%	9.0	8.8%

Source: Departamento Nacional de Planeación (2005d, 3) based on the 1993 census and the 2003 household survey by the National Statistics Department (DANE).
*Wells, cisterns and public standpipes.
**Includes piped water only; information not available for other types of technologies.

(90.2% in 2003 as compared to 81.8% in 1993). Concerning the number of new beneficiaries between 1993 and 2003 (19.1 million in total), 14.4 million corresponded to urban population and 4.7 million to rural population. Of those households who were lacking access to improved water services in 2003 (approximately 4.5 million persons),[3] 86.5% lived in rural areas and 13.5% in urban areas (Meléndez 2004, 51).

Coverage with WS services varies with household income. Table A5.1 (appendix) presents coverage levels with improved water and improved sanitation services for the year 2003 by income quintiles and by rural, urban, and total areas. On the aggregate level (total of rural and urban areas), there are considerable differences between households belonging to the lowest income quintile (water: 83.5%; sanitation: 83%) and those belonging to the highest income quintile (water: 96.8%; sanitation: 99.1%). When looking at the disaggregate figures for rural and urban areas only, it becomes evident that variance of coverage levels is high in rural areas (lowest income quintile: 62.7% and 63.4%; highest income quintile: 72.4% and 88.6% for water and sanitation respectively) and relatively low in urban areas (lowest income quintile: 97.5% and 96.2%; highest income quintile: 98.3% and 99.8% for water and sanitation respectively).

All in all, it can be stated that coverage levels have evolved positively during the last decade. Considerable coverage gaps persist in rural areas, especially among low-income households.

5.1.2.2. Service Quality

The coverage figures previously presented are not corrected for deficiencies in service quality, like frequent service interruptions or the delivery of contaminated or polluted water and, thus, give only a partial picture of the service situation.

Continuity

According to the available data, the continuity of water services seems to be guaranteed in the major Colombian cities. For the year 2000, Superintendencia de Servicios Públicos Domiciliarios (SSPD; 2002, 53) reports an average continuity of 90% (sample of 42 providers). The continuity of services roughly decreases with the size of the city:

- Cities above 600,000 habitants: 100%;
- Cities between 100,000 and 600,000 habitants: 97%; and
- Cities between 50,000 and 100,000 habitants 77%.[4]

This pattern is confirmed by a recent study for the year 2005 (SSPD 2006, section 5.3.2). There are, however, notable exceptions to the rule that users from bigger cities enjoy more continuous water services. The *Empresa*

Industrial y Comercial from Cúcuta, the sixth biggest Colombian city with more than 700,000 habitants, in 2005 presented a continuity of 43.75% only, which, on average, corresponds to 10.5 hours per day.

Drinking Water Quality

The standards for drinking water quality that every WS service provider has to meet are defined in *Decreto No. 475* (Ministerio de Salud 1998). These standards refer to the physical, chemical, and microbiologic parameters of the water delivered, and set thresholds below which water is considered not suitable for human consumption.

Based on the data reported by the provincial and district health authorities, SSPD (2006, Chapter 6) informs that in 2005, in 64% of the districts for which information was available (312 in total), the water delivered did not meet the legal standards. Similar to the situation with respect to service continuity, drinking water quality is, in general, lower in smaller districts. Because the bulk of the population is concentrated in big districts with typically higher levels of drinking water quality, the share of the population that received water considered not suitable for human consumption was "only" 32% (total sample size: 28,500,787, which corresponds to the population of the 312 districts for which information was available).[5]

5.1.2.3. Internal Efficiency Indicators

Common indicators for the internal efficiency of WS service providers used by the Colombian regulatory authorities are the following:

- Share of unaccounted-for water[6] (UFW), which is defined as:

   UFW = (WP—WB) / WP   (E5.1)

   [WP = amount of drinking water produced (m³); WB = amount of drinking water billed (m³)]

- Collection rate (CR), which is defined as:

   CR = CL / BL   (E5.2)

   [CL = amount of money collected from customers ($); BL = amount of money billed to customers ($)]

Average UFW in Colombia has remained on a high level, as compared to the national standard set by the Regulatory Commission for Water and Sanitation (*Comisión de Regulación de Agua Potable y Saneamiento Básico–CRA*), which is 30%.[7] According to the data presented by Fernández (2004, 36), average UFW has not improved between 1990 (40.6%) and 2001 (40.3%).[8] The information for 2001 is largely confirmed by Domínguez Torres and Uribe Botero (2005, 55), who report an average UFW of 39.43%,[9] and by SSPD (2002, 57), who reports 43%.[10] According to a recent publication by

SSPD (2006, section 5.3.1), UFW in 2005 was 39% on average for the three major providers, 51% for a sample of 7 big to intermediate providers, and 53% for a sample of 19 intermediate providers.

Just like UFW, CR is one of the indicators defined by CRA in order to assess the internal efficiency of WS service providers. According to the data presented by Fernández (2004, 99–100), the CR (water services) for a sample of service providers from big and intermediate cities in 2001 was on average 80.9% (in 2002, 85.7%).[11] However, CR varies largely among WS service providers. Some firms show a CR of (close to) 100%, and others show a CR of below 60%. CR and UFW of Colombian WS service providers are investigated in more detail in section 5.5 when assessing the influence of PSP on the internal efficiency of providers.

All in all, with respect to service quality and internal efficiency indicators, it can be stated that there persist major deficiencies, particularly in smaller and rural districts. The concentration of deficiencies regarding service quality in smaller districts could be related to the atomised industry structure[12] (on the industry structure see sub-section 5.3.4). Moreover, it is especially remarkable that average UFW has not improved since 1990, and that even the major providers show relatively high water losses. This could be related to the fact that regulation until 2005 did provide only very weak incentives to improve internal efficiency (for more details see subsections 5.4.1 and 5.4.5).

The types of delivery models existing in the Colombian WS service industry with an emphasis on the scope of PSP are described in detail in subsection 5.3.4.

5.1.3. Procedure and Methodology

The procedure followed in this chapter results from the two complementary purposes previously stated. Sections 5.2 to 5.4 serve the first purpose, i.e., to describe and assess the key factors on the national or sectoral level that according to the framework developed in Chapters 2 and 3 affect service delivery that takes place at the local level. The perspective taken in this first step is a national or sector-wide perspective. In detail, the following dimensions are described and assessed:

- Key elements of the political governance, i.e., main actors and institutions of the policy-making process (section 5.2);
- Key elements of WS governance, i.e., horizontal and vertical articulation (including user participation), institutional design of regulation and institutional design of service delivery (section 5.3); and
- Key elements of the regulatory, subsidy, and public investment policies (section 5.4).

The main sources of information used in this first step are academic papers and policy papers (mainly produced by government organisations), as well as, in part, the interviews[13] conducted by the author with government organisations, experts, service providers, and user representatives in Bogotá and the four provincial capitals of Manizales, Santa Marta, Tunja, and Villavicencio in June and July 2005.

This first step lays the foundations for the second purpose (sections 5.5 and 5.6), which is to explore the sources of sub-national variation in WS service provider performance by focusing on two different explanatory factors: PSP and the quality of local governance. This is done in two steps, using both quantitative and qualitative empirical approaches.[14]

- The quantitative analysis in section 5.5 focuses on capturing the effect of the delivery model (PSP versus purely public) on internal efficiency and coverage with WS services. It uses a data set that comprises 30 urban WS service providers from 30 districts and contains cross-sectional data for the years 1998 to 2003. The procedure applied is a multivariate regression analysis. The dataset has the drawback that it does not include data on local governance because comprehensive and reliable information on governance characteristics is not available for the local level. Therefore, the influence of the quality of local governance on provider performance cannot be analysed by quantitative means.
- The qualitative analysis in section 5.6 attempts to capture the influence of local governance factors on WS service performance while "controlling" for the effect of PSP. The main portion of the information used was gained in the interviews previously mentioned. The centrepiece is a comparison of the WS service providers of the four provincial capitals of Manizales, Santa Marta, Tunja, and Villavicencio. These four cases were purposefully selected so that they were compatible with the main supposition that local governance factors can dominate the expected positive effects of PSP on internal efficiency, and thus contribute to explaining well performing public delivery models, as well as badly performing PSP delivery models.

The methodological details regarding the two empirical approaches are explained in the respective sections 5.5 and 5.6.

5.2. BRIEF HISTORY AND KEY FEATURES OF POLITICAL GOVERNANCE

5.2.1. Brief Political and Economic History

Although this is a sweeping simplification, it is reasonable to say that recent Colombian political and economic history is marked by a turning point in the late 1980s and early 1990s. This turning point is characterised by three major reforms (Edwards and Steiner 2000; Cárdenas, Junguito, and Pachón 2006):

- The initiation of the decentralisation process in 1986;
- The enactment of the new Constitution in 1991; and
- The implementation of market-oriented economic reforms, including trade liberalisation, between 1989 and 1991.

5.2.1.1. Political Context of the Reform Period

Although Colombia showed quite a remarkable macroeconomic stability during and before this reform period (at least as compared to many other Latin American countries[15]), the country was undergoing a political and institutional crisis in the late 1980s (Edwards and Steiner 2000, 461–65; Cárdenas, Junguito, and Pachón 2006, 8–11):

In 1958, as a reaction to one decade of political violence between the two traditional parties (Liberal Party and Conservative Party), the parties' leaders agreed to share government power. This agreement considerably restricted the competitiveness of democratic elections. The period of power sharing, the so-called *Frente Nacional*, lasted formally from 1958 to 1974. However, many elements of the logic of power sharing between the Liberal and the Conservative Party remained in place even after the formal end of the agreement. One consequence of the *Frente Nacional* was the exclusion of the left from the political process. Thanks to the exclusionary nature of the system and the lack of authority of the state in some regions of the country, guerilla groups and social movements gained momentum, and the popular support of the two traditional parties eroded, as became evident from high rates of abstention. The growth of drug trafficking activities in the 1980s went hand-in-hand with an escalation of the crisis at the end of that decade. Figure A5.1 (appendix) depicts the evolution of the Political Rights and Civil Liberties Indexes (Freedom House), which both show a trend to deteriorate. The level of violence increased steeply[16] and the political system further lost credibility due to the entrance of drug money into the political process, to patronage and corruption. After the assassination of three presidential candidates in 1989, the idea of a Constitutional Assembly in order to reform the political system and to enhance broader popular participation gained support. After a positive referendum and the election of a Constituent Assembly, the new Constitution was adopted on 4 July 1991. The adoption of the Constitution did, however, not halt drug trafficking or guerilla and paramilitary groups[17] operations (in what follows, guerrilla and paramilitary groups are referred to as *non-state armed groups*).

The Constitution of 1991 contains two elements that shape governance structures with respect to the provision of WS services and which are going to be further discussed in this chapter:

   i. Comprehensive administrative and political decentralisation; and
  ii. The groundwork of a public services regime based on the principles of equity, efficiency and PSP.

The bulk of the market-oriented economic reforms were implemented at the beginning of the administration of President César Gaviria, who in 1990 had comfortably won the presidential elections. This success in the presidential elections and the fact that 87% of the voters had approved the convening of the Constituent Assembly, provided the new President with a major mandate for change. Gaviria used the window of opportunity (reform mood prevalent; high popular support of the President; discredited Congress; public attention focused on the *political* reforms and on the government's negotiations with the guerrilla and the drug cartels) to pass a broad *economic* reform programme through Congress: foreign exchange statute, financial sector, tax, and labour reform. In addition, trade liberalisation was enhanced through presidential decrees.

5.2.1.2. Macroeconomic Performance Before and After the Reform Period

Cárdenas, Junguito, and Pachón (2006) call attention to the change in behaviour of macroeconomic indicators since the reform period and analyse the relation between this change in behaviour and the new rules of the political game prevalent since the enactment of the Constitution in 1991. Figure 5.1 shows the evolution of government deficit, government consumption expenditure, real GDP growth rate, and inflation rate between 1980 and 2003. It becomes evident that government deficit and government consumption expenditure show a clear trend to increase since 1991 (the "small" peak of the central government deficit between 1982 and 1984 can

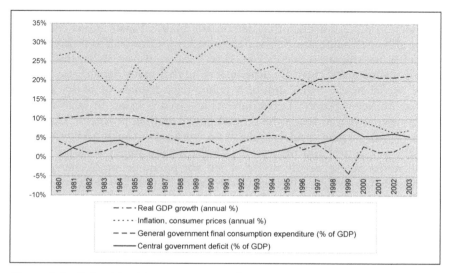

Figure 5.1 Colombia: Macroeconomic indicators 1980 to 2003. Sources: World Development Indicators 2005, World Bank (CD-ROM); Departamento Nacional de Planeación (www.dnp.gov.co, accessed October 13, 2006).

be explained by the Latin American debt crisis, which affected Colombia much less than other countries of the region[18]). At the same time, GDP growth has been, on average, lower and more volatile since the mid-1990s, showing a remarkable recession in 1999. The inflation rate, finally, shows a clear tendency to fall since 1991.

The 1991 Constitution includes very detailed rules concerning key components of public expenditures, above all earmarked fiscal transfers from the central government to sub-national governments for public services, such as education, health, and WS services (see sub-section 5.4.3). According to Cárdenas, Junguito, and Pachón (2006, 5–8) the structural fiscal deficit since the mid-1990s is related to this "hard-wiring" of public expenditures in the Constitution, which provides the central government with little flexibility to adapt fiscal policy to changes in macroeconomic conditions. In particular, the structural deficit restricts the adoption of a countercyclical fiscal policy. This fact may partially explain the severity of the recession in 1999. Changing public expenditure rules is very hard, because it involves a high number of effective vetoes: (i) changes require a Constitutional amendment; (ii) sub-national governments typically will oppose a reduction or flexibilisation of fiscal transfers. According to the data made available on-line by the National Planning Department (*Departamento Nacional de Planeación*–DNP),[19] transfers from the central government to subnational governments have increased from around 30% (in 1990) to around 40% (in 2002) of total central government receipts.

5.2.2. Key Features of the Policy-Making Process

Sub-section 3.2.2.1 argued that democratic political institutions compared favourably with autocratic political institutions with respect to their effect on the public-regardedness of policy making. It did, however, also mention that, among democracies, there are differences and that many democratic regimes show "deficiencies"[20] that diminish public-regardedness of policy making and commitment power of governments to given policies. In what follows, the key elements that shape the general policy-making process in Colombia are reviewed, putting special emphasis on working out such "deficiencies."

First, key actors and institutions of the formal policy-making process on the national level are discussed. Then, the phenomenon of clientelism is addressed, followed by a brief characterisation of political decentralisation. Finally, some conclusions are drawn.

5.2.2.1. Key Actors and Institutions of the Policy-Making Process[21]

Key actors of the formal policy-making process on the national level addressed in the following are the President, the Constitutional Court (*Corte Constitucional*), the bicameral Congress (consisting of the Senate—*Senado*—and House of Representatives—*Cámara de Representantes*), the political parties, the technocracy, and civil society organisations.

As is typical for presidential systems, the *President* of Colombia—who is both head of the state and chief executive—is the main agenda-setter in most policy areas. Although the 1991 Constitution reduced the presidential powers in a number of dimensions, the President is provided with powers that make him *the* proactive force in the Colombian policy-making process, e.g. he can use extraordinary legislative powers by declaring (for a predetermined limited period in time) a state of internal commotion or of economic emergency.[22] However, the Constitutional Court may revoke the presidential decrees issued during that period (including the declaration of commotion or emergency) if they are deemed unconstitutional. Further noteworthy powers of the President are (i) the control over the Congress agenda using the discharge or urgency petition, (ii) the exclusive right to introduce bills concerning some important policy areas (e.g. salaries of public employees, national budget), and (iii) the right to veto legislation (which, however, can be overrun by Congress with a simple majority). The president is directly elected in national elections for a four-year office term (majority run-off rule). Since the constitutional amendment achieved by the President Álvaro Uribe in 2004, the President can be re-elected for consecutive terms.

As has become evident, the presidential powers are checked by the Constitutional Court and the Congress. The *Constitutional Court* is considered an important veto player in the Colombian policy-making process since its creation in 1991. This is due to its extensive powers to review important statutes, treaties and bills (Cárdenas, Junguito, and Pachón 2006, 24–25). Since 1991, the Constitutional Court has issued 2,923 rulings, the majority of which have resulted from citizens' use of their right to demand a constitutional review (*acción pública de inconstitucionalidad*). The powers of the Constitutional Court are further enhanced by the fact that many policy issues have been elevated to the constitutional rank through the 1991 Constitution. The nomination procedure grants the Constitutional Court a good degree of independence. The magistrates are elected by the Senate from lists presented by the President, the Supreme Court (*Corte Suprema*), and the High Administrative Court (*Consejo de Estado*), for an eight-year office term.

The Colombian *Congress* can be considered as being fragmented and showing a tendency to push private- rather than public-regarding policies (Kugler and Rosental 2000; Cárdenas, Junguito, and Pachón 2006, 17–23). This is related to (i) the candidate-centred electoral system and (ii) the characteristics of political party organisation.

i. Congress is made out of two symmetric chambers. Both senators and representatives are elected for a four-year office term. The electoral formula applied is one of largest remainders (or "Hare system") without representation thresholds.[23] This system contributes to a proliferation of lists that compete in congressional elections. The candidates from the bigger parties have incentives to fragment into various factions with separate lists, because this enhances their chance to win a seat. This system encourages the election of candidates who have either narrow geographical bases or narrow special interest bases (Kugler and Rosental 2000, 14) and makes it hard for the government to push public-regarding policies (see the discussion of candidate-centred electoral systems in sub-section 3.2.2.1). Candidate-centredness is further reinforced by state electoral campaign funding that is given directly to candidates (and not to the parties), as well as by the tradition of clientelism in Colombia (see the following).

ii. Although the party structure is still marked by the two traditional parties (Liberal Party and Conservative Party), there is a high degree of intra-party competition or factionalisation within these two parties (there are several "movements" that compete in elections with separate lists). In general, there is a trend to an increasing fragmentation of the party structure, which several analysts attribute to (i) the electoral system described previously, in combination with (ii) political decentralisation (see the following). "The degree of fragmentation has increased largely because regional and local political machines do not require centralized political parties, and parties no longer have the means to control the career paths of their local leaders in the local areas" (Cárdenas, Junguito, and Pachón 2006, 21). This means that the political parties in Colombia manage only partially to aggregate the preferences of elected legislators in Congress (i.e., to achieve a certain degree of "unity of purpose"—see sub-section 3.2.2.1).

According to various analysts, *technocrats*[24]—who are typically not directly linked to a political party—have had some influence on policy formulation in the economic policy areas (Edwards and Steiner 2000, 458–61; Cárdenas, Junguito, and Pachón 2006, 25–26). Important organisations or actors shaped by the technocracy are the Ministry of Finance, the National Planning Department (DNP)—the head of which has a cabinet level position—and the Central Bank.

The 1991 Constitution defines the Colombian state as "democratic, participative and pluralist" (Asamblea Nacional Constituyente 1991, article 1). Accordingly, it includes several formal institutions for the participation of citizens and the civil society. Concerning participation via elected representatives, the most important element that complements national elections are sub-national elections (see political decentralisation in the following). In addition, the Constitution and further legislation define a whole set of mechanisms for direct participation in (i) political decision making (e.g. referendums and plebiscites) and in (ii) controlling the activities of the public administration and the respect of the citizens' rights (e.g. right to demand a constitutional review—as explained previously, tutelary action—*acción de tutela*, civic oversight committees—*veedurías*; Departamento Administrativo de la Función Pública 2003). However, several analysts conclude that these mechanisms have not been widely used, and that civic participation remains limited in Colombia, among other things due to the rigidity of these mechanisms and to weaknesses in civil society organisation (Maldonado and Vargas Forero 2001, 288–93; Nickson 2001, 9–11; Transparencia por Colombia 2004, 65–70).

5.2.2.2. The Tradition of Clientelism

One prominently discussed issue in the Latin American context that is related to deficiencies in emerging democracies is the tradition of *clientelism*.[25] According to many scholars, the Colombian policy-making process has been clearly marked by clientelism.[26] Clientelism can very briefly be characterised as a vertically structured exchange relation between a politician (patron) and his electoral supporters (clients) in which the patron secures his political support by delivering particularistic benefits or private goods to its clients (instead of public goods that would benefit the broad majority of citizens; Wills Herrera 2002, 392; Robinson 2005, 8–9).

Consequently, clientelism typically diminishes public-regardedness of policy making: (i) particularistic benefits are allocated to rather narrow constituencies (the clients) and (ii) public goods are undersupplied. Keefer (2002) establishes a relation between clientelism and the ability of politicians to make credible commitments. The author argues that clientelism is a rationale strategy for politicians and voters in institutional environments in which candidates can make no credible pre-electoral promises to all voters. In such an institutional environment patrons—thanks to their personal ties to their clients and thanks to the particularistic benefits they offer—*can* make credible agreements with their clients.

Moreover, Keefer (2002, 26–27) argues that the relatively high level of corruption[27] in emerging democracies is linked to clientelism. The close relation between clientelism and corruption is confirmed by Wills Herrera (2002) in a study on Colombia.

The clientelistic system in Colombia has consequences for the local public administration (which is responsible for delivering WS services) and for public service providers (Nickson 2001, 7).[28] The case study literature reports that elected mayors (patrons) commonly use the posts in the public administration and in the service company to reward their clients. This practice implies frequent staff rotation in tandem with political leadership and prevents establishing a career civil service. Moreover, at the end of his office the incumbent mayor may target WS investments to those parts of the city where votes are most needed in order to provide support for its chosen successor (mayors cannot be re-elected). This renders a long-term investment planning unfeasible and, in the worst case, means that "white elephants" (i.e., unworkable infrastructure) are built instead of useful infrastructure. In this study, it is argued that the prevalence of such clientelistic interventions varies with the ownership of the provider (PSP delivery models make such interventions more difficult) and with the quality of local governance (transparency and participation in local administration also prevent clientelistic interventions).[29]

5.2.2.3. Political Decentralisation

Regarding the concept of decentralisation, the literature often distinguishes between political and administrative decentralisation (e.g. Departamento Nacional de Planeación 2002, 15–17):

- *Political decentralisation* means the transfer from the national government to sub-national entities of the rights (i) to elect their governments and (ii) to formulate and implement policies within the scope of their sub-national responsibility.
- *Administrative decentralisation* means the transfer from the national government to subnational entities of (i) functions (e.g. the provision of public services like WS), (ii) resources (the transfer of financial resources is often conceived as a separate dimension and termed *fiscal decentralisation*), and (iii) decision making power.

The Colombian state is characterised by both dimensions of decentralisation. The fundamental norms to this respect are fixed in the 1991 Constitution. The next section, 5.3, discusses, in some detail, the administrative decentralisation within the WS sector. Here, the political decentralisation is briefly touched.

The political decentralisation in Colombia comprises basically two sub-national levels (Departamento Nacional de Planeación 2005a, 63–74): (i) provinces (*departamentos*) and (ii) districts (*municipios*). In Colombia as of 2005, there existed 32 provinces and 1,098 districts (see the map in Figure A5.5 for the Colombian provinces). At the provincial level, citizens directly elect the governor (*gobernador*) and the representatives of the provincial assembly (*asamblea departamental*). At the district level, citizens directly elect the mayor (*alcalde*) and the representatives of the district council (*concejo municipal*). The Constitution of 1991 (Asamblea Nacional Constituyente 1991, article 311) defines the districts as the "fundamental territorial entities" of the sub-national division. Mayors and representatives of the district assemblies are elected for four-year office terms. Unlike district council members, mayors cannot be re-elected for consecutive terms. Among other things, the district governments have the responsibilities

- to deliver WS and other public services with an emphasis on eliminating unsatisfied needs,
- to further local development via territorial planning and investment in local infrastructure, and
- to promote the participation of citizens.

In addition, democratic participation via representation can occur on a sub-district level. District governments can further subdivide their territory (into so-called *comunas* in urban areas and so-called *corregimientos* in rural areas). Citizens in *comunas* and *corregimientos* elect Local Administrative

Councils (*Juntas Administradoras Locales*)[30] that carry out administrative functions delegated by the district government and that shall participate in the enhancement of local economic and social development.

5.2.2.3. Conclusions

In conclusion from the review above the following general "deficiencies" that affect the political governance in Colombia shall be highlighted:

- Until the 1980s, democratic participation was restricted to a certain degree due to the agreement between the two traditional parties to share government power (*Frente Nacional*), which limited competitiveness and plurality of the political process. This restriction has been overcome at the latest with the 1991 Constitution that enhanced competitiveness and plurality.
- Since the 1980s, democratic participation has become, to a certain degree, restricted due to periodical escalations of the armed conflicts amongst non-state armed groups and between non-state armed groups and the state security forces. In this context, civilian authorities have not always managed to effectively control state security forces that, in some instances, have acted in violation of state policy (United States Department of State 2006). This general situation has had negative consequences for civil liberties (e.g. intimidation and homicide of journalists and members of civic organisations) and political rights (e.g. intimidation and homicides of electoral candidates and workers' union leaders) as shown by the deterioration of the political rights and civil liberties indexes (see Figure A5.1), as well as by the deterioration of the freedom of the press index.[31]
- In addition, corruption is considered to be endemic in Colombia in both the public and the private sector (Wills Herrera 2002; United States Department of State 2006). Figure A5.2 (appendix) shows the evolution of the corruption perception index (Transparency International). In 2005, according to that index, Colombia occupied rank 55 (out of 158 countries).
- Some elements of the political governance (candidate-centred electoral system, tradition of clientelism) suggest that policy making is biased towards private-regardedness, rather than towards public-regardedness.

5.3. KEY FEATURES OF WS GOVERNANCE

Two major reforms have shaped the governance structure of the Colombian WS sector in the recent past: (i) Administrative decentralisation and (ii) public utilities reform (Maldonado and Vargas Forero 2001; Fernández 2004):

i. Through the decentralisation process—initiated in 1986 and enhanced by the 1991 Constitution—the responsibility for WS service delivery and the ownership of infrastructure assets were transferred to districts. Before, there had been a mixed responsibility: The major cities typically had been served by district-owned public enterprises and the remaining urban and rural areas by national government-owned providers managed by the National Institute for District Promotion (*Instituto Nacional de Fomento Municipal–INSFOPAL*).

ii. Based on the principles of a public services regime contained in the Constitution (Asamblea Nacional Constituyente 1991, articles 365 to 370), the Public Utilities Law (Congreso de Colombia 1994) introduced major institutional changes in the WS sector. The most important changes were (a) the establishment of regulatory agencies at the national level with the mandate to regulate tariffs and enhance competition, (b) the introduction of the principle of cost covering tariffs, (c) corporatisation of service providers and promotion of PSP, as well as (d) the creation of institutions for consumer participation. The Public Utilities Law confirmed (e) the principle of solidarity prescribing cross-subsidies between socio-economic groups and declaring the covering of unmet needs for WS services a priority.

The remaining sub-sections describe and briefly assess the key features of the Colombian WS governance: horizontal articulation of roles and actors (5.3.1), vertical articulation (5.3.2), institutional design of regulation (5.3.3) and institutional design of service delivery (5.3.4). For this purpose it is referred to the respective concepts developed in Chapter 3.

5.3.1. Horizontal Articulation of Roles and Actors

Table 5.2 shows the horizontal articulation (see subsection 3.2.3.1) of roles and actors in the Colombian WS sector. Thanks to administrative decentralisation, the three horizontal roles of (a) policy making, (b) regulation (and control),[32] and (c) service delivery are distributed among the three levels of territorial organisation: (i) nation, (ii) province, and (iii) district (Fernández 2004, 27–30).

5.3.1.1. Policy Making

i. The Ministry of Environment, Housing and Development (*Ministerio de Ambiente, Vivienda y Desarrollo Territorial–MAVDT*) is responsible for defining the national policies regarding WS service provision (e.g. institutional structure, national priorities, allocation of national funds, enhancement of PSP, technical assistance) as well

Table 5.2 Horizontal Articulation of Roles and Actors in the Colombian WS Sector

Role	Nation	Province	District
Policy making	Ministry of Environment, Housing and Development (MAVDT): *Strategic WS service policy; Allocation of national funds; Environmental policy*	Autonomous Regional Body (CAR): *Environmental policy*	Mayor / District council: *Urban planning; WS investment priorities; Ownership of assets; Allocation of district funds for investments and of user subsidies*
			Mayor: *Socio-economic stratification*
Regulation	Regulatory Commission for Water and Sanitation (CRA): *Economic regulation*	Autonomous Regional Body (CAR): *Environmental regulation*	
Control	Superintendency of Public Utility Services (SSPD): *Economic control*	Autonomous Regional Body (CAR): *Environmental control*	District health authority: *Health-related control of drinking water quality*
Service delivery		Provincial administration: *Technical assistance*; Provincial enterprise: *Service delivery (exception)*	District administration or District enterprise or Private enterprise: *Service delivery (rule)*

Source: Based on Fernández (2004, 28), modified by the author

as the national environmental policies. This task is partially complemented by the DNP, especially with respect to the allocation and monitoring of national funds.

ii. Within the legal and policy framework set on the national level, the Autonomous Regional Bodies (*Corporaciones Autónomas Regionales–CARs*)[33] set the policies regarding the water resource management of river basins. For this purpose, they dispose of own budgets and sources of revenues. Policy instruments that immediately affect WS service providers are permits and fees for water abstraction and waste water discharge.

iii. At the district level, it is the mayor (partially with approval of the district council) who is responsible for urban (and rural) planning, defining local WS investment priorities, deciding on the allocation of district funds and guaranteeing the subsidisation of households from low socio-economic groups. Moreover, he decides on the delivery model, i.e., whether services are delivered directly through the district administration, a public district-owned enterprise, or a PSP delivery model. In case of the former two delivery models, the mayor also appoints the manager and the board of directors and bears, thus, responsibility for important management decisions.

5.3.1.2. Regulation and Control

i. The economic regulation of WS services is accomplished by two national regulatory agencies. Colombia is a special case as compared to international practice because responsibility for economic regulation is split. The task of defining tariff and quality of service levels is done by CRA, whereas control and sanctioning is accomplished by SSPD.

ii. It is the CARs at the provincial level that are responsible for regulating and controlling the environmental policies set by themselves. This involves e.g. defining and monitoring discharge parameters and setting abstraction and discharge fees.

iii. Relying on the standards for drinking water quality defined by the Ministry of Social Protection (Ministerio de Protección Social), the district health authorities are responsible for controlling whether the water delivered by service providers meets these standards. Test results are reported to SSPD, which makes the national reporting of drinking water quality (SSPD 2005c, 8–9). Moreover, the mayor is responsible for classifying neighbourhoods into socio-economic groups (socio-economic stratification). Classification decides on whether a certain household will benefit from cross-subsidies or whether it will have to pay a surcharge (for more details on the cross-subsidy scheme, see section 5.4).

5.3.1.3. Service Delivery

i. The central state bears no direct responsibility for delivering WS services.

ii. Provinces play just a minor role in service delivery. Provincial administrations have created WS support units that provide technical assistance to districts. Moreover, three provincial enterprises (owned by provincial governments), that deliver WS services to various districts within their province have "survived" the decentralisation process (provinces of Caldas, Quindío, and Valle del Cauca).

iii. It is the districts that are responsible for delivering WS services to their citizens. This is done either directly through the district administration, a public district-owned enterprise, or a PSP delivery model.[34]

Besides the key actors listed in Table 5.2, there are some further noteworthy public actors responsible for upholding the rule of law within the public sector—including the WS sector: (i) The Procurator General (*Procurador General*),[35] through its regional and local offices, is responsible for controlling the respect for the Constitution and the laws, protecting the public interest against abuses from public officials, disciplinary control of public officials, and watching over the duly and effective functioning of public administration. (ii) The Auditor General (*Contralor General*) is responsible for the fiscal control of the funds of the Nation. This is a relevant function in the context discussed here, because the national budget is a substantial source of finance for the WS service industry, especially in smaller districts (see sub-section 5.4.3). Provincial and district auditors accomplish the same function, but with respect to provincial funds and district funds (Departamento Nacional de Planeación 2005a, 53–58).

In general, it can be said that the institutional design of the WS sector respects, to some degree, the principle of horizontal separation of roles. However, the separation of roles is absent or weak at the district level in case of public service delivery. More details regarding the institutions that govern regulation and service delivery are addressed in the sub-sections on institutional design of regulation (5.3.3) and institutional design of service delivery (5.3.4).

5.3.2. Vertical Articulation: User Participation

There are only few academic and policy papers available that treat user participation in WS services in Colombia. Therefore, the information gained in interviews with user representatives and experts is rather important for this sub-section.

5.3.2.1. Main Organisations and Institutions of User Participation

Committees for Social Development and Control

In the same tenor of the formal mechanisms for civic participation included in the Constitution, the Public Services Law (Congreso de Colombia 1994, articles 62 to 66) defines, in some detail, the mechanisms for user participation in public services.[36] The main vehicle for user participation—which was newly created by the law—are the Committees for Social Development and Control (*Comités de Desarrollo y Control Social; CDCSs*). CDCSs are formed via a constituent assembly of (actual and potential) public services users. The constituent assembly elects the members of the CDCS (minimum number of members: 50; in the case of Bogotá, 200) and a spokesman (*Vocal de Control*) who represents the CDCS. In every district there has to exist at least one CDCS. The election of the CDCS and of the spokesman has to be recognised by the mayor and is notified to the local service provider and to SSPD. The main functions of the CDCS and the spokesman according to legislation are the following (SSPD 2004c; SSPD 2004d):

- Facilitate the exchange of information between service users and the service provider, represent the interests of the users and make propositions to the service provider how to improve services;
- Support the users in the exercise of their consumer rights and regarding complaint procedures;
- Monitor the decisions taken by the Committee for Stratification (*Comité Permanente de Estratificación*; CPE); the CPE is responsible for reviewing and monitoring the classification of neighbourhoods into socio-economic strata carried out by the mayor;
- Monitor the delivery of the subsidies the district provides to users from low socio-economic strata;
- Spokesman: Be a member of the board of directors of district-owned service providers (so-called *Empresas Industriales y Comerciales del Estado*; EICEs) and of the CPE, provided he is appointed by the mayor among the eligible user representatives.[37]

Spokesmen are not remunerated and they and their family members are not allowed to be employees of (or maintain a contractual relationship with) the service provider they monitor or the national regulatory agencies (SSPD, CRA).

According to an empirical investigation, by the year 2000 there existed active CDCSs in just 40% of the districts (Maldonado and Vargas Forero 2001, 291). Buitrago Restrepo (2001) and Consumidores Colombia (2005) point at the barriers that exist for creating a CDCS: (i) many users and local leaders do not know about their right to form a CDCS and (ii) the creation is a quite complicated and bureaucratic act. In the recent past, SSPD has put emphasis on providing information (e.g. brochures and manuals) and pro-actively encouraging the formation of CDCSs through workshops. According to SSPD,[38] by 2005 there existed 632 CDCSs covering WS services.

Others

Besides the formal mechanism of user participation via CDCSs introduced by the Public Services Law, participation of users in service delivery (e.g. exchange of information, user education, coordination of construction activities, settlement of disputes) occurs in practice also via other mechanisms.[39] These mechanisms build on the existing structures of civil society organisation, above all on the Committees for Community Action (*Juntas de Acción Comunal*; JACs). JACs are the most widespread form of local community organisations in Colombia.[40]

5.3.2.2. Assessment

The main area of the existing structures for user participation is clearly the *local level*:

- *Participation in services delivery* (relation users–local service provider): This is the main area of participation regulated in the law. With respect to the degrees of participation defined in sub-section 3.2.3.1 (consultation, representation, influence), it can be said that the emphasis lies on *consultation*. In practice, it seems that the bulk of work for spokesmen is to assist users in managing their complaints,[41] i.e., to carry out activities in the field of consumer protection. In the case of public district-owned service providers (EICEs) participation takes, in addition, the form of *representation* in the board of directors via the spokesmen.
- *Participation in local regulation* (relation users–local authorities engaged with regulatory functions regarding tariffs and subsidies): Although the main regulatory functions are carried out by the national agencies (CRA, SSPD), the mayor plays a certain role in this context. He is responsible for carrying out the socio-economic stratification and assuring the delivery of subsidies to low socio-economic strata:
  - o The stratification study—which is the basis for classifying neighbourhoods into socio-economic strata—has to use the methodology provided by the National Statistics Department (*Departamento Administrativo Nacional de Estadística*; DANE). This methodology is based on "objective" criteria related to the characteristics of the dwelling (Meléndez 2004, 25–26). The participation of users, via their representatives in the CPE, is limited to reviewing the application of the methodology and the results of the stratification study. Moreover, CPEs are the second instance for complaints against classification decisions (the first instance is the mayor).

o CDCSs are supposed to monitor the delivery of subsidies to low socio-economic strata. The Colombian subsidy scheme is based on cross-subsidies, which means that subsidies are not directly paid to users but delivered indirectly through tariff discounts (see section 5.4). The resources to cover the tariff discounts of low socio-economic strata come partially from the surcharge paid by high socio-economic strata and partially from funds transferred from the district to the service provider. Monitoring the amount of subsidies delivered is complicated because it requires detailed accounting information, as well as legal and accounting knowledge. This means that, in practice, CDCSs and their spokesmen are not able to carry out this monitoring.

Participation of users in regulation on the *national level* is, in general, weak. This is especially true for the activities carried out by CRA, i.e., the development of new and the adaptation of existing regulatory norms. The main mechanisms for participation in this context are public hearings (*consultas públicas*) carried out by CRA (Consumidores Colombia 2005). Although the big service providers, either through their own staff or through the staff of their National Association (ANDESCO),[42] manage to dialogue with the staff of CRA on a technical level in such events and to make propositions to change regulatory projects, this is not the case for the spokesmen of the CDCSs or other user representatives. User representatives generally lack the necessary legal, technical, and economic knowledge to do so. This has to do with the low degree of organisation of user representatives in Colombia, who lack a strong national association with the financial and technical means to effectively participate in regulation.[43]

5.3.3. Institutional Design of Regulation[44]

In Colombia, regulation of WS services follows the Anglo-American model of an own specialised regulatory body that acts within a set of general rules (Public Services Law) and that enjoys a certain level of discretion with respect to the formulation of the detailed regulatory norms it issues. As has been said, there are two regulatory agencies in Colombia: CRA[45] is responsible for the definition of the norms regarding monopoly regulation and SSPD[46] is responsible for controlling and sanctioning the compliance with these norms, as well as with further legal regulations.

5.3.3.1. Comisión de Regulación de Agua Potable y Saneamiento Básico (CRA)

CRA, which is based in Bogotá, was created by the President in 1992 but started to work effectively only after the enactment of the Public Services

Law in 1994, which set the legal framework for its functioning and responsibilities. The tutelary oversight of CRA is accomplished by the responsible ministry—the MAVDT.

The decision-making body of CRA is a board consisting of seven members in 2005. The board takes its decisions by simple majority vote. All members are appointed by the President:

- four "experts" in regulation appointed for a four-year office term,
- two ministers (MAVDT and Ministry of Social Protection), and
- the director of DNP.

There are no specific legal requirements concerning the experts' professional qualification or working experience, and posts are not awarded via public advertisements. According to information gained in an interview, political criteria prevail over technical criteria for the appointment of experts in regulation. According to Consumidores Colombia (2005), it is common that ex-managers of WS service providers are appointed as regulatory experts. There exist no legal restrictions concerning the causes for removal of the experts. Moreover, like with all other ministers, the President is free to remove the three members of the regulatory board that represent the government at any time (i.e., the two ministers and the director of DNP).

CRA is financed by a levy on the turnover of the regulated service providers. Because CRA has no own legal identity (unlike SSPD), its budget is a part of the budget of MAVDT and, thus, subject to revision by this ministry. However, according to information given by a representative of CRA, the budgets approved so far always have been sufficient to cover the costs associated with its functioning. As of July 2005, CRA had a staff of 56 persons, including support staff.

Concerning transparency and participation procedures, the justifications of the norms issued are not regularly published. The instrument of public hearings for the discussion of new regulations is not legally prescribed. Since a decision of the Constitutional Court in 2003 that demanded the embodiment of participation into the regulatory process, public hearings have been used more regularly, in particular in order to prepare the introduction of the new tariff regulation methodology, which has become effective in 2005[47] (CRA 2005, 25).

5.3.3.2. *Superintendencia de Servicios Públicos Domiciliarios (SSPD)*

Unlike CRA, SSPD was created by the Constitution (Asamblea Nacional Constituyente 1991, article 370), and just like CRA, the legal framework for its functioning and responsibilities is given basically by the Public Services Law and complementary regulation. The director of SSPD is appointed by the President and can be removed at any time. Similar to CRA, SSPD is financed through a levy on the turnover of the regulated enterprises.

SSPD is divided into three departments: (a) water, sanitation, and waste disposal; (b) telecommunications; and (c) electricity and liquefied petroleum gas. Moreover, besides its headquarters in Bogotá, SSPD has branch offices in the most important regional capitals. The technical department for WS services by 2005 had a staff of 25 professionals (exclusive of support staff). In addition, in the department for investigation, ten professionals were taking care of WS services.[48]

To accomplish its functions of control and sanctioning, SSPD has a series of faculties: among other things (i) to require information from the regulated providers and to conduct investigations, as well as (ii) to levy fines and to intervene in the management of service providers in order revitalise or liquidate them. Moreover, SSPD is the second instance for resolving user complaints (the first instance is the service provider). Due to the considerable volume of work associated especially with this latter function, SSPD has been absolutely overloaded with work in 2002 and 2003, which has implied enormous delays in the processing of the complaints. By 2005, the situation regarding the processing of complaints had improved considerably.[49]

5.3.3.3. Assessment

The review of the literature on institutional design of regulation in subsection 3.2.3.2 has yielded a list of typical recommendations regarding design characteristics that support the independence and the accountability of regulatory agencies (see Table 3.1). Although some of the institutional characteristics of CRA and SSPD *are in line* with these recommendations:

- "Autonomous source of finance" via a levy on the industry turnover, "responsibility for various utility sectors" (in the case of SSPD only), "distinct legal mandate" defined in the Public Services Law;

others *are not*:

- "Freedom of ministerial control," "appointment for fixed terms," "specify causes of removal," "involve execute *and* legislative branch in appointment process," "prescribe professional criteria for appointment," and "publication of decisions *and* justifications."

From these latter design characteristics, it can be concluded that formal independence from the executive is, at best, partial and that, therefore, there is a risk of state capture. On the other hand, there are two factors that may reduce, somewhat, this risk: (i) Thanks to the system of separation of powers, the two institutional veto players (Congress and Constitutional Court) are, in principle, able to control the capture of the regulator by the executive. (ii) The public officials that have the greatest incentives to influence regulatory decisions are the mayors, because they are responsible for WS service delivery. However, perhaps with the exception of the mayor of Bogotá, mayors have only little political influence on CRA and SSPD, since the agencies depend directly on the President and the National Minister (MAVDT).

There is also some risk of industry capture due to shortcomings regarding transparency (justifications are not regularly published) and due to the weakness of user advocacy organisations. The risk of industry capture may be compounded if regulatory experts are appointed primarily amongst professionals that have a WS industry background.

In what concerns the credibility of the regulatory framework of the WS sector, there is one element that enhances credibility and commitment power: the fundamental norms for regulation are defined in the Public Services Law that cannot very easily be changed, not least thanks to the existence of institutional veto players like the Constitutional Court. However, according to Fernández (2004, 81–83), the practical performance of CRA in the past has diminished the credibility of regulation. CRA has remarkably delayed the revision of the old methodology for tariff regulation, which should have been completed by 2001 but actually was implemented only in 2005. The way the revision of the tariff methodology was handled raised some doubts concerning the professionalism and the political independence of CRA.

Finally, both regulatory agencies are confronted with the structural problem of information asymmetry. This problem is compounded in Colombia by the atomisation of the provider structure (there are many small providers—see sub-section 5.3.4) and the low reliability of the information provided by many, especially smaller, service providers due to low accounting standards. Both agencies have made big efforts during the last years to improve information.

5.3.4. Institutional Design of Service Delivery and Industry Structure

The reforms of the WS sector in the late 1980s and early 1990s had two somehow opposing consequences for the structure and organisation of service providers:

- The decentralisation of the WS sector led to an atomisation of the enterprise structure and to a proliferation of service delivery directly by the district administrations, because many district administrations in small urban centres began to operate the existing systems—which formerly had been operated by INSFOPAL—with their own staff (Fernández 2004, 9–11).

- The Public Services Law put strong emphasis on the aspect of internal efficiency of public service providers prescribing a corporatisation of the entities delivering public services as the norm (Congreso de Colombia, 1994, articles 6 to 20), and, in general, the Law paved the way for PSP in service delivery.

The regulations contained in the Public Services Law meant that many districts had to engage in a process of corporatisation.[50] The two options of corporate organisation defined as the norm—which are, by the way, also the two most relevant ones with respect to the share of the population served—are

i. the public enterprise (*Empresa Industrial y Comercial del Estado*; EICE), which is always entirely owned by the district; and
ii. the stock corporation (*Sociedad Anónima / Empresa de Servicios Públicos*; ESP), which can either be public (0% of the shares owned by the private sector), mixed (1% to 49% owned by the private sector), or private (50% or more owned by the private sector).[51]

In what follows, first the industry structure with respect to corporate form, ownership and size is characterised, then the institutional design of EICEs and ESPs is compared and, finally the institutional design and the scope of PSP are discussed.

5.3.4.1. Industry Structure

The structure of the WS industry regarding the corporate form of service providers is described in Table 5.3. It becomes evident that the most frequent corporate form is the (i) authorised organisation (which is a generic term that mainly applies to user associations, cooperatives etc.), followed

Table 5.3   Structure of the Water and Sanitation Industry: Corporate Form of Entities Providing Water and/or Sanitation Services

Corporate Form	Number	%
Authorised Organisations (user associations, cooperatives, etc.)	339	41.5
District	190	23.2
Public Enterprise (*EICE*)	179	21.9
Stock Corporation (*ESP*)	97	11.9
Others	12	1.5
*Total**	*817*	*100*

*Total of entities registered with SSPD by 31 December 2003.
Source: Fernández (2004, 10); modified by the author.

by (ii) districts, (iii) EICEs and (iv) ESPs. The figures are limited to those entities that were officially registered with SSPD by the end of 2003 (817 entities). It is estimated that the total number of entities providing WS services in Colombia is far bigger: around 1,500 in urban areas and 12,000 in rural areas (Fernández 2004, 10).

If, however, the corporate form of service providers is looked at in relation to the inhabitants potentially[52] served, the picture is the following (SSPD 2002, 35–39; Fernández 2004, 9–11):

- Regarding the *big and intermediate urban areas*, it can be said that all of the big cities (over 600,000 inhabitants)[53] and almost all of the intermediate cities (between 100,000 and 600,000 inhabitants) are served either by EICEs or by ESPs (see also Table A5.2 in the appendix).[54] The cities from these two groups (60 in total) concentrate approximately 75% of the urban and 55% of the total population of Colombia. Because some of the service providers (e.g. *Empresas Públicas de Medellín*), in addition to their home district, serve the population of neighbouring districts, the market share attended by service providers based in the big and intermediate cities is even greater.
- Concerning the *smaller urban areas* (cities below 100,000 inhabitants), it can be said that the smaller the cities, the more frequently WS services are delivered directly through the district administration.
- Finally, the majority of the *rural* population is served by user associations, cooperatives etc. (authorised organisations).

The figures presented here illustrate a concern raised by several analysts (e.g. Foster 2001b; Fernández 2004), which is the atomisation of the enterprise structure in the Colombian WS sector. There are many small service providers (mainly districts and authorised organisations) that serve only a small number of users each (mainly in small urban centres and in rural areas). The major concerns to this respect are that (i) organisational economies of scale are lost driving up costs of service and compromising quality of service and that (ii) it is practically infeasible for the two national agencies CRA and SSPD to regulate the large number of small providers.[55] The discussion of these two important concerns is, however, beyond the scope of this study.

5.3.4.2. Comparison and Assessment of the Institutional Design of EICEs and ESPs

The features EICEs—as well as public, mixed, and private ESPs—have in common are (i) an own legal identity, (ii) administrative autonomy, and (iii) an own budget (Departamento Nacional de Planeación without year-a, 3). Moreover, the Public Services Law (Congreso de Colombia 1994) is applicable to all of them and, for instance, in article 27 prescribes: "The authorities of the territorial entities [. . .] guarantee administrative autonomy to the public enterprises of public services as well as continuity to effective and efficient managements. No other interests shall be given priority to managerial continuity except the delivery of good services."[56]

However, EICEs, and public, mixed, and private ESPs also show some important institutional differences, which are listed in Table 5.4 and which, especially in the cases of EICES and public ESPs, partially contradict the spirit of the law:

- The *political independence* depends on who appoints the board of directors and the general manager. In the case of the EICEs, it is the mayor who appoints directly both the board members[57] and the general manager. In the case of ESPs, in which the district holds all or nearly all the shares, the mayor directly appoints the board of directors, which then appoints the general manager,[58] i.e., in both cases the mayor has full or nearly full control of the appointment of the most important positions. This fact, together with the tradition of clientelism (see sub-section 5.2.2), raises doubts regarding the political independence of the management in these cases.
- The importance of the *profit motive* is closely related to the balance of ownership between public and private shareholders and the political independence. It is strong in private ESPs and typically absent in public ESPs and EICEs where other (political) objectives are very likely to dominate the profit motive.
- Regarding the relation between *autonomy* on the one hand and *responsibility and accountability* on the other hand, Departamento Nacional de Planeación (without year-a, 18–19) concludes that in the cases of EICEs and public ESPs, this relation is characterised by imbalance. The managers of these enterprises have much more autonomy than, e.g. directors of the public administration with respect to wage negotiations with workers' unions and credit operations but bear only little responsibility for the financial consequences[59] of their management decisions because deficits are commonly covered with transfers from the public budgets. Such a behaviour, which disregards financial sustainability, may even be encouraged by the mayor, who may want to use posts and contracts to reward its political clients.
- Whereas, in the case of EICEs and public ESPs, the *applicable labour law* is the one for public employees, in the case of mixed and private ESPs it is the private sector labour law (*Código Sustantivo de Trabajo*; SSPD 2004a). Regarding this point, it is interesting to note that the Constitutional Court has ruled that the salaries of public employees have to be adjusted upward at least equivalently to the increase of the consumer price index (Cuéllar 2005, 18–21).

Table 5.4 Comparison of Institutional Characteristics of EICE and ESP

Corporate Form (Ownership)	Political Independence?	Profit Motive?	Balance Between Autonomy and Accountability?	Applicable Labour Law
EICE	Low: Mayor appoints directly the board of directors and the general manager	No	No (high autonomy but low accountability)	Public sector labour law
Public ESP (0% privately owned)	Low: Mayor appoints the board of directors; the latter appoints the general manager	No (depends on the character of the public share holders)	Limited	Public sector labour law
Mixed ESP (1%-49% privately owned)	To an increasing degree: Depends on the balance of share holders	Partially/ Yes (depends on the balance of share holders)	To an increasing degree	Private sector labour law
Private ESP (≥ 50% privately owned)	Almost completely/ completely: Depends on the balance of share holders	Yes	Yes (management is held accountable by private share holders)	Private sector labour law

Source: Author; inspired by Foster (2001b, 307).

To sum up, it can be said that the institutional characteristics of EICEs, public ESPs, and partially also of mixed ESPs, compromise (a) the incentives and the ability of the management to pursue the profit motive and, thus, internal efficiency and (b) the susceptibility of the management to respond to regulatory instruments that build on the profit motive (see also subsection 5.4.5).

5.3.4.3. Institutional Design and Scope of PSP

Institutional Design

Although the majority of the substantive PSP experiences in Colombia have been initiated after the enactment of the Public Services Law in 1994, there have been some prior PSP experiences (Ochoa 1996). Amongst them is the case of Barranquilla (initiated in 1990), which is the most important PSP delivery model in relation to the number of population served. PSP in the Colombian WS sector has taken basically three forms:

- *Concession contract* implying privately financed expansion investments (less frequent—one of the cases is Tunja; see section 5.6);
- A *combination of lease and management contract* (the so-called *empresa mixta*) implying no privately financed expansion investments but privately financed rehabilitation investments (more frequent—one of the cases is Santa Marta; see section 5.6); and
- *Service contract* (common).

In this study, just the former two PSP delivery models are considered. The details of these two models are described in section 5.6 when addressing the cases of Tunja and Santa Marta. Here, it shall suffice to clarify that the fact that mixed ESPs are quite common in the Colombian WS sector does not necessarily imply that the capital contributed by the private share holders to these mixed ESPs can be used to finance expansion investments. The typical model is the combination of a lease and a management contract in which an ESP (major shareholders: (i) district and (ii) specialised private operator) with a rather small amount of equity capital is founded that leases the assets from the district. The ESP is responsible for the operation and the rehabilitation of the infrastructure but not for its expansion, a responsibility that stays with the district. The management is subcontracted via a management contract to the specialised private operator, who earns a management fee.[60]

Scope

Table A5.2 (appendix) shows the corporate form and the ownership of the WS service providers serving the most important Colombian cities. Out of the 34 providers listed, 18 are fully public-owned (13 EICEs and 5 public ESPs), 7 are mixed ESPs (of which only *Aguas de Cartagena* presents a substantial [≥ 25%] portion of privately owned shares) and 9 are private ESPs (> 50% privately owned shares). It is noted that the three big capitals with populations above 2 millions (Bogotá, Cali, and Medellín) are all served by EICEs. The three most important PSP delivery models with respect to the population potentially served are the providers of the Caribbean cities of Barranquilla, Cartagena, and Santa Marta, which all correspond to the model that combines a lease and a management contract.

According to Fernández (2004, 31, 74–76), the private sector in Colombia has shown a clear preference for these lease and management contracts, i.e., models that do not entail the responsibility for major expansion investments to be financed on the private capital market and, thus, bear less risk than concession models. Still, depending on the initial conditions of assets, a lease contract may require notable private rehabilitation investments in order to improve services and thus increase collection of tariffs—which is the source of revenue for the leaseholder.

Nevertheless, there are some noteworthy concessions in intermediate and smaller cities, implying privately financed expansion investments that are, however, to a substantial part co-financed by the public sector. Examples are the contracts of Montería, Riohacha, Maicao, and Tunja, among others (Departamento Nacional de Planeación 2005c, 29–34). According to this latter source, between 1993 and 2003 investment projects in the WS sector[61] have reached financial closure involving private investments for an amount of 1,180 billion Colombian Pesos (approximately 518 million US Dollars).[62] This corresponds to 15% of the total volume of investment projects in the sector.

5.4. REGULATORY, SUBSIDY AND PUBLIC INVESTMENT POLICIES

This section describes and assesses the key policies that, besides the political and WS governance factors treated earlier, influence WS service performance: tariff regulation, cross-subsidy policy, and public investment policy. In order to describe and assess these policies, the section draws on the categories developed in Chapter 2.

A good introduction to these issues is a brief review of important principles set in the Public Services Law to this respect. The Public Services Law (Congreso de Colombia 1994, article 87) prescribes that CRA and the further involved government actors have to respect the following principles for tariff regulation:[63]

- (i)"Economic efficiency"[64] and (ii) "financial sufficiency,"[65] which according to the Public Services Law means (i) that tariffs shall approximate to those that would result in a competitive market and

(ii) that tariffs shall cover the full costs, i.e., operation, replacement *and* expansion costs of an efficient provision.

- "Solidarity and redistribution," which according to the Public Services Law means that the tariff regulation has to implement a system that, via the tariff contributions made by residential users from higher socio-economic strata and by commercial and industrial users, shall contribute to lower the tariffs that users from low socio-economic strata have to pay for their basic needs (cross-subsidy system).
- (i) "Simplicity" and (ii) "transparency," which according to the Public Services Law means (i) that tariff formulae shall be designed in a way that eases comprehension, application and control and (ii) that the tariff regime shall be explicit and the related information easily available to the broad public.
- Moreover, regarding the expansion of services, the Public Services Law (article 2) says that the state has to ensure (i) that the coverage of services is continuously expanded and (ii) that priority is given to covering unmet needs for WS services.

Taking all together, this means that policies shall be guided by the three normative principles discussed in sections 2.2 to 2.4: equity, allocative efficiency, and internal efficiency.

The remainder of this section describes and assesses the key WS policies. Sub-section 5.4.1 deals with tariff regulation, sub-section 5.4.2 with the cross-subsidy policy, sub-section 5.4.3 with public investment, and sub-section 5.4.4 with control and sanctioning. Finally, sub-section 5.4.5 draws some conclusions.

5.4.1. Tariff Regulation

5.4.1.1. Initial Situation Regarding the Relation of Tariffs and Costs

The tariff regulation by CRA within the new legal framework was initiated in 1995. The general picture with respect to WS tariffs and costs at the beginning of the 1990s was as follows: (i) Tariffs were "too" low, because average tariffs of all main service providers were far lower than average full costs (according to the definition of financial sufficiency given in the Public Services Law). (ii) Costs were "too" high because they reflected inefficiencies in the production of services.

On average, the service providers of the 12 main cities in 1996 presented tariffs that were 46% below the reference costs recognised by CRA (see the following for the term *reference costs*). Tariffs for residential users from low socio-economic strata were especially low, reaching implicit subsidy levels of 70% to 90% in relation to reference costs. Related to the imbalance of tariffs and costs, many of the service providers were financially strained, did not sufficiently invest in expansion, rehabilitation, and maintenance of the systems, and showed high levels of water losses and a low service quality with respect to continuity, pressure, and drinking water quality (Ángel Gómez and Aguilera 2002, 16–23). Related to the low tariffs, water consumption was irrationally high: on average, more than 200 litres per capita per day in 1992. Ten years later (2002), after substantial tariff increases, average water consumption had fallen to 135 litres per capita per day (Domínguez Torres and Uribe Botero 2005, 15).[66]

Based on the tariff formulae that have been applied by CRA since 1995, tariff regulation can be divided into two periods (cf., e.g. CRA 2006):

- 1996 to 2005: Pure cost-of-service regulation with gradual tariff increases in order to meet the reference cost level.
- Since 2005: Gradual incorporation of elements of incentive regulation into the cost-of-service regulation in order to target inefficiencies in the production of services.

The following review focuses on the former because the data analysed and discussed in sections 5.5 to 5.6 fall within this first period.[67]

5.4.1.2. 1996 to 2005: *Pure Cost-of-Service Regulation*

To come to the point right away, it can be said that, regarding the balance between the two legal principles of "economic efficiency" and "financial sufficiency," during the first period, CRA put a clear emphasis on the latter principle. This contributed to close the gap between tariffs and costs but (i) did not address the problem of low internal efficiency presented by many service providers and (ii) was associated with considerable tariff increases, especially for the residential strata 1 and 2 (Figure 5.2). With the initiation of the second regulatory period in 2005, CRA has started to target the internal inefficiencies in the production of services and to incorporate mechanisms that are designed to avoid that these inefficiencies are passed on to consumers.

Tariff Formula

The "old" tariff formula (from now on *the* tariff formula) requires tariff receipts to be equal to total reference costs. The methodology for calculating the authorised tariffs[68] for the different user classes, which became effective in 1996, can be divided into three steps:[69] (i) Calculation of total reference costs, (ii) calculation of the individual reference tariff, (iii) adaptation of the individual reference tariff for the various user classes in order to account for cross-subsidies.

i. Total reference costs were calculated as follows:

$$RC = ADC + OC + IC \qquad\qquad (E5.3)$$

[RC = reference costs; ADC = administrative costs; OC = operation costs; IC = investment costs]

- IC were calculated for a perspective of at least 15 years and include the following (fixed) costs: (i) investment costs for the replacement of the existing system assets, (ii) investment costs for necessary system expansions estimated relying on a least-cost investment plan to attend the projected future demand, (iii) interests on the inverted capital in the order of 9% to 14% p.a.
- OC include all variable costs incurred to operate the system
- ADC include the fixed administrative and commercialisation costs.

With the exception of the investment costs for future expansions, RC correspond to historical or actual costs. RC were authorised by CRA based on the audited cost studies (base year 1994) presented by the service providers.

ii. RC were converted into a two-part individual reference tariff t (m^3), which depends on the amount of cubic metres (m^3) consumed:

$$t\,(m^3) = f + v * m^3 \tag{E5.4}$$

$$[f = ADC\,/\,\text{number of users}; v = OC\,/\,m^3 + IC\,/\,m^3]$$

The individual reference tariff allows the service provider to pass total reference costs on to the users, i.e., the formula contains no incentives for the service provider to reduce those costs that are due to internal inefficiencies. The only exception is the maximum percentage of unaccounted-for water[70] (30%) that is allowed to be discounted in order to calculate v.

iii. Finally, the individual reference tariff was adapted in order to account for the legally prescribed system of cross-subsidisation. There are four user classes: Industrial, commercial, official, and residential. Residential users are divided in up to six socio-economic strata with, 1 being the lowest and 6 the highest. According to legislation, the "basic consumption"[71] (20 m^3 per month per connection) of residential users of the strata 1, 2, 3 shall be subsidised via surcharges paid by (i) industrial and commercial users and (ii) residential users of the strata 5 and 6. The legal upper limits for the subsidies are set at 70% (stratum 1), 40% (stratum 2), and 15% (stratum 3) of the average reference costs. Legislation—and even more practice (see sub-section 5.4.2)—is ambiguous with respect to the limits of surcharges that can be levied to finance these subsidies. The Public Services Law (Congreso de Colombia 1994, article 89) sets the *maximum* limits for surcharges at 20% of average reference costs. A recent decree by MAVDT (2006), however, requires surcharges to be set at *minimum* at 30% (industrial), 50% (commercial and residential stratum 5) and 60% (residential stratum 6).

Tariff Transition Period

Since the tariffs charged by service providers in 1996 were well below reference tariffs adjusted for maximum subsidies allowed, it was politically unfeasible to increase tariffs to the reference levels in one go. Therefore, it was established that reference tariffs had to be reached by each service provider only by the end of a transition period in 2001 (Congreso de Colombia 1996). However, the transition period was prolonged until December 2005 (Congreso de Colombia 2000), because in 2000 actual tariffs charged were still well below the reference levels adjusted for maximum subsidies allowed. In addition, real incomes of households had been hit by the economic recession of the year 1999, which meant that considerable tariff increases would have had further diminished real incomes and, thus, would have been associated with high political costs (SSPD 2002, 81–82). Figure 5.2 shows average tariff increases between 2001 and 2004 for a sample of the major service providers. It becomes evident that stratum 1 has been faced with the highest increases.

5.4.2. Cross-Subsidy Policy

5.4.2.1. *User Structure: Relation Between Subsidees and Contributors*

The cross-subsidy scheme that has already been briefly described is characterised by a considerable financial deficit because the amounts of contributions raised via tariff surcharges systematically fall short of the amounts of subsidies granted via tariff discounts (SSPD 2005a). One of the roots of

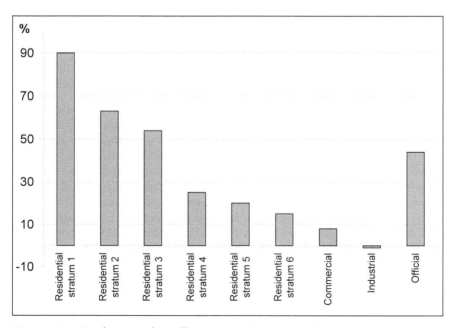

Figure 5.2 Total nominal tariff increases (2001–2004) by user classes. Source: Superintendencia de Servicios Públicos Domiciliarios (2005a, 64), adapted by the author. Data sample: Four major capitals.

this problem is the user structure in Colombia, which is such that there are much more users that are eligible for receiving subsidies than users that can be surcharged in order to finance these subsidies. Table A5.3 (appendix) shows the relation between the user classes for different district classes. It becomes evident that the relation between subsidees and contributors is very asymmetric, even for the four major capitals (69.4% to 17.4%). In small districts, however, almost all users are subsidees (the relation is 92.7% to 6%). The relevant geographical area for balancing contributions and subsidies is the area served by the respective service provider. For small districts, this means that the portion of subsidies that can be financed via tariff contributions is practically insignificant.

In this context, it has been argued that mayors are not applying the methodology for socio-economic stratification (cf. sub-sections 5.3.1, 5.3.2, and Meléndez 2004, 25–26) in an objective way, but that they are using the socio-economic classification to pursue short-term political goals. For instance, in a press report the Superintendent for Public Services, Evamaría Uribe Tobón, stated that mayors were discretionally reclassifying residential users from high strata to low strata, contributing this way to widen the gap between tariff contributions and tariff subsidies (Federación Colombiana de Municipios 2005). In a statistical analysis based on data from household surveys Meléndez (2004, 27–30) confirms that the proportion of non-subsidees (strata 4, 5 and 6) among urban residential users has fallen during the last decade (1993: 25%; 2003: 12%). However, she finds no statistically significant evidence, that actual classifications are systematically contradicting the objective "need criteria" established in the methodology, i.e. that mayors use their discretion for classification.

5.4.2.2. Deficits Between Tariff Contributions and Tariff Subsidies

District governments are not only responsible for the socio-economic stratification, but also for determining the tariff subsidy and surcharge levels and for administrating the balance of contributions and subsidies (SSPD 2001). For this purpose, each district administration has to create a balance account called Solidarity Fund (*Fondo de Solidaridad y Redistribuición de Ingresos*) in which the amount of subsidies granted and the amount of contributions levied are registered. However, until recently there were still many districts that had not even created Solidarity Funds, and, amongst the Solidarity Funds created, only a minority was operating (Meléndez 2004, 17).

According to the laws and regulations, Solidarity Funds have to be in balance.[72] Only if the Solidarity Fund is in balance, the respective service provider earns a tariff that covers the full reference costs. However, because only very few Solidarity Funds have been operating, this legal norm has been of limited practical relevance so far. The imbalance and inoperation of the Solidarity Funds is related to three factors:

  i. District governments have been reluctant to cut tariff discounts for the residential users of the strata 1 to 3 to the maxima allowed (discussed previously) and even more to reduce discounts below these maxima.

  ii. They have also been reluctant to transfer funds from the district budget to the Solidarity Fund in order to compensate for the deficit. Instead, district governments have preferred to allocate their spending for WS services directly and not via the Solidarity Fund (Departamento Nacional de Planeación 2004, 11–15).

  iii. The possibility to compensate for the deficit by raising more contributions via tariff surcharges is limited due to various reasons: (a) The small portion of contributing users (see previous discussion). (b) Legal restrictions: The *maximum* surcharge allowed in the Public Services Law was 20%.[73] (c) Economic reasons: The demand for WS services—and thus the amount of contributions that can be collected—decreases with price increases.[74] By the way, a considerable number of industrial users—55,000—have already exited the regulated market and have opted for self-supply with WS services (Echeverri 2001, 287).

Figure 5.3 shows the overall deficit (2001 to 2004) between (i) tariff subsidies, (ii) tariff contributions, and (iii) district government spending for WS services for a sample of 41 districts. The deficit amounts to a sum of

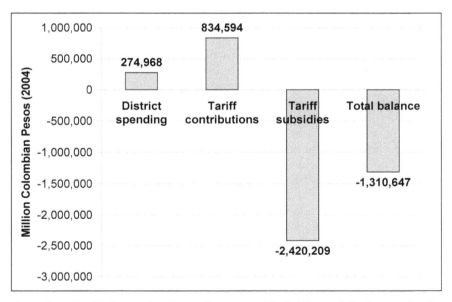

Figure 5.3　Total balance of tariff contributions, tariff subsidies, and district spending for WS (2001–2004). Source: Superintendencia de Servicios Públicos Domiciliarios (2005a, 68), adapted by the author. Data sample: 41 big, intermediate and small districts.

1,310,647 million Colombian pesos.[75] It is emphasised here that the district government spending considered in Figure 5.3 (274,968 million Colombian pesos) corresponds only to a very small portion to transfers to Solidarity Funds.[76] The bulk of the district government spending corresponds to direct investments in WS assets (for more details, see sub-section 5.4.3). Thanks to the gradual tariff increases that have been implemented during the last years, the annual deficits have shown a clear trend to diminish between 2001 (488,100 million Colombian pesos) and 2004 (181,774 million Colombian pesos; SSPD 2005a, 69).

5.4.2.3. Targeting Quality and Distributive Impact

Meléndez (2004, 22–23) investigates the ability of the existing cross-subsidy scheme to target subsidies to those households in need and to redistribute income. As the criterion for assessing the targeting quality, she assumes that only the poorest 40% of the country shall be eligible for a discount in WS tariffs. This criterion of eligibility corresponds to the national poverty line in Colombia. According to the results of the study, the targeting quality of the cross-subsidy scheme can be considered low because the error of inclusion is high: 51% of consumers that receive a tariff subsidy have an income that lies above the national poverty line. The positive thing about the scheme is that the error of exclusion is extremely low: only 0.7% of the *connected* households with an income below the poverty line do not receive a tariff subsidy. The share of income paid in 2003 by the poorest quintile for water and sanitation services together is estimated in around 7% (Meléndez 2004, 53). It, thus, exceeds the internationally recommended threshold of 5%.[77] Concerning the distributive impact, the study finds that the cross-subsidy scheme does not redistribute income from rich to poor households but, instead, is slightly regressive.

The high error of inclusion does not seem desirable, because considerable amounts of subsidies are allocated to non-poor households, a situation that hardly can be justified on equity grounds. From an equity point of view, it would seem preferable to improve the targeting quality of the cross-subsidy scheme and to use the funds "saved" for subsidising coverage expansion to those households that lack access to improved WS services and that, due to the fact that they are not served by an official service provider, do not receive WS subsidies at all. The price per m³ of water paid by households that have to rely on informal water vendors is between 8 and 25 times higher than the price paid by households from stratum 1 served by an official provider (Departamento Nacional de Planeación 2004, 24; SSPD 2005b, 3). In Santa Marta, the former pay approximately 45,000 Colombian pesos[78] for 2 m³ per month, whereas the latter pay between 15,000 and 18,000 Colombian pesos for 18 to 20 m³ per month.

5.4.3. Public Investment Policy

According to the Public Services Law, public officials have to prioritise the satisfaction of unmet basic WS service needs, which means to prioritise coverage expansion to households that lack access to improved WS services. This priority is in line with the normative discussion in section 2.2, which has identified the lack of access to improved WS services as the most pressing problem from an equity perspective. In accordance to the logic of political and administrative decentralisation in Colombia, the main responsibility for prioritising and coordinating coverage expansion lies with district governments (see sub-sections 5.2.2 and 5.3.1). The two key policy areas to this respect are (i) territorial planning and (ii) public investment policy.

5.4.3.1. Territorial Planning

Investment projects in WS services and the eventual allocation of public funds to these projects occur within a context of territorial planning. The question of whether the district government will give a high priority to WS service expansion, especially to poor households, will, in general, depend on the magnitude of the problem, the financial resources available and the institutional and political factors affecting the planning process.

According to legislation, the two main instruments for territorial planning are (i) the district development plan (*plan de desarrollo municipal*) and (ii) the land use plan (*plan de ordenamiento territorial*):

i. The district development plan shall express the priorities for local development and address relevant local development problems. Moreover, the plan shall be elaborated with the participation of citizens and civil society organisations.
ii. The land use plan can be seen as the translation of the development plan into the (urban) space. It guides all construction activities and, e.g. delimits residential and industrial zones, zones of urban expansion, and risk zones. Like the development plan, the land use plan shall be elaborated in a participative manner (Departamento Nacional de Planeación 2005b, 39–44).

From a legal perspective, there are several links between the territorial planning process and the construction of WS assets. In order to benefit from funds stemming from the national budget (explained in the following), WS investment projects have to be part of the district development plan (SSPD 2005a, 6). Moreover, they have to follow the standards established in the technical regulation for the WS sector (*Reglamento Técnico para el sector de Agua Potable y Saneamiento Básico*; RAS).[79] The RAS demands that WS constructions have to comply with land use plans and prioritises the expansion of the water system over the expansion of the sewer system.

The land use plan is also important for another reason. It is the basis for defining the service perimeter and, thus, for defining the responsibilities of the WS service provider in terms of coverage. This is of special relevance in PSP delivery models that require a very clear definition of responsibilities in terms of rehabilitation, reposition, and expansion investments and their deployment in space. In this context, it is important to realise that coverage expansion in the context of "orderly" urban growth is not related to major investments in water and sewer pipes for the WS service provider, because these costs are borne by the company that develops the new construction plots.[80] By contrast, system expansions into existing squatter settlements *are* related to major expenses for water and sewer pipes, which makes a big difference from the perspective of a service provider or a district government that has to bear these costs. This means that there are special (financial) obstacles for expanding improved WS services to poor urban areas and that these obstacles require a targeted strategy to be overcome.

Concerning the state of affairs of territorial planning in Colombia, González Salas (2002) reports, in an empirical study, that the introduction of district development plans and land use plans has helped to render the territorial planning process on the district level more systematic. However, the author finds that this process, in general, is plagued with several weaknesses: (i) low qualification and reduced number of the district staff responsible for planning activities, (ii) low importance given to citizen participation in practice, and (iii) deficiencies in implementation: from a representative sample of 162 districts, by 2001 55% had elaborated a land use plan but only 3.5% had approved it. Weaknesses are greater or more numerous in smaller districts.

5.4.3.2. Public Investment Financing

Important amounts of public funds[81] are allocated to the WS sector by district governments (the vast majority) and by the national government (a smaller fraction) that, in principle, could be used to pursue the objective of expanding WS services, especially to low-income households. The bulk of these resources stems from the national budget (Departamento Nacional de Planeación 2004, 7–11).

Table 5.5 shows the funds stemming from the national budget that have been allocated to the environmental services sector (WS services, waste water treatment, solid waste disposal) between 1998 and 2002. It can be seen that earmarked regular transfers[82] from the nation to districts within the framework of the Decentralisation Law (Congreso de Colombia 2001) are, by far, the most important source with a share of 86%. These transfers are earmarked to be used for the environmental services sector but the administration of these funds and the spending decision is made by district governments. The formula for distributing transfers among the 1,098 districts considers poverty and unsatisfied basic needs as important

Table 5.5 Public Spending for Water and Sanitation, Waste Water Treatment and Solid Waste Disposal Stemming From the National Budget (1998–2002)

Source	Thousands US Dollars 2003		
	Total Amount 5 Years	Average per Year	Proportion (%)
Transfers to districts (Decentralisation Law)	1,195,716	239,143	86
National Royalties Fund	56,234	11,247	4
Ministry for Economic Development	84,410	16,882	6
Other	54,220	10,843	4
Total	*1,390,579*	*278,116*	*100*

Source: Fernández (2004, 62).

criteria. This means that, in practice, poorer and smaller districts receive higher transfers per capita than richer and bigger districts. These regular earmarked transfers are not only the most important source of public spending in the sector; they are important even when compared to the value added of the whole sector: 33.5% on average as measured in current prices for the years 1994–2003.[83]

At the first glance, it seems incoherent and contradictory to allocate grants to the WS sector, given the fact that tariff regulation is designed such that service providers earn a tariff that covers the full costs, including the investment costs for system expansion. However, as has been explained, in practice tariffs have been below reference costs. So, as long as deficits between subsidies and contributions persist, assuming that deficits are not due to internal inefficiencies, and accepting the logic of the tariff regulation and the cross-subsidy scheme, allocating grants to the sector in order to cover these deficits is coherent with the overall system.[84]

The focus in the following is on public investment policy of districts. District governments are allowed to use the earmarked transfers from the national budget (i) either for financing the deficits between contributions and subsidies (ii) or for investments in WS assets (Departamento Nacional de Planeación 2004, 6–7). There are two alternative channels for allocating the public funds to the WS sector:

i. In the first case, public funds are allocated via the WS service provider. This is probably an effective way to allocate public funds in order to achieve coverage expansion if the service provider is professionally and efficiently managed, if it has a problem-oriented investment plan that focuses on coverage expansion and if the investment plan is coordinated with the priorities defined in the territorial planning process (e.g. system expansion to poor neighbourhoods); otherwise probably not.

ii. In the second case, funds are allocated directly by the district administration. This requires a very close coordination with the investment plan of the service provider because investments have to be compatible with the existing system and the new components have to be operated by the provider after the completion of construction. If this condition, as well as the conditions previously mentioned, hold, this might be an effective way to allocate public funds in order to expand coverage—otherwise, probably not. In general, districts have preferred this second channel.

In an evaluation of the public spending of districts in the WS sector, Departamento Nacional de Planeación (2004) reaches the following findings:

- There is a positive correlation between the amounts transferred within the framework of the Decentralisation Law and the coverage gap of districts, i.e., districts with lower coverage receive higher per capita transfers.
- There are indications that public funds have not been effectively used for expanding services in order to satisfy unmet WS needs. Assuming standard expansion costs, the coverage in 2003 with piped water connections should have been 92% (instead of actually 88%) and with sewer connections 76% (instead of actually 74%), given the total amount of public spending for the WS sector between 1996 and 2003 (Departamento Nacional de Planeación 2004, 17–18). The authors offer several explanations for this result:
  o In many cases in which the districts allocate the funds directly, there is a lack of coordination with the investment plan of the provider; moreover, investment projects in several cases do not meet the necessary economic and technical criteria, which means that unworkable or useless assets are built;
  o Several providers, especially those that have not undergone a process of corporatisation and commercialisation, may lack the capacities to execute expansion investments effectively (refers to cases in which the funds are channelled via the provider);
  o If, in addition, tariff levels are low when compared to inefficiently high administrative and operation costs, the public funds transferred to these service providers are consumed and cannot be used for investments;
  o In districts where there is a substantial investment backlog, public funds may have to be used for necessary replacement investments first, in order to keep the system going, before they can be used to expand coverage;
  o The atomisation and dispersion that characterises the provider structure for the smaller districts implies that economies of scale in the development of investment projects, as well as in construction supervision are wasted, which means that more funds than necessary are consumed in overheads.

Finally, an additional point is made here:

- Awarding construction contracts is an activity that is prone to be used for rewarding clients within a clientelistic strategy and that is prone to corruption. If these are important forces at work when awarding construction contracts, formal criteria like cost effectiveness, needs-orientation, and prioritisation of service expansion for poor parts of the town may loose their practical importance.[85]

5.4.4. Control and Sanctioning

The main organisation responsible for control and sanctioning in the WS sector is SSPD (see sub-sections 5.3.1 and 5.3.3). Control and sanctioning is complemented by the Procurator General and the Auditor General that monitor the compliance with public sector laws and the effective use of public funds. Control and sanctioning are important in order to render the regulations issued by CRA and other authorities effective.

In this respect, it is important to note that CRA has not only issued regulations concerning tariffs (see sub-section 5.4.1). CRA has also defined internal efficiency and service quality indicators and has authorised investment plans. The problem, however, is that the regulation issued by CRA has not established an explicit relation between tariffs authorised on the one hand and service quality, internal efficiency and investment indicators on the other hand (Fernández 2004, 82–84). According to Fernández, SSPD, therefore, has not been able to adequately control and sanction service providers. Another factor that has hampered effective control by SSPD is the low quality of information provided (especially by smaller providers) and the atomisation of the provider structure. Still another factor that has complicated control and sanctioning is that, for most service providers, tariff earnings have been well below their reference costs because tariff levels have not been increased or because Solidarity Funds have generated deficits. This situation makes it difficult to call the providers to attention and to sanction them for missing service quality standards or investment targets. Those mainly responsible for the low tariff levels and for the deficits of the Solidarity Funds are the district governments. This means that, in many cases, SSPD should sanction the district governments for not complying with the tariff regulation and for not covering the deficits of the Solidarity Funds. However, SSPD lacks the authority and the capacity to do so. Recently, SSPD and the Procurator General have established a closer collaboration in order to render control and sanctioning of district governments more effective.

Control of drinking water standards in practice also shows some weaknesses. SSPD is not directly responsible for controlling drinking water standards. Nevertheless, SSPD reports the results of the controls carried out by district and provincial health authorities and possibly sanctions providers that do not meet the standards. WS service providers have repeatedly called into question the quality of the tests carried out by health authorities and the quality of the information reported by SSPD.[86]

5.4.5. Conclusions

This sub-section summarises the most relevant aspects of the WS policies previously assessed and draws some conclusions. With respect to the policies aiming at the equity goal the following points are emphasised:

- A substantial amount of public funds are allocated to the WS sector that can, in principle, be used for expanding services to those households that lack access to improved WS services. However, there is evidence that a portion of these funds is not effectively used for expanding services. Factors that seem to be related to this problem are (i) reduced territorial planning capacities of districts, as well as lacking civic participation in the planning process; (ii) lack of coordination between the service provider's investment plan and the investments carried out by the district; (iii) lack of transparency and control in the awarding of construction contracts; (iv) atomisation of the provider structure ending up in high overheads for investment projects; and (v) financially strained or internally inefficient service providers that require the available public funds to keep the existing systems running.
- The poorest quintile spends a slightly higher proportion of income on WS services than 5%, which is the common threshold used to judge affordability. The cross-subsidy system shows the well-known defect that it reaches only those households that are connected to a regulated service provider. Furthermore, the targeting quality of the system can be considered low, because more than half of the households that are subsidised have an income that lies above the national poverty line. Finally, contributions raised through tariff surcharges systematically have been falling short of subsidies granted through tariff discounts, a situation that generates deficits. These deficits have complicated regulation aimed at improving efficiency and financial sustainability.
- An option for overcoming some of the problems related to the subsidy system, is to abolish cross-subsidies and to introduce a Chilean-like subsidy system in which means-tested subsidies are given directly to users.[87]

Concerning the policies aiming at allocative and internal efficiency the following aspects are highlighted:

- Until 2005, tariff regulation has unilaterally focused on improving financial sustainability of service providers by increasing tariff levels to cost levels. Until 2005, tariff regulation did not include mechanisms designed to avoid that internal inefficiencies—which manifested in high historical costs—could to a great extent be passed on to users.

- The low level and the low quality of information provided by, especially, the smaller service providers have hampered regulation. This problem has been exacerbated by the big number of small providers existing in Colombia. The information deficit of the regulatory authorities partially explains why more demanding regulation techniques have not been adopted earlier.
- The structure of the WS service industry renders regulation extremely demanding. Bigger and profit-oriented providers should be treated differently from smaller non-profit providers.
- The articulation of roles between district governments that are responsible for defining cross-subsidies and public investments and SSPD that is responsible for sanctioning WS service providers does not seem to be perfect. By not cutting down tariff discounts to the legally prescribed maximum levels, district governments can compromise financial sustainability and probably performance of WS service providers. However, SSPD lacks the authority to sanction district governments for this behaviour.
- Tariff regulations in combination with the regulations concerning cross-subsidies are far from being "simple" and "transparent" as required in the Public Services Law and thus complicate comprehension and monitoring by the broad public.

5.5. THE INFLUENCE OF PSP ON WS SERVICE PROVIDER PERFORMANCE: A QUANTITATIVE ANALYSIS

In accordance with the first purpose of this chapter, sections 5.2 to 5.4 have characterised, from a national perspective, the political governance (5.2), the WS governance (5.3) and the main WS policies (5.4) in Colombia. Building on these preceding sections, this section starts to work on the second purpose of this chapter, which is to explore the determinants of the sub-national variation in WS service provider performance. Drawing on data from a sample of 30 Colombian providers, it analyses, by econometric means, the influence of the delivery model (PSP versus purely public) on provider performance. The quantitative analysis of this section is complemented by the qualitative analysis of section 5.6, which investigates the importance of the quality of local governance for explaining sub-national variation in provider performance.

There are two papers available that investigate by econometric means the influence of PSP on WS service provision in Colombia (Barrera-Osorio and Olivera 2007; Gómez-Lobo and Meléndez 2007). Both papers use household level data from the Living Standard Survey (*Encuesta de Calidad de Vida*) by DANE and differences-in-differences estimations in order to analyse the impact of PSP.[88] The authors consistently find a robust positive effect of PSP on the quality of water services. Moreover, both papers report that user payments of the low income quintiles increase with PSP, although this effect is not robust in the case of Gómez-Lobo and Meléndez (2007). With respect to access to services, the results are more ambiguous. Barrera-Osorio and Olivera (2007) find a positive influence of PSP on access to water services in urban areas, whereas this effect is markedly negative in rural areas. Using a similar estimation technique, but without separating urban and rural households, Gómez-Lobo and Meléndez (2007) report that the effect of PSP is not statistically significant. Finally, Barrera-Osorio and Olivera (2007) find an interaction effect between the technical capacity of district governments and the influence of PSP leading to greater access, better quality and lower user payments.

This section uses provider-level data and follows an econometric approach that is similar to the model used in Chapter 4 (see the following for the details). The specific purpose is to investigate the relation of PSP and

- the evolution of the internal efficiency of the provider (as measured by the indicator unaccounted-for water[89]—UFW)
- the evolution of access to piped water and sewerage connections (as measured by the coverage rates).

The remainder of this section is organised as follows. First the data (5.5.1) and the expected effects of PSP in the Colombian context (5.5.2) are briefly discussed. Then the econometric model and the estimation results are presented (5.5.3) and, finally, some conclusions are drawn (5.5.4).

5.5.1. Data

The data set comprises 30 urban service providers from 30 districts. It contains cross-sectional data for the years 1998 and 2003 (Table A5.2 in the appendix lists the service providers and districts contained in the sample, see column "Coding of the variable PRIVATE"). The 30 districts contained in the sample have a total population of 20,266,535 (by 2003), which corresponds to almost half of the population of Colombia. The main portion of the data was made available by the regulatory agencies SSPD and CRA: coverage levels for piped water and sewerage, number of connections, UFW, collection rate (CR),[90] corporate form and ownership. This information was complemented with data from DANE (population), DNP (poverty indicator),[91] and the National Institute of Hydrology, Meteorology and Environmental Studies—IDEAM (water resources vulnerability index; see Table A5.4 in the appendix for a description of the variables used and the respective data sources). The dataset has the drawback that it does not include information on local governance because such indicators are not available on the district level. This means that governance has to be neglected in the quantitative analysis performed here (see the following qualitative analysis in section 5.6, which focuses on the effects of local governance).

Because the data sample is very short (1998 to 2003) a cross-sectional approach is preferred. According to Clarke, Kosec, and Wallsten (2004, 4), a cross-sectional approach is principally able to provide a rigorous test of the effect of PSP. PSP is modelled as a dummy variable (for more details on the model, see sub-section 5.5.3). All service providers contained in the sample are either ESPs or EICEs. In order to draw a line of distinction between "public" (variable PRIVATE = 0) and "private" delivery models (variable PRIVATE = 1), the following criteria have been used:

- Private: All ESPs with a share held by the private sector of ≥ 25%
- Public: (i) All ESPs with a share held by the private sector of < 25%; (ii) all EICEs

PSP delivery models were not further differentiated in concession, lease or management contracts. The sample contains 10 cases classified as private and 20 cases classified as public (see Table A5.2 for more details). Concerning the year of PSP engagement, in 8 cases engagement occurred prior to 1998, and in two cases (Montería and Tuluá) it falls within the period analysed (the year 2000 for both cases).

5.5.2. Expected Effects of PSP

What are the expected effects of PSP on internal efficiency and coverage indicators in the Colombian context?

- *Internal efficiency indicators*: It is to expect that PSP delivery models will show a better performance with respect to the internal efficiency indicator than public providers.
  - o The managements of EICEs and public ESPs depend on the district government and are likely to give a relatively low priority to internal efficiency improvements because, in general, they do not have a strong profit motive. Moreover, mayors may use posts in the company for rewarding clients in the context of a clientelistic strategy which negatively affects internal efficiency (for more arguments see sub-section 5.4.3).
  - o In addition, internal efficiency amongst public providers is expected to be low because tariff regulation, so far, has not provided strong incentives for improving internal efficiency (sub-section 5.4.1) and control and sanctioning has proved to be especially difficult when dealing with public providers (see sub-section 5.4.4).
  - o Although tariff regulation has been the same for private providers, thanks to the monitoring of private shareholders, the managements of private providers do have incentives to improve internal efficiency, whenever this improves the cash flow. Private providers are, therefore, expected to show a better performance with respect to the internal efficiency indicator.

- *Coverage indicators*: The expected effect of PSP on the expansion of coverage is not clear:
  - The first argument is a methodological one: In principle, PSP can contribute directly and indirectly to spur coverage expansion. A direct effect can occur only in case of PSP models that entail private expansion investments (concessions). Lease and management contracts can contribute only indirectly to spur coverage expansion (see second argument). The empirical approach chosen here is not able to capture the direct effect because (i) the data set does not include information on investments, and (ii) the ownership variable does not distinguish between concession models and further PSP models in order to keep the regressions as simple as possible.[92]
  - A potential indirect effect of PSP on coverage expansion occurs if (i) the management of private providers is more effective in planning system expansions and in awarding and supervising construction activities than the management of public service providers, and/ or if (ii) the PSP engagement gives rise to internal efficiency gains (relative to public providers) and thus to higher cash flows that are used for financing *replacement* investments[93] which, by consequence, means that a higher proportion of the external financing can be used for *expansion* investments. These indirect effects depend, among other things, on the channel used for allocating the public funds (via the provider *versus* via the district government) and on the coordination between the district government and the service provider (see sub-section 5.4.3).

5.5.3. Multivariate Regression Analysis[94]

5.5.3.1. The Models

In what follows, two very similar econometric models are used:

- UFW is regressed using the model described in E5.5. The structure of the model is identical to the one used in Chapter 4 (see sub-section 4.3.1 for a thorough discussion). The dependent variable is the value of UFW by 2003 (UFW03). UFW03 is regressed on UFW98 (the value of UFW by 1998), PRIVATE ("0" in case of public providers; "1" in case of private providers) and a vector of control variables (see the following for the control variables used).

$$UFW03_i = \beta_0 + \beta_j\,UFW98_i + \beta_j\,PRIVATE_i + \beta_j\,CON_{j,i} + U_i \qquad (E5.5)$$
$$(i = 1,\ldots m;\, j = 1,\ldots n)$$

- For estimating the evolution of coverage with piped water (WAT) and sewer connections (SEW), the model is slightly modified (see E5.6).

Unlike the model used in Chapter 4, the dependent variable is not COV03 (which stands for both WAT03 and SEW03), but CHCOV. CHCOV is the change in coverage between 1998 and 2003 (CHCOV = COV03/COV98).[95] The independent variables are COV98, COV98SQ (which is the square of COV98),[96] PRIVATE, and further control variables (CONj).

$$CHCOV_i = \beta_0 + \beta_j\,COV98_i + \beta_j\,COV98SQ_i + \beta_j\,PRIVATE_i + \beta_j\,CON_{j,i} + U_i \qquad (E5.6)$$
$$(i = 1,...m; j = 1,...n)$$

Just like in Chapter 4, the models are initially estimated using OLS. In case of evidence for heteroscedasticity in the error terms, estimation procedures with (White-) heteroscedasticity-robust standard errors (HRSE) are used. Outlier analysis suggests that the results may be sensitive to single influential data points. Therefore, all models are re-estimated using the "robust regression" (RR) procedure in order to check the sensitivity of the results (see also sub-section 4.3.2 on this matter). The summary statistics of all variables used in the regression analysis is given in Table A5.5 (appendix).

Table 5.6 Results of Regression Estimates: Dependent Variable UFW03

Independent Variables	Coefficients and t-Statistics [†]	
	Model UFWa	*Model UFWb*[##]
UFW98	0.617	0.630
	(5.11)***	(6.78)***
PRIVATE	−0.069	−0.053
	(−2.83)***	(−2.83)***
CR	−0.389	−0.475
	(−3.85)***	(−6.11)***
POP	0.297	−0.027
	(1.06)	(−0.12)
VULWAT	−0.035	−0.011
	(−2.13)**	(−0.84)
INTERCEPT	0.321	0.654
	(0.88)	(2.34)*
N	29	29
$\bar{R}^2$	0.736	
F	16.6***	24.24***

[†]t-statistics in brackets. ***$p < 0.01$; **$p < 0.05$; *$p < 0.1$.
[##]Robust regression (RR; command *rreg* in STATA).

5.5.3.2. Results for UFW03

The results for the regression of UFW03 are reported in Table 5.6. The independent variables[97] included in the model, besides UFW98 and PRIVATE, which were already touched on previously, are

- CR, which is the average collection rate for the period 1998 to 2003;
- POP, which is the population growth of the district calculated by dividing the population in 2003 by the population in 1998; and
- VULWAT, which is an ordinally scaled indicator that expresses the vulnerability of water resources at the district level and which takes values between 1 = low vulnerability and 5 = high vulnerability (see Table A5.4 for a description of all variables used in the analysis).

In addition, the variable POV has been tested which, however, proved not to be statistically significant and has been dropped from the model. POV (*Índice de Necesidades Básicas Insatisfechas*)[98] is a multidimensional poverty index that measures the share of persons whose basic needs (housing, public services, education, income generation capacity) are not satisfied (the higher the index the higher the incidence of poverty). The values used correspond to the year 1993, which is the most recent year for which the index is available at the district level.

Model UFWa has been estimated using OLS and yielded an $\bar{R}^2$ of 0.736. The estimations for UFW98, PRIVATE, CR, and VULAGUA are statistically significant and the slope parameters show the expected sign: UFW98 has a positive effect (the lower the initial value of UFW the lower UFW03), PRIVATE has a negative effect (PSP is associated with a lower UFW03), CR is also negative (the higher the collection rate the lower UFW03), just like VULWAT (the higher the vulnerability of water resources the lower UFW03). Population growth (POP) shows no statistically significant effect. The *robust regression* estimation procedure (model UFWb) largely confirms these results with the exception of VULWAT, whose effect loses statistical significance.[99]

5.5.3.3. Results for CHWAT

The case of "Villavicencio" is dropped for regressing coverage expansion with piped water connections (CHWAT) because it shows an unplausibly high decrease in coverage.[100] The results for CHWAT are reported in Table 5.7. Besides the independent variables already touched upon, UFWAV (average unaccounted-for water for the period 1998 to 2003) is included in the model.

OLS estimation (model CHWATa) yields an $\bar{R}^2$ of 0.896. A large portion of the high R^2 is explained by the two variables that stand for the initial coverage level in 1998 (WAT98 and WAT98SQ).[101] The estimated overall

Table 5.7   Results of Regression Estimates: Dependent Variables CHWAT and CHSEW

Independent Variables	Coefficients and t-Statistics [†]			
	Model CHWATa	Model CHWATb[##]	Model CHSEWa[#]	Model CHSEWb[##]
WAT98	−3.220 (−3.65)***	−4.649 (2.87)***		
WAT98SQ	1.382 (2.62)**	2.173 (2.37)**		
SEW98			1.641 (2.58)**	1.80 (2.33)**
SEW98SQ			−1.373 (−3.27)***	−1.425 (−2.79)**
PRIVATE	−0.001 (−0.10)	−0.013 (−1.00)	−0.043 (−1.18)	−0.017 (−0.61)
UFWAV	−0.212 (−1.98)*	−0.168 (−1.75)*	−0.329 (−2.48)**	−0.290 (−1.67)
POP	−0.379 (−2.11)**	−0.211 (−1.27)	−0.928 (−3.13)***	−0.826 (−2.29)**
POV	0.0007 (0.55)	0.0003 (0.23)	0.0031 (1.73)*	0.0023 (1.03)
INTERCEPT	3.324 (9.71)***	3.778 (5.67)***	1.759 (4.23)***	1.541 (4.04)***
N	28	27	29	29
$\bar{R}^2$	0.896		0.540	
F	39.71***	24.12***	6.74***	5.33***

[†]t-statistics in brackets. ***$p < 0.01$; **$p < 0.05$, *$p < 0.1$.
#Heteroscedasticity-robust standard errors (HRSE).
##Robust regression (RR; command *rreg* in STATA).

effect of the initial coverage level on CHWAT is negative and convex (see Figure A5.3 in the appendix for a depiction of the estimated functional form). The test of joint significance of WAT98 and WAT98SQ yields an F of 85.11 (highly significant). In addition to the reported variables, the influence of VULWAT and CR was tested which proved, however, to be not statistically significant.

The slope parameter of PRIVATE is negative (which means that PSP is associated with a lower coverage expansion) but the effect is far from being statistically significant. In order to preclude that this lack of significance is due to multicollinearity[102] problems, the model has been re-estimated after dropping UFWAV, POP, and POV. Nevertheless, the effect of PRIVATE remained statistically not significant.

By contrast, the variables UFWAV and POP show statistically significant coefficients: the higher unaccounted-for water, the lower coverage expansion, and the greater population growth, the lower coverage expansion. However, the magnitude of the latter result is sensitive to influential data points: Estimation with RR renders the coefficient of POP statistically not significant (see model CHWATb).

5.5.3.4. Results for CHSEW

For CHSEW (coverage expansion with sewer connections) estimation procedures with (White-) heteroscedasticity-robust standard errors (HRSE) are used. Results (see model CHSEWa in Table 5.7) are similar to those for piped water connections. However, it is remarkable that the $\bar{R}^2$ is considerably lower (0.540), just as the F value for the whole model (6.74) which is, however, still significant at $p < 0.01$.

Again the joint effect of SEW98 and SEW98SQ is highly significant ($F = 11.44$). The estimated functional form of the relation CHSEW → F(SEW98, SEW98SQ) is depicted in Figure A5.4 (appendix). The overall effect of the initial coverage on CHSEW is positive until a value of 0.6, and then becomes negative (i.e., it is negative for the vast majority of the cases contained in the sample, because the vast majority shows values > 0.6 for SEW98). Just like for CHWAT, the negative effect of PRIVATE is not statistically significant. The remaining variables, UFWAV, POP, and POV, are statistically significant and the slope parameters have the same sign, like above. Again, these results are not integrally confirmed by the RR estimation procedure (see model CHSEWb). The effect of POV loses statistical significance, just like the effect of UFWAV. The result is confirmed for POP, which shows a robust and statistically significant negative effect on CHSEW.

5.5.4. Conclusions

The results of the regressions previously presented should be interpreted with care. First, the data quality of the performance indicators has improved only recently, and reliability is still not very high for smaller districts. This means that the data quality, especially for the year 1998, could be lower than desirable. Second, some independent variables that are supposed to have an influence on the dependent variables could not be included in the models because data at the district level is not available or could not be gathered (e.g. governance, per capita income). Supposing that these variables—for instance, governance—matter, the results are likely to be biased. These are quite important limitations and the points summarised in what follows should, therefore, be taken as preliminary results to be confirmed with new and more reliable data:

- PSP shows a positive influence on lowering UFW. This effect is robust and statistically significant. The finding supports the supposition that PSP delivery models perform better than public delivery models with respect to internal efficiency achievements.
- PSP shows no statistically significant association with coverage expansion. Interestingly, low UFW shows a statistically significant positive effect on coverage expansion (this effect is robust for piped water only). Since PSP is related to lower UFW, there could be an indirect positive effect of PSP on coverage expansion via higher internal efficiency. This seems to be an interesting conjecture that would require further research.
- As is expected, population growth is negatively associated with coverage expansion (this effect is robust for sewer connections only).

Finally, the main result of the regression analysis—the higher internal efficiency of PSP delivery models—is interpreted, drawing on the findings of the preceding sections 5.2 to 5.4. Households do not immediately benefit from a higher internal efficiency of service providers, as explained in the following:

- Benefits for households that are already connected to the service emerge only if the higher internal efficiency translates into better and/or cheaper services. Whether this happens depends a lot on tariff and quality-of-service regulation. However, as has been discussed in section 5.4, tariff regulation, until recently, did not include mechanisms that encourage providers to pass on possible internal efficiency gains to households. Moreover, control and sanctioning mechanisms remain weak, and the quality of services, with respect to continuity and drinking water standards, shows considerable deficiencies, especially in intermediate and small districts (sub-section 5.1.2). This means that, in the Colombian context, it cannot be taken for granted that connected households actually benefit notably from internal efficiency gains achieved through PSP.
- Benefits for households that lack access to services emerge only if the higher internal efficiency and the associated higher cash-flow translate into higher replacement investments and thus—given a fixed amount of public funds to be allocated in the sector—into higher total investments (private and public together). Higher total investments mean that a higher portion can be used for expansion investments. Again, this effect depends on the regulation and on the coordination between the public investment policy of the district and the investment plan of the service provider (see section 5.4). Because 86.5% of the population without services live in rural areas, it would be desirable for this effect to materialise especially in rural areas. However, conditions in rural areas are especially adverse: Private providers are typically not

interested in serving rural areas, due to, among other things, the high atomisation of the industry and, especially, the low tariff levels. Moreover, capacity of district governments to conceive and implement (i) well designed PSP delivery models and (ii) sensible public investment policies are typically limited in rural areas.

It makes, therefore, a difference whether policy succeeds in spurring internal efficiency by encouraging PSP (which is a necessary, but not sufficient, condition for welfare improvements of households) or whether, in addition, policy succeeds in translating these internal efficiency gains into better or cheaper services and into a greater coverage with services, by using public-regarding regulatory and investment promotion instruments. This section has presented some evidence that the former effect takes place in Colombia. However, bearing in mind the weaknesses worked out in the preceding sections, 5.2 to 5.4, it can be doubted that governance structures and WS policies in Colombia are fully appropriate to bring around the second effect.

5.6. THE INFLUENCE OF LOCAL GOVERNANCE ON WS SERVICE PROVIDER PERFORMANCE: A COMPARISON OF MANIZALES, SANTA MARTA, TUNJA, AND VILLAVICENCIO

Because there is no comprehensive and reliable governance data available on the local level, the role of local governance for explaining the variation in WS service provider performance could not be studied in the preceding quantitative analysis. Therefore, this section investigates, with a qualitative approach, the influence of local governance for a sample of four cases for which the author has collected information on WS service performance, local governance and further important dimensions that can affect local service performance.

The main portion of the information was collected by the author during interviews in the four cities of Manizales, Santa Marta, Tunja, and Villavicencio in July 2005 (see the following for the selection criteria). The interviews were conducted with representatives of the main organisations involved in the provision and consumption of WS services in each city: service providers, district governments, spokesmen of CDCSs and other user representatives, chambers of commerce, CARs, and experts. The complete list of the organisations interviewed is given in Table A5.6 (appendix). The interviews, as well as the additional material (e.g. annual reports of the service providers), provided by the interview partners are the main sources of information used for this section. Whenever other sources of information are used in the following analysis, this is made explicit by citing the respective source. In order to validate the information gained in interviews or from the additional material provided by interviewees, this information has been cross-checked with other sources—whenever possible.

5.6.1. Case Selection, Research Question and Procedure

5.6.1.1. Selection of the Four Cases

The sample has been purposefully selected:

i. The four cases have been chosen on the dependent variable so that there is variation in service performance (i.e., two good performers and two bad performers have been chosen). This procedure prevents a selection bias that is common in qualitative research.[103]

ii. The ownership of the providers has been intentionally selected so that it is unrelated to the variation in the performance, i.e. amongst the two good providers chosen there is one public and one private, just as amongst the two bad providers there is one public and one private.

iii. The four cases are relatively similar with respect to the size of the cities (they have been chosen amongst the group of intermediate cities). This precludes, largely, a systematic effect of system size on service performance.

The intention behind this selection procedure is to avoid having the variation in two important control variables (ownership, size) causing variation in service performance. This eases the endeavour of capturing the supposed effect of local governance on service performance. Such a selection procedure is well suited to explore the supposed causal relation between two variables and to gain information about the empirical plausibility of such a causal relation (King, Keohane, and Verba 1994, 141–42).

The exact selection procedure was the following: Relying on the data on WS service performance and ownership available in advance of the field stay, the four cases have been selected amongst the group of intermediate cities contained in the data set described in subsection 5.5.1[104] (see Table A5.7 in the appendix for the 24 cities considered). Besides the intention of "holding the city size fix," there was also a pragmatic reason for concentrating on intermediate cities. Interviewing the relevant stakeholders and representatives from the organisations involved in the provision and consumption of WS services within the limited time available seemed easier to be accomplished when avoiding the big capitals where there are more actors involved and the institutional structures are more complex.

Eight indicators have been considered for assessing the quality of performance:[105] (i) average coverage with piped water connections 1998–2003, (ii) average coverage with sewer connections 1998–2003, (iii) average UFW 1998–2003, (iv) average CR 1998–2003, (v) change in coverage with piped water connections between 1998 and 2003, (vi) change in coverage with sewer connections between 1998 and 2003, (vii) change in UFW between 1998 and 2003, (viii) change in CR between 1998 and 2003. The 24 cases were ranked for each indicator, ranking the "best" performer highest and the "worst" performer lowest. For each indicator, cases received scores equal to their rank position (i.e., the case ranked first received one score and the case ranked last received 24 scores). After, total scores for each case were calculated by adding the scores for the eight indicators. Finally, cases were ranked according to their total scores yielding the rank order listed in Table A5.7. The eight cases ranked highest were considered "good" performers and the eight cases ranked lowest were considered "bad" performers (the remaining eight cases were considered "average" performers).

Amongst the eight good performers, the cases of Manizales (public provider "Aguas de Manizales") and Tunja (private provider "Sera QA") were selected, and amongst the eight bad performers the cases of Santa Marta (private provider "Metroagua") and Villavicencio (public provider "Empresa de Acueducto y Alcantarillado de Villavicencio–EAAV") were selected. Besides the intentional selection on ownership previously addressed, the following additional selection criteria have been applied in this second step: (i) security recommendations of GTZ (German Agency for Technical Co-operation) in Colombia that advised not travelling to certain regions of the country and (ii) availability of contacts to the main actors involved in the local provision and consumption of WS services. The four cities are on the map in Figure A5.5 (appendix).

5.6.1.2. Research Question and Procedure

The main supposition explored in this section is that the variation in service performance of public, as well as private, providers can be explained by the variation in the quality of local governance. Resuming the expected effects of ownership on internal efficiency and coverage with services, the following can be said (see sub-section 5.5.2 for the detailed argumentation):

    i. Internal efficiency: Private providers are expected to show a better performance with respect to internal efficiency indicators. The preliminary statistical results obtained in 5.5.3 support this hypothesis.
   ii. Coverage: The effect of ownership on coverage expansion is more ambiguous and is expected to depend on the specifics of the delivery model, on the local public investment policy and on the local political governance.

Thanks to the purposeful case selection, the ownership of the provider is unrelated to the variation in performance, i.e., amongst the four cases chosen there are (i) two cases that clearly contradict the first statement and (ii) two cases that confirm it:

    i. Aguas de Manizales (public) shows good internal efficiency (as well as coverage) indicators and Metroagua Santa Marta (private) shows bad internal efficiency (as well as coverage) indicators;

ii. Sera QA Tunja (private) shows good internal efficiency (as well as coverage) indicators and EAA Villavicencio (public) shows bad internal efficiency (as well as coverage) indicators.

This section investigates whether (a) the unexpected performance of Aguas de Manizales and Metroagua Santa Marta with respect to internal efficiency can be explained by local governance factors and whether (b) local governance factors also can explain the good (respective bad) performance with respect to coverage. For this purpose, the section proceeds in the following way. It describes the patterns of variation amongst the four cases for the dependent variables (performance indicators), the explanatory variables of interest (local governance), as well as further explanatory variables that are likely to affect the service performance and, finally, draws conclusions regarding the main supposition.

Sub-section 5.6.2 describes, in detail, the service performance of the four companies. This is done by using the information provided by the companies themselves (instead of the information given by SSPD and CRA). Moreover, some basic characteristics of the respective WS systems are described, in order to identify technical reasons that may contribute to explain the variation in the performance indicators. Sub-section 5.6.3 briefly discusses the variation in socio-economic conditions, which may be related to the variation in the performance. Sub-section 5.6.4 enters into the details of the four delivery models in order to check whether the variation in the performance amongst the two public (two private) cases are rooted in institutional differences between the two public (two private) delivery models. For instance, Aguas de Manizales is an ESP, whereas EAA Villavicencio is an EICE, and Sera QA Tunja is a concession model, whereas Metroagua Santa Marta is a lease model. After having assessed the technical and socio-economic context, as well as the delivery model characteristics, sub-section 5.6.5 concentrates on analysing the main supposition previously stated, i.e., whether the variation in the performance can be explained by local governance factors. Finally, subsection 5.6.6 concludes.

5.6.2. WS Service Performance and System Characteristics

Table 5.8 summarises important performance indicators for the four cases, as well as some basic system characteristics. The information reported stems from the service companies and was either provided on request of the author or taken from the companies' annual and monitoring reports. This information partially differs from the information provided by SSPD and CRA, on which the case selection was based.

The information gathered largely confirms the classification in underperforming and outperforming cases as far as the levels of the four indicators used for the case selection are concerned (coverage with water and sewer connections, UFW and CR). Aguas de Manizales and Sera QA Tunja show clearly[106] better values than EAA Villavicencio and Metroagua Santa Marta with respect to these indicators. The picture is not that clear cut with respect to change over time of these indicators and as far as some additional indicators reported in the table are concerned. In the following service performance, basic system characteristics and main investment needs are discussed for each of the cases.

One important context information is given in advance. Relatively recent environmental legislation provides environmental authorities (CARs) with the authority to levy considerable wastewater discharge fees on WS service providers. Fees depend on the degree of contamination of the effluents. This explains why investments in wastewater collection and treatment are given a great attention in the cities discussed.

5.6.2.1. Aguas de Manizales

Amongst the four cases chosen, the public provider Aguas de Manizales was ranked highest according to the data of SSPD and CRA (see Table A5.7). This relative position is confirmed by the information reported in Table 5.8, according to which Aguas de Manizales outperforms the other three cases.

Between 2000 and 2004, the company has maintained or improved performance indicators on a high level, notably coverage with water and sewer connections, which is close to 100%.[107] Aguas de Manizales presents the lowest UFW and the highest CR. Coverage with meters is 100%. Labour efficiency (number of workers per 1,000 connections) is comparable to the two private providers (3.5 in 2004). The continuity of water service reported is 24 hours per day and, according to the information given by the company, the water delivered has continuously met legal drinking water quality standards. This latter point is corroborated by the reports on drinking water quality published by SSPD (2004b; 2005c) and by the statements of two user representatives.

These very positive figures have to be judged considering the initial situation, as well as the technical characteristics of the system. Unlike the other three cases, Aguas de Manizales shows very favourable initial values for all performance indicators. The high initial coverage levels could be maintained by expanding the number of water connections by a very moderate annual growth rate of 1.3%.[108] Moreover, water consumption per connection has been decreasing during the last years and installed drinking water production capacity lies well above the capacity needed to meet demand.[109] Taken altogether, this means very low, or even absent, investment needs for system expansion. The management could, thus, concentrate efforts and financial means on improving the already high technical and commercial efficiency. An additional advantage is rooted in the water distribution system that is integrally gravity fed. This implies lower production

Table 5.8 Main Indicators and Characteristics of the Four Cases (Information Given by Enterprises)

	Aguas de Manizales		Sera QA Tunja		EAA Villavicencio		Metroagua S. Marta	
	2000	2004	1998	2004	2001	2004	1999	2004
Performance indicators								
Coverage* water	99.5%	99.5%	98%	100%	53.3%**	58.5%	79%	88%
Coverage* sewer	98.8%	98.2%	95.8%	98.2%	57.6%**	60.5%	69%	74%
UFW	32.3%	29.7%	48%	42%	77.5%	67.5%	62%	48%
Collection rate	97.7%	99.4%	87%	93%	86%	91%	n.a.	70%#
Continuity water	24h/day	24h/day	17.7h/day	24h/day	20.5h/day	23.7h/day	n.a.	22h/day#
Coverage meters	100%	100%	98%	100%	48.3%	82.7%	n.a.	62%
Workers/1,000 water connections	3.6	3.5	n.a.	3.5	6.8	4.2	4	3.2
Production data and system characteristics								
Water connections	76,637	80,737	25,353	30,993	53,547	63,922	56,724	69,231
Water produced/ connection (m³/month)†	n.a.	30.5	n.a.	25.8	n.a.	58.0	n.a.	41.5
Vulnerability of water resources††	High		High		Low		High	
Pumping required	No		Yes		Most part of the year/ main system: No		Yes	
Sewer system	Wastewater and storm-water (partially separate)		Wastewater and storm-water (combined)		Wastewater and storm-water (combined)		Wastewater only (no stormwater)	
Wastewater treatment	No		No		No		Yes (submarine wastewater diffuser)	
Ownership	Public		Private		Public		Private	

* Refers to urban areas.
**Estimated by the author based on the available coverage figures (new definition of measurement) for 2004, the number of water and sewer connections (2001, 2004) and population (2001, 2004). Coverage in 2001 according to the old definition of service area was: 77% (water); 85% (sewer).
#May 2005.
†Author's calculations based on water production data.
††Source: IDEAM (without year: cuadro 5); scale of the indicator: very low, low, middle, high, very high
Source: Information provided directly by the enterprises or contained in their annual reports.

costs because no investments in pumps are required and no energy costs for pumping have to be incurred.

The most pressing problems and investment needs are related to the environmental dimension. Except for a very small pilot plant, wastewater is not treated. The wastewater includes industrial effluents, which are an important source of contamination of the Chinchiná River. The construction of interceptor sewers for the collection of wastewater is in progress. The fact that the sewer system partially separates storm and wastewater eases this endeavour. The technology to be used for wastewater treatment had still to be defined by end of 2005.

According to IDEAM (without year: cuadro 5), the vulnerability of water resources in Manizales (conditions of a dry year) is high,[110] just like in Tunja and Santa Marta, but unlike in Villavicencio (low). The provincial environmental authority (CORPOCALDAS) has engaged in a strategy for the management and conservation of the up-river water sources that feed the city of Manizales. There seemed to be a close cooperation between CORPOCALDAS, Aguas de Manizales, and the district government to this respect.

5.6.2.2. Sera QA Tunja

The private provider Sera QA Tunja is the second company classified as a good performer. By 2004, it shows values for the indicators coverage with water and sewer connections, coverage with meters, continuity of water service and labour efficiency that are just as good as those shown by Aguas de Manizales. UFW (42%) and CR (93%) are worse, but still the second best of the sample. As far as drinking water standards are concerned, the company states that the water delivered meets legal standards. However, according to the information published by SSPD (2004b; 2005c), during 2003 and 2004, the water did not meet legal standards. These reports have been called into question by Sera QA Tunja. In this context, it has to be reminded that the reliability of the information on drinking water quality reported by SSPD has been repeatedly disputed by service providers (see sub-section 5.4.4).

Sera QA Tunja presents less favourable initial values with respect to the values of the indicators UFW, CR, and continuity of service than Aguas de Manizales. The company managed to improve these indicators and to maintain the high levels of coverage during the period in question while facing a growth of water connections corresponding to an annual rate of 3.4%.[111] The improvement of the continuity of the water service seems especially remarkable, because for decades Tunja has had a bad reputation in Colombia for the discontinuity and lack of water service (Tunja shared this bad reputation with Villavicencio). The improvements have been associated with important intellectual and physical investments during the period in question, e.g. in an inventory of pipes, a sectorisation of the water distribution network, the interconnection of the two main water sources of the city (superficial source and aquifer), the replacement of old water pipes, and the construction and installation of additional storage tanks and pumps. Unlike Manizales, which integrally relies on (up to now reliable) superficial water sources, Tunja faces a shortage of superficial water sources and has to use both superficial sources and the aquifer. This means that the company has to rely on pumping during the whole year.

Similar to Manizales, by 2005 the most important problems and future investment needs are related to wastewater collection and treatment and to the management and protection of water sources. Construction activities with respect to separating storm and wastewater sewers and to installing interceptor sewers for the collection of wastewater are in an advanced stage and the project for the construction of the first module of a wastewater treatment plant is ready. Concerning protection and management of the up-stream superficial water sources, according to information gained in an interview with a representative of the responsible environmental authority (Corporación Autónoma Regional de Boyacá, CORPOBOYACÁ), the district of Tunja and Sera QA are not willing to financially support necessary conservation activities planned by CORPOBOYACÁ.

5.6.2.3. EAA Villavicencio

Based on the data reported by SSPD and CRA (years 1998 and 2003), the public service provider EAA Villavicencio had been ranked worst of the four cases because it not only showed unfavourable average values, but also worsening of some indicators. This gloomy picture is not integrally confirmed by the information available from the company, according to which performance indicators have improved between 2001 and 2004.

Nevertheless, all indicators show a poor performance by 2001, particularly UFW (77.5%), labour efficiency (6.8 workers per 1,000 connections), and coverage with water (53.3%) and sewer (57.6%)[112] connections. The situation with respect to coverage with water and sewer services is very particular in Villavicencio and needs to be commented on. Because, for many years, the company has been delivering discontinuous and bad water service, in the context of the construction of new neighbourhoods, there have been founded several private water providers that typically exploit the aquifer and serve their neighbourhood only.[113] This history partially explains the ambiguity of the available information on service coverage. According to the "old" coverage definition, these neighbourhoods were not considered when calculating coverage because they did not belong to the service area of EAA Villavicencio. However, by request of SSPD, since 2003 the whole urban area has to be considered when calculating coverage, which explains the extremely low figures reported in Table 5.8. According to the "old" definition, coverage in 2001 was 77% (water) and 85% (sewer). The apparently low coverage with services in Villavicencio implies that many households have to rely on unsafe or expensive sources for their domestic water supply.

Starting from a low level and according to the data presented in the table, the company has achieved major improvements between 2001 and 2004, particularly with respect to continuity of service, coverage with meters and labour efficiency. The annual growth rate of water connections (6.1%)[114] is the highest amongst the four cases. However, the biggest portion of the increase in connections does not correspond to new connections but to the acquisition of two private water providers in 2002 and 2003 by EAA Villavicencio. The improvements in continuity have only become possible since the completion of a new surface water captation system in 1998. This has considerably increased raw water availability and has made it possible to feed the system most time of the year by gravity without having to rely on pumping from the Guaitiquía River. Before 1998, service interruption was rather the rule than the exception for the users of EAA Villavicencio.

However, UFW is still on a very high level in 2004 (67.5%) pointing at major incentive problems with regard to internal efficiency. The great technical and commercial[115] water losses imply unnecessary drinking water treatment costs (EAA Villavicencio produces more than double of drinking water per connection than Sera QA Tunja). Similar to the case of Tunja, the available information regarding the water quality is ambiguous: according to the reports of EAA Villavicencio, the water delivered has been meeting the legal standards, whereas, according to the report published by SSPD (2005c), it did not in 2004. Doubts concerning the water quality are corroborated by a report of the district auditor of Villavicencio in 2005 who establishes the bad condition and maintenance of the main drinking water treatment plant.[116] Moreover, according to information reported by Veeduría de Servicios Públicos (2003), there have been major service interruptions in 2002 and 2003 of more than 2 weeks in each case. This is in spite of the abundance and low vulnerability of water sources in the district of Villavicencio, which presents the most advantageous natural conditions of the four districts.

The problems sketched show that there is a major need for improvements and suggest that efforts and investments should be concentrated on reducing the existing coverage gap and on improving UFW, continuity, and quality of service. Besides, there seems to be a need for starting to face the problem of wastewater effluents that until today are released into the water body without any treatment. By 2005, the management of EAA Villavicencio and the district government were clearly prioritising the latter point, concentrating attention and financial means on a very ambitious project comprising the construction of interceptor sewers for wastewater collection and the construction of a wastewater treatment plant with a planned investment volume (2003–2010) of 233,350 million Colombian Pesos.[117]

5.6.2.4. Metroagua Santa Marta

The private provider Metroagua Santa Marta is the second company classified as a bad performer. Similar to EAA Villavicencio, the company shows very unfavourable initial values for coverage with water (79%) and sewer (69%) connections and UFW (62%) in 1999.[118] The company managed to improve these indicators considerably until 2004, particularly coverage with water connections (88%) and UFW (48%). Consistent with the increase in coverage, the annual growth rate of water connections is the second highest of the sample (4.1%).[119] However, the coverage gap by 2004 is still great implying that many families, especially those living in the poor peri-urban settlements of Santa Marta, are without safe water and sewer services (see the following). Moreover, continuity of water service (22 hours/day) and coverage with meters (62%) present low values. The collection rate (70%) is remarkably poor for a private provider and is, by far, the worst of the four cases. Only the indicator for labour efficiency presents a favourable value (3.2 workers per 1,000 connections). Unlike in the other three cities, in Santa Marta there is no stormwater sewer system, implying frequent flooding of the streets during the rainy season.

Again, the information on drinking water quality is ambiguous, with the company stating that the water released into the distribution network meets legal standards, but SSPD (2005c) reporting that it did not in 2004. The statements of several users corroborate problems with drinking water quality. Moreover, according to these users, the discontinuity of service and the lack of pressure seem to be considerably more pronounced than the value of the continuity indicator suggests. In various neighbourhoods, it is common that the water service is available only during some hours between midnight and the early morning. In other cases, when the water service is interrupted for longer periods, households have to rely on water vendors or tanker trucks. These deficiencies may partially explain the extremely low collection rate of Metroagua Santa Marta.[120]

With regard to the deficiencies in service quality, it has to be commented on the particular social conditions in Santa Marta. Unlike in Manizales and in Tunja, and to a greater extent than in Villavicencio, in Santa Marta there is a growing number of poor peri-urban settlements. These settlements typically have been built on state property without any regulation and without any WS or other infrastructure. In order to have access to water, the dwellers of many of these settlements have connected themselves illegally and in a non-professional way to the water network operated by Metroagua (approximately 10,000 dwellings are connected in such conditions, according to information given by the company). Several of the settlements have been built on the hills above the storage tanks of the distribution system and dwellers use motor pumps to transport the water to their homes. According to Metroagua Santa Marta, apart from causing high UFW, the illegal connections and the use of motor pumps

give rise to a drop in pressure in the distribution network and to a contamination of the water, which negatively affects the quality of service
for all users.

A further problem that is related to the discontinuity and low quality
of service is the low captation capacity from superficial water sources
(water flows have been shrinking during the last years). This means that
raw water production has to rely heavily on the aquifer (60% of the water
produced during the dry season and 40% during the rest of the year) and
thus implies relatively high energy costs for pumping and service interruptions in case of power failures (which are relatively common in Santa
Marta). The limited raw water availability is compounded by the relatively low drinking water production capacity (1,080 litres per second)
and the high UFW.

The problems explained make clear that there are big challenges that need
to be faced which involve major investments, above all expanding coverage
with services and improving their continuity and, related to this, reducing
UFW and possibly expanding raw, as well as drinking water production
capacity. By 2005, the district and the company were working on these
issues. The major investment projects planned or recently initiated were
the construction of new domestic water and sewer connections, a project
for augmenting surface water captation capacity and the construction of a
major rainwater collector sewer in order to prevent flooding. Finally, there
is an urgent need for designing and implementing an integrated management of the up-stream water resources stemming from the Sierra Nevada
because quality and quantity of these resources have considerably diminished during the last years.

5.6.2.5. Summary

Summing up and neglecting the aspects related to wastewater treatment
and up-stream water resource management and protection, it can be stated
that in the period of analysis

- Aguas de Manizales (i) maintained all performance indicators on a high
  level, (ii) presented a low growth rate in the number of connections, and
  (iii) benefited from favourable technical conditions (no pumping);
- Sera QA Tunja (i) maintained coverage with services and coverage
  with meters on a high level; (ii) improved the remaining indicators,
  particularly continuity of water services; (iii) showed an intermediate
  growth rate in the number of connections; and (iv) operated a system
  that relies on pumping during the whole year;
- EAA Villavicencio (i) improved performance indicators starting
  from low levels; (ii) presented a high growth rate in the number of
  connections which is, however, mainly explained by the acquisition
  of existing private providers; (iii) by 2004, still showed important

performance deficiencies, particularly with respect to UFW (which is extremely high), coverage with meters and coverage with services; and (iv) operated a system that relies only partially on pumping;

- Metroagua Santa Marta (i) improved performance indicators starting from a low level; (ii) showed relatively high growth in new connections; (iii) by 2004 still showed important performance deficiencies, particularly with respect to the collection rate, coverage with services, coverage with meters and continuity; and (iv) operated a system that relies on pumping during the whole year.

5.6.3. Socio-Economic Conditions

Before describing and analysing the institutional design of service delivery (5.6.4) and the local governance factors (5.6.5), the socio-economic context of the four cities is briefly touched.

Table 5.9 lists some basic indicators that illustrate the socio-economic context of the four cities in question. Unfortunately, data like GDP per capita, neonatal mortality, literacy, and housing deficit indicators are not available on the district level. This is why these indicators are reported for the provincial level, i.e., for Caldas (capital Manizales), Boyacá (capital Tunja), Meta (capital Villavicencio), and Magdalena (capital Santa Marta). Since the values for the provinces are to an important portion determined by their capitals, these indicators are used as proxies for describing the relative conditions in the capitals.

The demographic, health, and housing indicators present a pattern according to which Manizales shows the most favourable values, followed by Tunja, Villavicencio, and, finally, by Santa Marta (see annual population growth, number of displaced people as share of the population, neonatal mortality, share of households with housing deficits). Santa Marta received, by far, the greatest number of displaced[121] people between 1999 and 2005 (measured as share of the population in 2004) and presents the highest share of households with housing deficits. These indicators are in line with the information gained in the interviews according to which in Manizales and Tunja there were no families living in squatter settlements, in Villavicencio a moderate number and in Santa Marta a high number.

The remaining indicators listed show a more diverse picture. As far as illiteracy is concerned, Manizales (most favourable) and Santa Marta (least favourable) maintain their rank positions, whereas Villavicencio (second most favourable) and Tunja (second least favourable) change their positions. The GDP per capita is greatest in Villavicencio (which is, to a good degree, explained by the oil production that occurs in the Province of Meta), followed by Manizales, Tunja, and Santa Marta. The pattern with respect to the WS user structure is remarkable in so far as Santa Marta, which is one of the "bad" performers, presents the most favourable proportion of subsidees to contributors. It is followed by Manizales and Villavicencio.

Table 5.9   Socio-Economic Indicators

	Manizales (Caldas)	Tunja (Boyacá)	Villavicencio (Meta)	Santa Marta (Magdalena)
Population (2004)*	355,368	116,420	314,015	418,630
Annual population growth (1998–2004)**	1.04%	1.20%	2.83%	3.14%
No. of displaced people received 1999–2005 as share of the population in 2004***	2.25%	3.12%	8.79%	16.73%
Total annual receipts of district government per capita (thousands Colombian Pesos)#	351.85	394.39	354.81	308.14
User structure (proportion of subsidees per contributor by 2004)##	3.67	8.74	4.76	2.95
GDP per capita (2001) (constant million Col. Pesos 1994)†,###	1,473,030	1,382,306	2,058,516	936,466
Neonatal mortality (2000) (deaths /100,000 habitants)†,###	14.9	15.8	19.4	22.7
Illiteracy (2002)†,###	7.3%	9.9%	8.4%	11.9%
Share of households with housing deficit (2000)†,###	14.4%	22.5%	29.0%	39.2%

*DANE; www.dane.gov.co (accessed November 11, 2006): Urban area ("cabecera").
**Own calculations with data from DANE.
***Own calculations with data published in CODHES (2005).
#Average of the years 2001 to 2004 (current Col. Pesos); own calculations with data provided by DNP.
##Own calculations with data provided by the WS service providers.
###DNP, Información básica regional, Datos generales, www.dnp.gov.co/paginas_detalle. aspx?idp=197 (accessed November 8, 2006).
†Data refers to the provincial level, i.e. to Caldas, Boyacá, Meta, Magdalena.

Finally, Tunja presents, by far, the most unfavourable user structure: there are 8.74 subsidees per contributor. This is partially explained by the fact that, in Tunja, there is no residential stratum 6.

With regard to the financial situation of the districts, the figures reported in Table 5.9 show that total district government receipts[122] per capita are highest in Tunja, followed by Villavicencio and Manizales, that show very similar amounts, and finally by Santa Marta. Moreover, the district of Santa Marta is highly indebted. Under the mediation of the Ministry of Finance, in 2004 the district government has subscribed an agreement with its creditors in order to restructure its debt.[123] This agreement restricts the district's ability to issue new debt and demands for fiscal austerity.

To sum up, it can be said that the pattern of the demographic, health, and housing indicators corroborates the pattern of the WS performance indicators previously described, according to which Manizales and Tunja are the good performers and Villavicencio and Santa Marta the bad performers, and suggests that the WS performance may be related to these socio-economic dimensions. The picture for the remaining indicators is a little more diverse. Nevertheless, there is one striking feature: except for the user structure, Santa Marta shows the least favourable values for all indicators discussed, and, in addition, its district government had to subscribe an agreement for restructuring its unsustainable debt.

5.6.4. Institutional Design of Service Delivery and Financing

This sub-section describes and compares the main aspects of the institutional design of service delivery, as well as the related aspect of financing. The question to be asked here is whether the variation in the performance between the two public cases (between the two private cases) can be explained by differences in the specifics of the two public (of the two PSP) delivery models.

All four companies are members of the National Association of Public Service-Providing Companies (ANDESCO), which is the most important lobby organisation for service providers. Table 5.10 summarises important characteristics related to the institutional design (ownership, corporate form, contractual arrangement), the tariff level, and the profitability, which are discussed to more detail in what follows. First the two public, then the two PSP delivery models are treated.

5.6.4.1. *Aguas de Manizales*

Institutional Design of Service Delivery

Aguas de Manizales is a stock corporation (ESP) founded in 1996 in reaction to the Public Services Law (1994) that prescribed a corporatisation of service providers (see sub-section 5.3.4). Ninety-nine point eight percent of the shares are held by Instituto de Financiamiento, Promoción y Desarrollo de Manizales (INFIMANIZALES), which is a public enterprise that acts as a holding company owned to 100% by the district of Manizales. INFIMANIZALES is also the owner of all physical assets of the water and sewer system of Manizales. These assets are given in concession to Aguas de Manizales, which is responsible for the operation, rehabilitation, and expansion of the system, and that pays a royalty of 10% of the turnover to INFIMANIZALES. Since the transformation of the district water works into a stock corporation in 1996, the company has no workers' union and no important pension or labour liabilities.

The board of directors of Aguas de Manizales consists of five members who are appointed by the mayor, acting as representative of the district government and owner of INFIMANIZALES. Since the 1990s—i.e., since

Table 5.10 Institutional Characteristics of Service Providers, Tariffs and Returns on Sales

	Aguas de Manizales	EAA Villavicencio	Sera QA Tunja	Metroagua S. Marta
Ownership and corporate form	Public ESP (99.8%)	Public EICE (100%)	Private ESP (100%)	Private ESP (65%)
Contract (duration: end of contract)	Concession (30 years: 2026)	—	Concession (30 years: 2026)	Lease & management (20 + 6 years: 2017)
Foundation/change in corporate form (change of investor)	1996	1996	1996	1989 (1997, 2002)
Number of general managers 1998–2005	6	6	1	4
Members board of directors	3 public/2 private	4 public/1 private/1 user	All private	3 public/6 private
Monthly water + sewerage tariff by December 2004 (Colombian Pesos)*	961 + 628 = 1,589	1,032 + 1,062 = 2,094	1,521 + 761 = 2,282	1,416 + 799 = 2,215
Return on sales, average 2003/2004	28.8%	26.2%	12.5%	16.1%

*Tarifa media básica aplicada estrato 4 / m³: monthly amount per m³ paid by residential stratum 4 supposing a monthly consumption of 20 m³ (the amount comprises fixed and variable charge components).
Sources: Companies; supplemented with information provided by SSPD or taken from SSPD (2005b).

the local business elite has come to local political power in Manizales (see sub-section 5.6.5)—there has been an agreement between the respective mayor and the local business associations to appoint three directors amongst public officials representing the district government and two directors amongst the local business representing the private sector. Formally, it is the board of directors who chooses the general manager but, *de facto*, he is chosen by the mayor. The general manager of Aguas de Manizales has been changing in tandem with the mayor, i.e., there has been a great fluctuation. Between 1998 and July of 2005, the company has been directed by six general managers.

Financing

As has been said, Aguas de Manizales is responsible for the operation, rehabilitation, *and* expansion of the system, and thus for arranging the corresponding finance. By December, 2004, Aguas de Manizales offered the lowest water and sewerage tariff of the four companies (see Table 5.10). In spite of this, during the last years the company has been able to almost integrally finance its "traditional" activities[124] by tariff receipts (internal financing) and credit (external financing), and to achieve the highest return on sales (28.8%) of the sample. Aguas de Manizales has been assigned a very favourable credit risk rating of AA+ and, thus, enjoys privileged conditions in the capital market. Therefore, it can be stated that the company is in a financially sustainable situation (see sub-section 2.4.2). This is, in so far, remarkable, as the district government has only recently begun to cover a small portion (12.4%) of the accumulated deficit between subsidies and contributions in the Solidarity Fund.[125] The fact that the deficit is not covered by transfers implies either that the company has to cut down its investment plan on which the reference tariff authorised by CRA was based, or that actual costs lie well below reference costs, which means that deficits between subsidies and contributions are covered by the company's surplus. The relatively low tariffs and the good financial performance of Aguas de Manizales have to be judged in the context of the favourable technical conditions (no pumping required) and the relatively low investment needs.

The significant investments associated with the "non-traditional" activities of the company, i.e. the construction of collector and interceptor sewers in the context of the planned wastewater treatment, are financed relying on grants from CORPOCALDAS.

5.6.4.2. EAA Villavicencio

Institutional Design of Service Delivery

Just like Aguas de Manizales, EAA Villavicencio was founded in 1996. But unlike the former, EAA Villavicencio has the corporate form of an *Empresa*

Industrial y Comercial del Estado (EICE), which means that its equity capital is not divided into shares and that it is totally owned by the district of Villavicencio. There is no explicit concession contract between the district and the company. The general manager and the members of the board of directors are appointed directly by the mayor. Just like in the case of Aguas de Manizales, there has been a great fluctuation in the general management (six general managers between 1998 and 2005). By July 2005, the board of directors consisted of six members: four representatives of the district government (amongst them the mayor), one local representative of the business association FENALCO[126] and one user representative. Until 2004, the President of the Chamber of Commerce of Villavicencio had also been a member of the board of directors. The President left the board in 2004 because she did not agree with the way the company was managed (see the following).

The workers of the company are public employees, and there is a workers' union. According to BRC Investor Services S.A. (2004), the company was not faced with important pension or labour liabilities by 2004. The mayor regularly intervenes in the management of the company regarding staff decisions in order to arrange for posts for his clients. This creates uncertainty regarding career opportunities for the staff members. Employee motivation and identification with the company appeared to be low (see the following).

Financing

Table 5.10 shows that EAA Villavicencio has charged the second lowest water and sewerage tariff and has achieved the second highest return on sales of the sample. According to BRC Investor Services S.A. (2004), the company has lately shown satisfactory, although erratic, financial results. The financial results could be even better if they were not compromised by the technical deficiencies described in sub-section 5.6.2. The district government regularly has been transferring funds to cover the deficit between subsidies and contributions via the Solidarity Fund, notably increasing the operating income of the company. In 2004, the transfers to the Solidarity Fund amounted to 5,800 million Colombian Pesos,[127] corresponding to 19.8% of operating income. EAA Villavicencio has been assigned a credit risk rating of BBB (the lowest grade for which an investment is recommended).[128] This means that EAA Villavicencio has access to the private capital market, but enjoys less favourable conditions than Aguas de Manizales.

The financing scheme of EAA Villavicencio is shaped by the important investments in collector and interceptor sewers recently undertaken and projected for the future (as discussed previously). In 2004, total expenditures almost doubled operating income. The wastewater investments executed so far have been financed by credits raised by the company (16,000 million Colombian Pesos),[129] as well as by public grants from the district government (granted in addition to the funds transferred via the Solidarity Fund), the provincial government, and the national government.

5.6.4.3. Sera QA Tunja

Institutional Design of Service Delivery

Sera QA Tunja is a stock corporation (ESP) owned 94% by Proactiva Medioambiente SA,[130] the headquarters of which are in Madrid (Spain), and 5.8% by Proactiva Colombia SA. The members of the board of directors and the general manager are appointed by Proactiva Medioambiente SA. Since the foundation of Sera QA Tunja in 1996, the general manager has not been changed. The staff members seemed to be motivated and appeared to have a great feeling of identity with the company. This could partially be related to the training and career opportunities that an international group like Proactiva Medioambiente SA can offer. Sera QA Tunja has no workers' union.

The concession contract, with a duration of 30 years, was awarded through a public tender in which two competitors participated. The detailed and comprehensive concession contract includes the responsibility for operation, rehabilitation, and expansion of the system. It stipulates that the necessary investments associated with these activities are to be co-financed by the district of Tunja. In 2005, there were legal proceedings pending concerning the validity of the concession contract.

Financing

Sera QA Tunja charges the highest water and sewerage tariff of the sample and, at the same time, shows the lowest return on sales. The relatively high tariff level should be judged taking into consideration that the user structure of Tunja is the least favourable and that operating the system requires pumping. In order to finance its expenses for the operation, rehabilitation, and expansion of the water and sewer system, Sera QA Tunja relies on tariff receipts and on credits. During the first five years of the concession, the company has invested its own funds to an amount of approximately 7,000 million Colombian Pesos[131] in pipes, sewers, pumping stations, tanks, and master plans.

The district does not transfer money via the Solidarity Fund to the company in order to cover the deficit between subsidies and contributions. Instead, the district has made important commitments for financing investment activities, which are fixed in an agreement with Sera QA Tunja on the investment obligations of each party. These commitments exceed the transfers, earmarked for WS, that the district receives in the context of the decentralisation law. This means that the district has to arrange for additional funds. During the first five years of the concession, the district government has invested an amount of approximately 11,000 million Colombian Pesos,[132] and the national government a sum of 4,000 million Colombian Pesos.[133] The financing of investment activities by the district government has not always been problem-free. The predecessor of the mayor in office by July 2005 had delayed the committed financing by two years, hampering this way progress of construction activities.

By 2005, the investment activities are marked by the wastewater treatment project. The design and supervision of construction activities are made by Sera QA Tunja. The financing of the collector and interceptor sewers (16,473 million Colombian Pesos[134]) is provided by the district government and the national government, whereas Sera QA Tunja concentrates on investments in the water and sewer network and related assets. The project for the construction of the first module of a wastewater treatment plant is ready and a financial agreement (financiers: CORPOBOYACÁ, district, provincial, and national governments) is about to be signed. By 2005, Sera QA Tunja had important liabilities with CORPOBOYACÁ originated in the non-payment of wastewater discharge fees—there was a court decision pending on this issue.

5.6.4.4. Metroagua Santa Marta

Institutional Design of Service Delivery

Metroagua Santa Marta is one of the pioneer PSP experiences in Colombia. The company was founded in 1989, i.e., well before the public services reform. There was no public tender, but the contract was awarded by direct negotiations. At the beginning, the contractual scheme was a pure lease contract. This changed in 1997 when a specialised operator (Aguas de Barcelona) invested in Metroagua Santa Marta and started to operate the system. In 2000, AAA de Servicios SA[135] replaced Aguas de Barcelona as investor and operator. Since 1997, the contractual arrangement has been characterised by the combination of a lease and a management contract explained in what follows.

Metroagua—which is a stock corporation (ESP) owned 43% by AAA de Serivcios SA, 22% by local private investors, and 35% by the district of Santa Marta—leases the system assets from the district. The leasing fee paid by Metroagua to the district amounts to 2% of annual turnover. The responsibilities from the leasing contract include operation and rehabilitation of the system, but exclude expansion investments. Besides this leasing contract between Metroagua and the district of Santa Marta, there is a management contract between Metroagua and the operator AAA de Servicios SA. The operator earns a monthly management fee amounting to 4% of the turnover, plus 12% of the profit before taxes.

The board of directors of Metroagua consists of three members that are appointed by the mayor and that represent the district (amongst them the mayor, himself, who is the chair of the board), two members that represent the local private investors, and four members that represent the operator AAA de Servicios SA. The general manager is proposed by the operator. Between 1998 and 2005, the company has been directed by four general managers. Metroagua Santa Marta has no workers' union.

Financing

Metroagua Santa Marta charges the second highest water and sewerage tariff (only slightly lower than the tariff charged by Sera QA Tunja) and shows the second lowest return on sales (16.1 % on average for the years 2003 and 2004). Returns of the company have been positive since the engagement of AAA de Servicios SA in 2000. Between 1997 and 1999, the company had suffered losses. There is a contractual arrangement between Metroagua Santa Marta and the district to assure that the funds destined to cover the deficit between subsidies and contributions are transferred to the company (nevertheless, between 2001 and 2003, under the predecessor of the mayor in office by 2005, the district government failed to transfer a guaranteed amount of 15,000 million Colombian Pesos[136]). The company has elaborated a comprehensive study of the aquifer of Santa Marta and has invested in the modernisation or reposition of drinking water treatment plants, pumping stations, tanks, pipes, and sewers. Between 2001 and 2004, investments with its own funds amounted to 3,233 million Colombian Pesos.[137]

As has become evident from the deficiencies of the system described, there are not only required major investments in the rehabilitation but also in the expansion of the system. As of 2004, the projected expansion investments amounted to a total sum of 73,668 million Colombian Pesos.[138] Since the district is highly indebted, it is constrained in arranging for the necessary financial resources. Noteworthy expansion investments (water service and rainwater collection) for an amount of approximately 10,000 million Colombian Pesos[139] have been financed by resources stemming from the national government. The planned investments for augmenting the capacity for surface water captation, as well as the capacity of the drinking water treatment plants for a total amount of 17,630 million Colombian Pesos[140] are to be financed by the national government and by the district's transfers via the Solidarity Fund (years 2005 to 2008). According to Metroagua, there is no urgent need to invest in wastewater treatment in Santa Marta since the system is provided with a submarine wastewater diffuser.

5.6.4.5. Summary

The purpose of this sub-section was to analyse whether the institutional differences between the two public (the two private) delivery models may help explain the variation in their performance. With respect to the two public delivery models, the following points are highlighted:

- The difference in the corporate structure (ESP in case of Manizales and EICE in case of Villavicencio) does not seem to make a difference regarding the stability of the management (both companies had six general managers between 1998 and 2005).

- Unlike in Villavicencio, in Manizales there is an explicit concession contract between the district (more precisely: INFIMANIZALES) and the service provider. This explicit concession contract may contribute to strengthen the separation of roles between the district government and the company and, thus, the independence of the management, e.g. with respect to staffing decisions (for more aspects regarding government intervention see 5.6.5).

With respect to the two private delivery models, the following points seem especially relevant:

- The differences in the way of awarding the contracts could have had an impact on the performance. Unlike in Santa Marta, where the contract was awarded in direct negotiations, in Tunja a public tender was carried out—which was supported with technical assistance by the Ministry of Development and accompanied by consultancy and transaction advisory services. As compared to direct negotiations, public tenders have the advantages of stimulating competitive forces and of improving the informational basis, the transparency, and the quality of the contract.
- Tunja is a concession model, and Santa Marta is a combination of a lease and a management contract. This implies a greater responsibility and, thus, a greater risk borne by Sera QA as compared to Metroagua (or AAA de Servicios). But, at the same time, the concession implies a greater independence for achieving improvements (e.g. in service continuity and, thus, tariff receipts) because the company directly controls a greater portion of the investments. In the case of Santa Marta, service improvements depend, to a good degree, on expansion investments that, in turn, depend on the availability of public funds from the highly indebted district government. This district government has proved to be an unreliable financier in the past (see also 5.6.5).
- The differences in performance could also be related to the stability in the management. Whereas Metroagua has been directed by four general managers between 1998 and 2005, Sera QA Tunja in 2005 still was directed by its first general manager. The fluctuation in the case of Metroagua is partially explained by the change in the principal shareholder and operator in 2000.

All in all, these arguments seem more plausible for explaining the divergent performance in the case of the private delivery models than in the case of the public delivery models.

5.6.5. Local Governance Factors

The purpose of this sub-section is to identify local governance factors that contribute explaining the variation in the performance of the four cases.

This is, perhaps, the dimension that is most difficult to investigate empirically. Unfortunately, there are no standard indicators available that capture the level of democratic participation, the degree of separation of powers, the quality of the local bureaucracy, or the incidence of corruption for the sub-national level in Colombia. Therefore, building on the categories developed in sections 5.2 and 5.3, the analysis concentrates on describing and qualifying the following dimensions of local government:

  i. User and civil society participation in WS services;
  ii. Security situation and activities of non-state armed groups; and
  iii. Clientelistic strategies as well as corruption affecting the provision of WS services.

The investigation has to deal with the problem that the latter two dimensions are sensitive and could not be directly addressed in the interviews. Corruption, by definition, is an illegal phenomenon which, in addition, in Colombia is partially linked to the activities of non-state armed groups involved in drug trafficking and other criminal activities (see sub-sections 5.2.1 and 5.2.2). The information gained in interviews and informal conversations is, thus, likely to be fragmentary and biased. Therefore, apart from the information gained in interviews and informal conversations, this sub-section relies on the available quantitative indicators on the security situation, as well as on reports and news articles on non-state armed groups activities and corrupt practices (see the sources cited in the following).

5.6.5.1. User and Civil Society Participation

During the field stay, the attention has been concentrated on the role of the CDCSs. In each city, there have been conducted interviews with at least one CDCS spokesman. Information on the role of additional civil society organisations has been collected in a cursory manner. For a description of the functions and a general assessment of the CDCSs, see sub-section 5.3.2.

In none of the four cities did the CDCSs seem to have a significant impact on (i) monitoring the subsidies delivered by the district to users from low socio-economic strata and (ii) furthering the cooperation between users and the provider or making propositions for service improvements. In none of the cities was there a close cooperation between the CDCS and the district administration on the one hand, or between the CDCS and the service provider on the other hand. The most important function of the spokesmen was to assist users in managing their complaints (bad service, undue charges, differences with respect to metering) with the provider and with SSPD. With the exception of the spokesman of Villavicencio, all spokesmen interviewed were unemployed.

At the time of the field stay, there existed three CDCSs in Manizales, four in Tunja, four in Villavicencio, and 11 in Santa Marta (these numbers include not only the CDCSs responsible for WS, but also those responsible for fixed-line telecommunication, electricity, and gas).

Manizales

In Manizales, CDCSs seemed to keep a low profile. The district government did not support the work of the spokesmen. CDCSs received some support of the *Personero Municipal*.[141] Concerning user representation in the CPE, according to the information given by a user representative who participated in the CPE, the district government has refused to pay the legally prescribed fee to the user representative for participating in the CPE sessions. The user representative has not been able to influence any decision of the CPE regarding user complaints against their socio-economic classification in favour of the complainant.

A distinctive element of Manizales is that, as compared to the other three cities, the degree of organisation of the civil society appeared to be strong. Local entrepreneurs dominate civil society organisation in Manizales and shape local politics. Entrepreneurs were the driving force for the creation of the civic watchdog organisation *Corporación Cívica de Caldas* (CCC) in the 1980s. In the 1980s, the prevailing perception was that local governments in Manizales were embezzling public funds and badly managing public enterprises. CCC was founded in order to act as an organ of the civil society that could denounce this state of affairs and claim more transparency and civic participation. CCC now is an established organisation. Besides, there are strong business organisations in Manizales.[142] Since the 1990s, local entrepreneurs have entered formal party politics. Several mayors, including the one in office during the time of the field stay and his two predecessors, have come from the local business elite since then.

Tunja

Just like in Manizales, CDCSs in Tunja seemed to keep a low profile. There has not been a close communication or even co-operation maintained between the spokesman and Sera QA Tunja. According to the spokesman and user representative interviewed, the district government has supported the last two assemblies of the CDCSs with the intention of influencing the elections of the spokesmen and placing its favourite candidates. Besides the CDCSs, there is a so-called "user committee" in Tunja that has been created as a reaction against privatisation of WS services, and that has repeatedly organised public protests against tariff hikes. However, according to the spokesman and the user representative interviewed, the protagonists of this user committee have not been really concerned with the problems and interests of users, but have used the committee to make their marks for their personal political career. Interestingly, the spokesman and the user representative, as well as the representative from Sera QA Tunja, agreed that the politicisation of user representation, which has been common in Tunja, has harmed the users' cause.

Villavicencio

According to the information gained from a spokesman, CDCSs in Villavicencio had been created only recently (in 2004). EAA Villavicencio—because it is an EICE—is the only company that has a spokesman representing the users' interests in the board of directors. However, the spokesman interviewed could not tell in what kind of assembly or election this board member representing users had been elected. It was, for sure, not the same assembly in which the interviewee was elected which, according to himself, was organised as prescribed by the law (see sub-section 5.3.2). According to the interviewee, communication and co-operation with the service provider was good, because, in addition to being spokesman, he was a member of the *Junta de Acción Comunal* of his neighbourhood and, therefore, could use his network of personal relations within the company. In general, he succeeded in arranging agreements between users and the company when the former were not able to pay a bill, or were billed an atypically high consumption. According to the spokesman, the company has shown to be co-operative in such cases.

The Chamber of Commerce of Villavicencio, due to concerns regarding the way EAA Villavicencio has been managed and in order to control the company's investment activities in the area of wastewater collection and treatment, in 2004 established two civic watchdog committees (*veedurías*) that have produced various reports on the service situation and on the state of affairs of the construction activities. In addition, the Chamber of Commerce has arranged for an investigation of EAA Villavicencio by SSPD.

Santa Marta

As has been said, the number of CDCSs in Santa Marta (11) is higher than in the remaining cities. One possible explanation for the high number of CDCSs is the low quality of service in Santa Marta (as previously described). As compared to his colleagues from the remaining cities, the spokesman interviewed in Santa Marta seemed to be best informed, most engaged, and best organised.[143] Nevertheless, according to the interviewee, his influence on improving the service situation of users has been very low. He worked on informing users on their rights and regularly assisted users in submitting their complaints to SSPD. However, complaints with SSPD are laborious, and success is uncertain. The district government has not been supporting spokesmen in Santa Marta. They have received some support (workplace) from the *Personero Municipal* and have received political support from the workers' unions movement.

At request of the President of Colombia, around the year 2003, the Chamber of Commerce of Santa Marta engaged in a process of mediation between users and Metroagua Santa Marta. At that time, there were frequent public protests due to service interruptions and tariff hikes. In this mediation process, that had come to an end by mid 2005, users had been represented by local community leaders (presidents of *Juntas de Acción Comunal*, etc.). The spokesmen of the CDCSs had not been involved in the mediation process.

5.6.5.2. Security Situation and Activities of Non-State Armed Groups

The urban security situation can be described by the urban security index published by Fundación Seguridad y Democracia (2006, 51–54), which ranks the Colombian cities above 200,000 habitants (27 in total) according to the incidence rates of homicides, kidnapping and extortion, and crime against property. The sub-index that is most relevant for this section is the one on kidnapping and extortion because it is an indicator for the intensity of the criminal activities of non-state armed groups. A high intensity of these activities is likely to compromise the autonomy of the local governments, as well as democratic participation and, in addition, is likely to be linked with higher levels of corruption.[144]

Table 5.11 lists two indicators for the security situation and one for the risk of corruption. It shows that Villavicencio occupies rank 1 in the kidnapping and extortion index, which means that the city showed the highest incidence rate in 2005 of all 27 Colombian cities considered. Santa Marta occupies rank 8 and Manizales rank 9. Unfortunately, this index is available only for the year 2005 and does not include Tunja (because Tunja has less than 200,000 habitants). A look at the long-term averages of the homicide rates—which is another indicator that can be used as a proxy for the activities of the non-state armed groups—for the respective provinces shows very low values for Boyacá (capital Tunja). The highest rates are registered for Caldas (capital Manizales) and Meta (capital Villavicencio), followed by Magdalena (capital Santa Marta).

The additional sources of information[145] checked corroborate and complement the picture regarding the security situation and non-state armed groups' activities given by the two indicators discussed so far in the following sense:

- There are neither indications for a significant presence of non-state armed groups in the surroundings of Tunja nor indications for significant security problems in Tunja during the last years.
- There is evidence for the presence of non-state armed groups in the surroundings of Manizales (Observatorio del Programa Presidencial

Table 5.11   Security and Risk of Corruption Indicators

	Manizales (Caldas)	Tunja (Boyacá)	Villavicencio (Meta)	Santa Marta (Magdalena)
Rank position of the city in 2005: Urban Security Index; Subindex: Extortion and Kidnapping (best rank = 27; worst rank = 1)*	9	n.a.	1	8
Average annual homicide rate for the respective province (homicides per 100,000 habitants)**	98.2 (1998–2002) 61.2 (2002–2006)	18.9 (1998–2002) 18.1 (2002–2006)	65.2 (1998–2002) 91.2 (2002–2006)	52.7 (1998–2002) 36.6 (2002–2006)
Value of the Risk of Corruption Index of the Provincial Government; Average 2003/ 2004 (1 = high risk; 5 = low risk)***	3	3.5	2.5	2.5

"n.a." = not available.
Sources: *Fundación Seguridad y Democracia (2006); **Fundación Seguridad y Democracia (2004); ***Transparencia por Colombia (2005; without year).

de Derechos Humanos y DIH 2006a), Santa Marta (Observatorio del Programa Presidencial de Derechos Humanos y DIH 2006b), and Villavicencio (Observatorio del Programa Presidencial de Derechos Humanos y DIH 2005), as well as for the influence[146] of these groups in the urban zones of the three districts. The pattern of the security indicators varies slightly between the three cities. Manizales has, for years, shown high homicide rates (varying between 90 per 100,000 habitants in 2002 and 50 in 2005) but a relatively low incidence of kidnapping. Santa Marta has also shown relatively high homicide rates (varying between 67 per 100,000 habitants in 2001 and 41 in 2004) and a rising incidence of kidnapping (12 incidents in 2000 and 56 in 2004). Villavicencio has lately shown a homicide rate similar to Santa Marta (54 per 100,000 habitants in 2003 and 49 in 2004) and a high incidence of kidnapping (48 incidents in 2003 and 68 in 2004).

- Since 2004, the situation in Villavicencio seems to have worsened. In 2004, four local politicians have been assassinated, amongst them Omar López Robayo, the predecessor of the mayor in office at the time of the field stay. The assassinations are attributed to demobilised paramilitary groups.[147] In March 2006, the procurator Tomas Garzón Roa, who was investigating criminal activities in the areas of drug trafficking, paramilitarism, and corruption in Villavicencio, was assassinated.[148]

- The migratory pressure on Santa Marta that drives the uncontrolled growth of squatter settlements is due, to an important degree, to the activities of non-state armed groups, confrontations amongst these groups, or between them and the state security forces in the surroundings of Santa Marta.

Unfortunately, the indicator for the risk of corruption published by Transparencia por Colombia (2005; without year) is only available for the provincial governments.[149] A value of 1 denotes the highest risk, whereas a value of 5 denotes the lowest risk of corruption. The average of the indicator for the years 2003 and 2004 reported in Table 5.11 shows the most favourable value for Tunja (3.5), followed by Manizales (3), and by Santa Marta and Villavicencio (both 2.5), i.e., the two good performers show better indicators than the two bad performers.

5.6.5.3. Clientelistic Strategies and Corruption Affecting WS Services

The information collected on these dimensions yields the following overall picture: There is clear evidence that EAA Villavicencio has been negatively affected by clientelistic, and by corrupt, practices during the last years, whereas for the remaining cases there is no such clear evidence.[150] The details are presented in what follows.

Villavicencio

Concerning clientelistic strategies, and as has already been mentioned in the preceding sub-section, the mayor has regularly been intervening in staffing decisions of EAA Villavicencio (at least the mayor in office in July 2005 and his predecessor). This does not only concern the post of the general manager, but also middle and lower management posts. An important criterion in order to obtain a post in the company is to be a political supporter of the mayor in office. Consequently, career opportunities do not mainly depend on qualification and working performance. Moreover, it is common that staff members are asked to quit their job by the incoming mayor. These are adverse incentives that are likely to negatively affect the quality and the motivation of the personnel. The observation that the motivation of the staff members seemed to be relatively low and that the feeling of identity with the company seemed to be weak corroborates this.

Concerning corrupt practices, the author has gained information from sources not listed in Table A5.6 that the mayor in office at the time of the field stay, Franklin Germán Chaparro Carrillo, has been intervening in the awarding of construction contracts (wastewater infrastructure) for his personal benefit. This seems to be a trustworthy information because, in the meanwhile, the mayor has been faced with around 20 disciplinary charges by the Procurator General[151] and has been convicted in one case (irregularities in awarding health service contracts) with the consequence that he has been removed from office and is not allowed to hold public office for 10 years.[152] Taking together the information from these different sources, the author estimates that the mayor has been taking bribes in the range of 10% to 15% of the respective construction contract volumes. In 2004, EAA Villavicencio awarded contracts for the construction of waste-water interceptor sewers for a total amount of 17,170 million Colombian Pesos.[153] Assuming a bribe share of 10%, this would mean that the mayor would have received a sum of 1,717 million Colombian Pesos[154] in one year. The consequence for the investment projects is not only that there are 10% less of the total amount available for construction activities and that, thus, less assets are built. In addition, the infrastructure built is in a great risk of being unworkable because unqualified contractors are chosen or because contractors use cheaper, but unsuited, materials or machines in order to compensate for the lower "net" contract volume.

Moreover, there is evidence that business and accounting practice of EAA Villavicencio has been intransparent and irregular. According to information given by the President of the Chamber of Commerce, when she was still a member of the board of directors, she has been denied financial and accounting information she has asked for. Furthermore, EAA Villavicencio in 2005 has been investigated by the District Auditor (Contraloría Municipal de Villavicencio 2006, 14–15). The Auditor found irregular financial transactions for a total amount of 1,780 million Colombian Pesos,[155] implying disciplinary and criminal offences.

Santa Marta

There have been gathered no indications for clientelistic practices in Metroagua similar to those described for EAA Villavicencio. It is plausible that massive interventions by the mayor in staffing decisions have not occurred, because the institutional structure of the PSP delivery model in place in Santa Marta prevents such a practice. Neither there have been gathered indications for corrupt practices directly affecting WS services during the district government in office at the time of the field stay. However, corrupt district governments have been common in Santa Marta in the recent past. The predecessor of the mayor in office in July 2005, Hugo Gnecco Arregocés, had been involved in the embezzlement of public funds and had been removed from office in 2003.[156] The mismanagement and corruption under the government of Hugo Gnecco Arregocés has affected the provision of WS services in so far as the district failed to transfer 15,000 million Colombian Pesos[157] earmarked for investment in WS infrastructure to Metroagua. The history of mismanagement and corruption of district governments in Santa Marta raises certain doubts concerning the soundness of the lease and management contracts held by Metroagua and AAA de Servicios SA, which were awarded not in a public call for tenders but in direct negotiations.

The, perhaps, most striking feature of Santa Marta, as compared to the remaining three cities (especially Manizales and Tunja), is the lack of control of the urban space by the district administration. This is quite a complex issue, which is common in many cities of the developing world and which, in the case of Santa Marta, has been driven to an important degree by migrants that have been displaced due to non-state armed groups activities in the region of Santa Marta (see earlier discussion). However, it can be supposed that a part of this lack of control is related to corrupt practices in real estate speculation and is, in some way, "functional" for speculators that benefit from it. According to two different sources of information, it is quite common in Santa Marta that migrants are used by speculators in order to take advantage from the illegal occupation of plots owned by the district or provincial governments: The speculator "arranges" the occupation of a certain area. After a while, either the plots are regularised by the district (and possibly equipped with infrastructure) and can, thus, be sold with high profit; or the district makes a deal with the occupants in order to evacuate the area and, possibly, has to offer a compensation. This means that those deficiencies of the WS system that are related to illegal connections in squatter settlements (see previous sections) are partially enhanced by corrupt practices in real estate speculation.

Tunja

According to the information gained in the interviews, the district government has not intervened in staffing decisions of Sera QA Tunja which is, in fact, hardly possible, because the company is totally owned by the Proactiva group. Nevertheless, according to the general manager of the company, at the beginning of the concession, during election campaigns, several local politicians or persons with political ambitions have tried to obtain gifts-in-kinds (e.g. pipes, construction works) from the company for certain neighbourhoods. According to the general manager, resisting these proposals proved to be relatively easy thanks to the independence of Sera QA.

According to information given by Sera QA, the co-operation between the district government and the company has passed through various tense periods. Both mayors who succeeded in office the one who awarded the concession in 1996, had made an election campaign against the privatisation of WS services and had, thus, a negative attitude towards the concessionaire. The second successor delayed the promised investment financing for two years (see previous discussion). Nevertheless, all in all, the two parties always managed to continue co-operating and working on the improvement and expansion of the system. One factor that might have contributed to the stability of the co-operation could be the transparent way that the concession was awarded, the support of the awarding process by the Ministry of Development, and the thorough and careful concession contract itself.

The district government of Tunja has not been spared corruption in the past years.[158] However, the author could not gather information on corrupt practices related to the provision of WS services in the past years.

Manizales

There have been no indications for massive clientelistic interventions by the latest mayors in Aguas de Manizales. Certainly, the incoming mayors have changed the general manager, but they seem not to have intervened in the middle and lower management posts. The interesting question here is why? As said earlier (sub-section 5.6.4) one reason could lie in the explicit concession contract between the company and INFIMANIZALES, which may contribute to strengthen the independence of the management. Other plausible reasons are:

i. What could be called an "entrepreneurial policy approach" of the business elite from Manizales, which has been in local political power since the late 1990s. Public officials from the business elite may regularly apply business principles that they are familiarised with from the private sector to the management of the district-owned companies and, thus, put emphasis on the internal efficiency and the financial performance of these companies.
ii. The level of organisation and capacities of the civil society (including the business associations) of Manizales and the experience of mismanagement and corruption made in the 1980s. These factors may contribute to raising awareness of clientelistic practices in public companies and to denounce them publicly.

This latter point would also be an important factor for preventing corruption. The author has gathered no evidence for recent major cases of corruption linked to the provision of WS services in Manizales. However, there seem to have occurred irregularities in the awarding of contracts by Aguas de Manizales in 2003. This becomes evident from a survey on the transparency of the district administration of Manizales (United Nations Office on Drugs and Crime without year). The information has been corroborated by a representative from CCC.

5.6.5.4. Conclusions

Comparing and assessing the available information on the four cases regarding the local governance dimensions analysed—(i) user and civil society participation; (ii) security situation and non-state armed groups' activities; and (iiia) clientelistic and (iiib) corrupt practices—yields the following results:

a. Tunja compares positively with the remaining three cases concerning dimension (ii) and is neutral with respect to dimensions (i), (iiia), and (iiib).
b. Manizales compares positively with the remaining three cases with respect to dimension (i) due to the relative strength of civil society organisations; it is neutral with respect to dimension (iiia) and slightly negative with respect to dimension (iiib).[159] Manizales shows negative indicators with respect to dimension (ii).
c. Santa Marta is neutral with respect to dimensions (i) and (iiia); it shows slightly negative characteristics with respect to dimension (iiib) due to corrupt practices in real estate speculation and the widespread corruption under the predecessor of the mayor in office in 2005. Santa Marta shows negative characteristics with respect to dimension (ii).
d. Villavicencio is neutral with respect to dimension (i) and shows negative characteristics with respect to the remaining dimensions (ii), (iiia) and (iiib).

This sort of ranking (1 to 4) of the four cities with respect to their local governance characteristics is roughly in line with the main supposition that local governance contributes to explaining the variation in the performance of the four service providers: The two good performers are ranked higher than the two bad performers.

What can be concluded on the influence of governance in the two conspicuous cases—the public "good" performer Aguas de Manizales and the private "bad" performer Metroagua Santa Marta?

- The relative strength of civil society organisations in Manizales, together with an "entrepreneurial policy approach" of the local business elite that has been in local political power during the last years, appears to have contributed to curb clientelistic interventions in Aguas de Manizales and to encourage a professional management. This institutional setting seems to have been triggered by a negative experience with widespread corruption and mismanagement in local government in the late 1980s that has been mastered. It is plausible that these institutional characteristics also have contributed to curb the potentially negative influence of the non-state armed groups' presence in the area (see the following).
- WS service provision in Santa Marta is overwhelmed with various problems of which weaknesses in local governance seem to be one important factor. Low coverage and low quality of WS services are partially explained by the uncontrolled growth of squatter settlements driven by migrants displaced by non-state armed groups' activities and by the lack of control of the urban space. This lack of control of the urban space by the district administration seems to be, in part, functional to corruption in real estate speculation. Moreover, in the

past, substantial amounts of public funds that could have been used for improving and expanding WS infrastructure have been withdrawn due to corruption and mismanagement of the local government.

Finally, this sub-section presented indications that the presence and influence of non-state armed groups negatively affect local governance by undermining the rule of law and encouraging corrupt practices, e.g. through extorting and coopting local public officials. This is quite obvious in the case of Villavicencio and seems also to be an issue in Santa Marta. In Manizales, a supposed negative influence of non-state armed groups' presence is less obvious.

5.6.6. Conclusions

This section has analysed the influence of local governance on WS service performance by comparing two PSP and two public delivery models. The main supposition was that differences in the quality of local governance can explain the variation in performance amongst the public cases (Aguas de Manizales: "good;" EAA Villavicencio: "bad") and the PSP cases (Sera QA Tunja: "good;" Metroagua Santa Marta: "bad"). Besides governance, the dimensions technical characteristics, socio-economic conditions, and institutional design of service delivery and financing have been considered in order to get a complete picture of the local factors that potentially contribute to explain the variation in the performance.

The overall result is that there is some evidence that local governance factors contribute to explain the variation in the performance of the four cases. However, it is not possible to assess the strength or magnitude of this relation. Several aspects of the further dimensions considered also contribute to explain the variation in the performance, which is why it is not possible to establish a hierarchy amongst local governance and further influencing factors.

This overall result is illustrated for the two particularly interesting cases of (i) Aguas de Manizales—which shows positive internal efficiency indicators in spite of being a public provider—and (ii) Metroagua Santa Marta—which shows negative internal efficiency indicators in spite of being a provider with PSP. Aguas de Manizales compares positively with Metroagua Santa Marta regarding local governance factors. However, in addition, Aguas de Manizales compares positively with Metroagua Santa Marta with respect to several further factors, like historical performance levels, technical conditions (which do not require pumping), investment backlog, and socio-economic conditions (particularly the low prevalence of squatter settlements and illegal connections). This means that the local governance and the further local factors together seem to dominate the ownership effect.

The section is concluded by highlighting some more specific policy lessons for Colombia:

- PSP (concession or lease contracts) seems to be effective in preventing harmful clientelistic interventions of local governments in the company. In none of the two PSP cases were there indications of massive interventions. This result supports the view that the institutional characteristics of PSP, which limit the politicians' access to the financial and human resources of the company, make clientelistic interventions more difficult.
- Nevertheless, local governance is still relevant for successful PSP. Weaknesses such as intransparent and non-professional awarding of PSP contracts, default of delivering promised public finance due to mismanagement or embezzlement and lack of orderly territorial planning can seriously compromise the performance of PSP delivery models.
- Neutralising clientelistic interventions in companies and encouraging internal efficiency can also be achieved in public service providers, as shown by the case of Manizales. The institutional design of public service delivery, like corporatisation and explicit concession contracts, as well as good local governance, like strong civil society organisations and the involvement of business organisations in the control of the company, appear to contribute to these achievements. This result supports the view that clear institutional boundaries of public providers and good local governance can prevent harmful clientelistic interventions.
- User participation, which up to now builds almost exclusively on local CDCSs, is weak in Colombia. CDCSs should be complemented by a national user advocacy organisation that (i) disposes of sufficient human and financial resources to effectively dialogue with CRA, SSPD, MAVDT, and ANDESCO, and thus to participate in regulation and that (ii) provides technical backstopping and support for local spokesmen.

6 Summary and Conclusions

This study has investigated the influence of governance on the performance of WS services in developing countries. The motivation for choosing this subject was the insight that the focus on provider ownership (private versus public), which has dominated the academic and the political debate, was too narrow in order to explain success or failure in the provision of WS services. By shifting the attention towards the influence of governance, this study has worked out those political and sectoral institutions that are essential for the provision of WS services and has found empirical evidence for their influence on the access to services and the internal efficiency of providers. Democratic participation and checks and balances have a statistically significant positive impact on the coverage with WS services in developing countries. Moreover, for the Colombian context there was found some evidence that low quality governance of sub-national governments compromises the internal efficiency of service delivery and the widespread access to services. With regard to the role of provider ownership, it can be said that PSP is just one important institutional design characteristic of the WS sector among others. The results obtained have yielded some evidence that PSP contributes to enhance the internal efficiency of providers. However, the results also suggest that PSP is not necessary and even less sufficient for achieving widespread access to low-cost and good-quality services.

In what follows, the results of the different chapters are summarised and some overall conclusions are drawn.

6.1. SUMMARY OF THE RESULTS

Chapters 2 and 3 make up the conceptual framework for the investigation.

Chapter 2 has introduced the normative categories for assessing typical problems related to the provision of WS services and for justifying general policies that are conducive to equity, allocative efficiency, and internal efficiency.

From an equity perspective, it is a priority to strive for a situation where anybody is able to use adequate essential WS services, irrespective of his economic situation. This implies focusing policies on expanding WS services to those households that lack access and justifies subsidising expansion costs related to the connection of poor households. Furthermore, it can also justify subsidising the expenses of poor households for the consumption of WS services if society judges these expenses unaffordable.

From an allocative efficiency perspective, it is desirable to correct the market failures associated with the provision of WS services (natural monopoly, external effects). This requires the use of regulatory policies that are able to compensate for the lack of competition, such as competitive bidding procedures for allocating the right to serve a certain area or price and quality regulation. Moreover, this entails the use of environmental regulation in order to account for the external costs associated with the production and consumption of WS services, e.g. by levying or limiting the abstraction of raw water or the discharge of wastewater.

The internal efficiency of WS service providers is a necessary, but not sufficient, condition for achieving allocative efficiency. Promoting internal efficiency can be achieved by reducing the scope for public officials to appropriate the quasi-rents of WS service providers and by increasing the accountability of the management to clients and financiers, e.g. through PSP or corporatisation and commercialisation under public ownership.

Chapter 3 has developed the political-economic framework for explaining the effect of political governance (democratic participation, checks and balances, rule of law) and WS governance (institutional characteristics of the WS sector roles) on the performance of WS services. Governance factors—by shaping the WS sector roles of policy making, regulation, and service delivery—influence the equitability and the efficiency of WS services.

Concerning political governance, it is postulated that the fundamental institutions of democratic participation (competitive elections, political rights, and alternative information) have systematic effects on policy making. Other things being equal, democratic governments have greater incentives to design policies in response to the interests of the broad majority than autocratic governments. Democratic governments are, thus, more likely to implement the kind of public-regarding WS policies deduced in Chapter 2. A system of checks and balances and rule of law further enhances the accountability of public officials to the broad majority and, therefore, public-regardedness of policy making.

Important elements of WS governance are (i) the horizontal separation and the institutional design of the roles of WS policy making, regulation, and service delivery, and (ii) the level of user participation.

i. Horizontal separation of roles means that WS policy making, regulation, and service delivery are accomplished by different sets of actors with own responsibilities. The separation of roles enhances the accountability and the professionalism of the actors responsible for regulation and service delivery because day-to-day intervention of politicians in the technicalities of regulation and service delivery becomes more difficult. Whereas regulation is a public role, service delivery can be delegated to the private sector. The more comprehensive PSP in service delivery is, the stronger is the institutional separation of service delivery and policy making.

ii. User participation in regulation and service delivery is important in order to make regulators and service providers responsive to the interests and needs of users. User participation can take the forms of consultation, representation, or influence, and depends on the existence of strong user advocacy organisations.

It is important to note that political and WS governance factors jointly affect WS policy making, regulation, and service delivery and, thus, the performance of WS services. In a polity marked by a well functioning system of checks and balances and rule of law, it is easier to establish an independent and accountable regulatory body and to prevent harmful interventions of politicians in the management of public service providers than in a polity marked by a high concentration of government power and by a disrespect for the rule of law. Furthermore, user participation is more likely to succeed in making regulators responsive to user interests in a democracy, where fundamental political rights are respected, than in an autocracy.

Building on this conceptual framework, Chapters 4 and 5 have empirically analysed different aspects of the influence of governance on the performance of WS services, using both quantitative and qualitative empirical approaches.

Chapter 4 has investigated the influence of political governance on coverage with WS services, using a multivariate regression model and cross-sectional data from 69 developing countries. The dimensions of political governance analysed were (i) democratic participation, (ii) checks and balances (veto players), and (iii) rule of law. Following the literature, the analysis has controlled for variables that are likely to have an impact on coverage with WS services, such as GDP per capita, spatial population patterns, and availability of water resources. The regression estimates have yielded the following main results:

- There is a significant and robust positive effect of higher levels of democratic participation and more checks and balances on coverage with both water and sanitation services. This largely supports the hypotheses developed in Chapter 3 regarding the expected effects of democratic participation and checks and balances. The results do not change substantially when regional dummy variables are included in the regression in order to account for region-specific effects.
- For the case of sanitation services, the results show that the positive effect of democratic participation and checks and balances is strongest for countries with low GDP per capita and becomes weaker for countries with high GDP per capita. A possible explanation for this

result is that non-accountable autocratic governments in poor countries are likely to make a bad use of scarce financial resources with respect to the provision of services. An improvement in democratic accountability may, thus, make a big difference for a poor country. This effect may become less strong the more financial resources per capita are available in an economy, because even if governments make a bad use of resources, on average there will be more resources left that can be invested in WS services.

These results underline the manifold benefits that arise from key elements of good political governance, such as democratic participation and checks and balances. Besides being crucial achievements that permit citizens to freely elect their governors and that provide protection against despotism, democratic participation and checks and balances seem to enhance the material well-being of the broad citizenry in an essential dimension such as access to WS services.

Chapter 5 has investigated the provision of WS services in Colombia with two purposes. First, it has described and assessed the key elements of political governance, WS governance, and WS policies in Colombia from a national perspective. Second, and building on the results of the first purpose, it has analysed the factors on the sub-national level that are able to explain the variation in the performance of Colombian WS service providers. The focus was set on the two factors local governance and delivery model (PSP versus purely public).

With regard to the **first purpose**, the analysis has focused on identifying potential weaknesses (and not so much the strengths) of governance characteristics and WS policies that may compromise equity and efficiency of WS services in Colombia.

As far as the *political governance* is concerned, certain features such as the candidate-centred electoral system and the tradition of clientelism suggest that policy making is biased towards private-regardedness rather than towards public-regardedness. Political rights and civil liberties have, to a certain degree, been compromised as a result of the influence of non-state armed groups and the periodical escalations of the armed conflicts amongst non-state armed groups and between these groups and the state security forces. Moreover, corruption is a widespread phenomenon in Colombia, which is likely to diminish the effectiveness of public spending in the WS sector.

Concerning *WS governance*, the institutional design of the roles of WS policy making, regulation, and service delivery respect, to a certain degree, the principle of horizontal separation. However, at the district level, separation of roles between the actors responsible for local WS policy making, local regulation and service delivery is weak—or even absent in case of public service provision. Mayors have a strong influence on the decision making of public providers, even when these are incorporated firms. This increases the probability of political interference in the management and tends to compromise the ability of the managers of public providers to improve internal efficiency and to respond to the regulatory instruments applied by the national regulatory authorities. At the same time, this aspect underlines the importance of the quality of local governance, because user participation and the availability of transparent information may prevent the mayors from misusing their strong influence for clientelistic or corrupt practices.

Another noteworthy result is that, in general, user participation in the area of WS services remains weak. This is especially true for user participation in regulation. Colombia lacks a strong user advocacy organisation on the national level that has the necessary human and financial resources to participate in regulation by maintaining a dialogue with the regulatory authorities on a technical level and that gives technical and logistic support to local user representatives for their daily work with service providers.

As far as the analysis of WS *policies* is concerned, the following results with respect to (i) public investment policy, (ii) subsidy policy, and (iii) tariff regulation are highlighted:

i. There is some evidence that a portion of the substantial public funds allocated to the WS sector is not effectively used for service expansion. The following factors contribute to this problem: Weak territorial planning capacities of districts and lacking civic participation in the planning process; lack of coordination between the service provider's investment plan and the investments carried out by the district; lack of transparency and control in the awarding of construction contracts; atomisation of the service provider structure ending up in high overheads for investment projects; financially strained or internally inefficient providers that consume the available public funds in order to keep the existing systems running.

ii. The cross-subsidy system has generated systematic deficits, which have complicated regulatory policies that aim at internal efficiency improvements and financial sustainability. Besides, the cross-subsidy system has the weakness that it reaches only those households that are connected to a regulated provider. Moreover, the targeting quality of the cross-subsidy system is low, because more than half of the households that are subsidised have an income that lies above the national poverty line.

iii. Until 2005, tariff regulation has unilaterally focused on improving financial sustainability of service providers by increasing tariff levels to cost levels. It has largely disregarded instruments that aim at improving internal efficiency and at avoiding the fact that inefficiencies are passed on to users. The delay in introducing more sophisticated regulatory instruments is partially explained by the low level and the poor quality of the information provided especially by the smaller service providers.

The **second purpose** of Chapter 5 was to analyse those determinants on the sub-national level that can explain the variation in service performance that is observed in Colombia. Because Colombia is marked by decentralisation and PSP in the WS sector, it offers the possibility to investigate both the influence of the delivery model (PSP versus purely public) and of local governance on service provision.

First, the effect of the delivery model on internal efficiency improvements (unaccounted-for water) and on coverage expansion (piped water and sewerage) has been analysed by means of a multivariate regression analysis using cross-sectional data from 30 Colombian WS service providers. Due to the lack of comprehensive data on governance on the local level, the analysis could not account for the quality of local governance. The regression estimates have yielded the following main results:

- PSP shows a significant positive influence on the reduction of unaccounted-for water. This result supports the supposition that PSP delivery models are superior to public ones with respect to internal efficiency.
- Low unaccounted-for water shows a significant positive effect on coverage expansion (this effect is robust for piped water only), whereas population growth is negatively associated with coverage expansion (this effect is robust for sewer connections only). The effect of PSP on coverage expansion is not statistically significant.

These results are in line with the argumentation followed in this study that PSP typically contributes to improve internal efficiency, but that more far-reaching effects such as significant contributions to coverage expansion or to improvements in allocative efficiency (i.e., to low-cost and good-quality services) depend on the quality of governance.

Second, the effect of local governance on the performance of WS service providers has been analysed by a qualitative approach, comparing the providers of the four provincial capitals of Manizales (public), Santa Marta (private), Tunja (private), and Villavicencio (public). The main supposition investigated was that the quality of local governance can dominate the expected effect of ownership and, therefore, explain unexpected results, such as a public provider with outstanding internal efficiency indicators (Manizales) or a private provider with poor internal efficiency indicators (Santa Marta). Based on the findings of the political and WS governance analysis reported, the dimensions used for assessing the quality of local governance were (i) user and civil society participation, (ii) security situation and influence of non-state armed groups, and (iii) prevalence of clientelistic, as well as corrupt, practices. Besides local governance, additional local factors (technical characteristics, socio-economic conditions, institutional design of service delivery, and financing) have been considered. The following results are highlighted:

- The overall result is that the quality of local governance is able to partially explain the performance pattern of the four cases with respect to internal efficiency and coverage indicators. However, it is not possible to establish a hierarchy between the influence of governance and the influence of further local factors, which are also able to partially explain the variation in performance.

• In none of the two PSP cases were there found indications for massive clientelistic interventions of local governments in the management of the companies. This result supports the view that the institutional characteristics of PSP (concession or lease contracts) make the politicians' access to the financial and human resources of the company more difficult and, thus, prevent clientelistic interventions.

• Nevertheless, local governance is still highly relevant for successful PSP, because weaknesses such as intransparent and non-professional awarding of PSP contracts, embezzlement of public funds earmarked for WS investments and discontrol of the urban space combined with corruption in real estate speculation can seriously compromise the performance of PSP delivery models.

• As evidenced by the case of Manizales, neutralising clientelistic interventions and encouraging internal efficiency can also be achieved in public companies. Good local governance (strong civil society organisations and involvement of business organisations in the control of the company) and the institutional design characteristics of service delivery (corporatisation, explicit concession contracts) appear to contribute to these achievements. This result supports the view that good local governance and clear institutional boundaries of public providers can prevent harmful interventions of politicians in the management.

6.2. CONCLUSIONS

What are the overall conclusions that can be drawn from this study, and what are the open issues that require further research?

The econometric results from the cross-country regression based on data from 69 developing countries have yielded evidence that higher levels of democratic participation and more checks and balances, which are key elements of good political governance, have a statistically significant positive effect on the access to WS services in developing countries. To the best knowledge of the author, this is an innovative result that has not been reported in research literature so far. By contrast, the variable used to measure the influence of PSP showed no statistically significant effect. It, thus, appears that good political governance is more relevant to achieve coverage expansion with WS services than PSP. However, the results regarding the influence of PSP may be biased because the available data on PSP in the WS sectors of developing countries is rather incomplete. A task for further research is, therefore, to replicate the analysis with new and more complete data on PSP in the WS sectors of developing countries. Moreover, because the arguments for the influence of political governance on coverage with WS services also apply to other public services, the econometric approach used in this study could be extended to analyse the coverage with other public services in developing countries, e.g. in the electricity or health sector.

The case study on Colombia has found some evidence that the quality of governance also plays a role for explaining the variation in service performance on the sub-national level. Strong civil society organisations, control of corruption and low levels of non-state armed groups' activities seem to further the efficiency of service delivery and the widespread access to WS services. A low quality of local governance appears to be able to dominate the positive effect of PSP on internal efficiency, for which statistical evidence was found in a regression analysis with data from 30 Colombian providers. Or, to put it differently, a good local governance and a sound institutional design of service delivery can be able to compensate for the disadvantages of public providers with respect to internal efficiency achievements. It, thus, appears that PSP is not a necessary condition for achieving internal efficiency improvements. Further research on this issue is desirable in order to confirm the results obtained here and to investigate whether the local governance factors identified as key also apply to different local contexts or whether they are location-specific.

This study is concluded by emphasising two lessons that emerge from the investigation: First, democratic participation and checks and balances do not "only" grant free elections and protection against despotism, but also seem to enhance the material well-being of citizens in an essential dimension such as the widespread access to WS services.

Second, the results from the Colombian case study show that successful WS sector reform requires much more than sound PSP. The analysis has found some evidence that PSP contributes to a higher internal efficiency of providers. This can be regarded as a partial success. However the analysis has also identified several weaknesses in governance characteristics and in WS policies that seem to hamper the translation of internal efficiency improvements into more far-reaching achievements such as significant coverage expansions. Therefore, it can be concluded that sound political and WS governance are necessary conditions to unfold and to reap the potential benefits of PSP. For policy makers, this means to keep in mind that adverse governance factors are likely to go against well-intentioned policies aiming at improving WS services and to render them useless in the end.

Appendix

Table A2.1   World Coverage With Water and Sanitation Services and
Efforts Required to Meet the Millenium Development Goal Targets

				Drinking Water		
Region	*Coverage in 1990 (%)*	*Coverage in 2004 (%)*	*Required Coverage in 2004 to be on Track to Reach MDG Target (%)*	*MDG Target (%) (Halving the Proportion of Unserved by 2015)*	*Average Annual Increase in Population Served 1990–2004 (Millions)*	*Average Annual Increase Required 2005–2015 to Reach the MDG Target (Millions)*
World	78	83	85	89	81.9	110.5
Developed regions	100	99	100	100	3.9	5.5
Developing regions	71	80	80	86	78.2	100.2
Developing regions						
Northern Africa	89	91	93	95	2.3	3.3
Sub-Saharan Africa	49	56	65	75	10.5	28.8
Latin America and the Caribbean	83	91	88	92	8.9	8.0
Eastern Asia	71	78	80	86	14.2	18.4
Southern Asia	72	85	80	86	30.5	24.7
South-eastern Asia	76	82	83	88	7.8	9.8
Western Asia	85	91	90	93	4.0	4.8
Oceania	51	50	66	76	0.1	0.4
Common-wealth of Independent States	92	92	94	96	−0.2	0.5

MDG = Millennium Development Goal.
Source: WHO and UNICEF (2006, 40).

			Sanitation		
Coverage in 1990 (%)	Coverage in 2004 (%)	Required Coverage in 2004 to be on Track to Reach MDG Target (%)	MDG Target (%) (Halving the Proportion of Unserved by 2015)	Average Annual Increase in Population Served 1990–2004 (Millions)	Average Annual Increase Required 2005–2015 to Reach the MDG Target (Millions)
49	59	65	75	80.5	163.7
100	99	100	100	4.4	4.8
35	50	55	68	76.2	146.3
65	77	76	83	2.7	3.3
32	37	52	66	7.1	34.5
68	77	78	84	8.6	10.4
24	45	47	62	22.2	28.8
20	38	44	60	22.1	50.8
49	67	65	75	9.9	10.2
81	84	87	91	3.5	5.6
54	53	68	77	0.1	0.3
82	83	87	91	0.0	1.8

Table A2.2 Key Problems, Underlying Reasons, Policy Implications, and Complementarities or Trade-Offs

Normative Perspective	Key Problem	Underlying Reason	Broad Policy Implication	Plausible Complementarities (+)/ Trade-Offs (−)
Equity	Households do not have access to adequate WS services	Households lack the income/creditworthiness to incur the necessary investment costs	Subsidise investment costs/connection costs for low-income households	Allocative efficiency (+) if social benefits from increased access to adequate WS services > social costs from increased costs of public funds Allocative efficiency (−) if vice versa Internal efficiency (−) if subsidy mechanism negatively affects the financial sustainability of service providers
		Households do not have access to property markets	Improve urban planning procedures; lower access barriers to property markets and improve transparency in these markets	Allocative efficiency (+)
	Households have access to WS services but do not use them	The optimal tariff in place (reflecting total social costs) for using adequate WS services is high relative to the willingness to pay	Subsidise consumption of an essential amount of adequate WS services for low-income households	Allocative efficiency (−) Internal efficiency (−) if subsidy mechanism affects negatively the financial sustainability of service providers
		The non-optimal tariff in place for using adequate WS services is high relative to the willingness to pay due to the abuse of monopolistic pricing	Introduce/improve tariff regulation	Allocative efficiency (+)

Allocative efficiency	Service providers take advantage of their market power by charging tariffs that are higher than private costs and/or providing bad quality services	WS services have a poor quality (continuity, pressure, water quality)	Introduce/improve regulation	Allocative efficiency (+)
		Households are not aware of the private benefits of adequate WS services (especially sanitation)	Raise awareness for the private benefits of using adequate WS services (especially sanitation)	Allocative efficiency (+)
	Natural monopoly markets due to economies of scale (scope) and high sunk costs		Economic regulation: competitive bidding procedures; tariff and quality of service regulation	Equity (+) if the number of low-income households that use adequate WS services increases thanks to regulation
	Water is not put to its socially most valuable use i.e. the resource is wasted/excessively contaminated	WS tariffs are below total social costs	Environmental regulation; increase WS tariffs	Internal efficiency (+) if WS tariffs were below private costs; Equity (–) if WS tariffs rise above the willingness to pay of low-income households
	Use of sanitation services is low relative to its social benefits	Households are not aware of the external benefits of sanitation services	Raise awareness for external benefits, subsidise sanitation services	Equity (+) if low-income households benefit from the external benefits of increased use of sanitation services
	Underinvestment in WS services by private investors	Availability of quasi-rents and inability of public officials to commit to abstain from capturing them	Reform political institutions that make commitments credible (e.g. independent judiciary; regulatory authority)	Internal efficiency (+); Equity (+) if the number of low-income households that use adequate WS services increases thanks to additional investments

(continued)

Table A2.2 (continued)

Normative Perspective	Key Problem	Underlying Reason	Broad Policy Implication	Plausible Complementarities (+)/ Trade-Offs (–)
Internal efficiency	Service providers do not produce a given quantity and quality at a minimum private cost	Managerial slack due to absent competition	Economic regulation: competitive bidding procedures; tariff and quality of service regulation	Equity (+) if the number of low-income households that use adequate WS services increases thanks to regulation; Allocative efficiency (+)
			Improve monitoring by owners through privatisation or corporatisation under public ownership	Allocative efficiency (+) if users benefit from improvements in internal efficiency (presupposes regulation/competition); Equity (+) if the number of low-income households that use adequate WS services increases thanks to improved quality/lower private costs (presupposes regulation)
		Managers of public service providers lack legal means to improve internal efficiency	Privatisation or corporatisation under public ownership	Idem
		Public officials induce managers to follow goals like the maximisation of employment, construction etc.	Privatisation or corporatisation under public ownership; improve regulation by public accounting offices; increase transparency of management decisions	Idem
	Receipts of the service provider are too low to cover private costs and thus the situation is financially unsustainable	Tariffs are set below private costs	Increase WS tariffs	Allocative efficiency (+); Equity (–) if WS tariffs rise above the willingness to pay of low-income households

Source: Author.

Table A4.1   Variables and Data Sources Used in the Statistical Analysis of Chapter 4

Variable Name	Variable Description	Data Source; Additional Information
Coverage variables (COV)		
WATTOT90; (WATTOT02)	Population using improved water supply services in 1990 (in 2002); percentage of total population	WHO and UNICEF Joint Monitoring Programme Database, http://www.wssinfo.org (accessed November 14, 2005); WHO and UNICEF (2000)
SANTOT90; (SANTOT02)	Population using improved sanitation services in 1990 (in 2002); percentage of total population	WHO and UNICEF Joint Monitoring Programme Database, http://www.wssinfo.org (accessed November 14, 2005); WHO and UNICEF (2000)
WATTOT90LN	LN (WATTOT90) = Natural logarithm of WATTOT90	
Political governance variables (GOV)		
POLITY	Index that measures the level of democracy (autocracy); original indicator "Polity;" average of available values 1990 to 2002; range of values: –10 to 10 (higher scores correspond to greater levels of democracy)	Polity IV Database, http://www.cidcm.umd.edu/inscr/polity/index.htm (accessed October 31, 2005); Marshall and Jaggers (2000); Jaggers and Gurr (1995)
POLRIGHTS	Index that measures the political rights situation; original indicator "political rights;" average of available values 1990 to 2002; range of values: 1 to 7 (higher scores correspond to greater political rights); the original indicator "political rights" has been transformed as follows: transformed values = original values * (–1) + 8	Freedom of the World Database provided by Freedom House, http://www.freedomhouse.org/template.cfm?page=15&year=2005 (accessed November 16, 2005); Freedom House (various years)
POLCON	Index that measures political constraints on the executive; original indicator "POLCONIII;" average of available values for 1990 to 2002; range of values: 0 to 1 (higher scores correspond to more constraints)	Database provided by W. J. Henisz, http://www-management.wharton.upenn.edu/henisz/ (accessed January 2, 2006); Henisz (2002)

(continued)

Table A4.1 (continued)

Variable Name	Variable Description	Data Source; Additional Information
CHECKS	Index that measures the number of effective veto points; original indicator "CHECKS;" average of available values 1990 to 2002; range of values: 1 to 18 (higher scores correspond to more veto points)	Database of Political Institutions (DPI2004), http://econ.worldbank.org/WBSITE/EXTERNAL/EXTDEC/EXTRESEARCH/0,,contentMDK:20649465~pagePK:6421482 5~piPK:64214943~theSitePK:469382,00.html (accessed February 6, 2006); Beck et al. (2001); Keefer (2005); Keefer and Stasavage (2003)
RULAW	Index that measures the respect of and the confidence in the rule of law; original indicator "rule of law"; average of available values 1996 to 2002; range of values: −2.5 to 2.5 (higher scores correspond to "better" performance)	Database of the World Bank Institute, Governance & Anti-Corruption, http://www.worldbank.org/wbi/governance/pdf/2004kkdata.xls (accessed November 22, 2005); Kaufmann, Kraay, and Mastruzzi (2004)
Control variables (CON)		
GDPCAP	Mean of annual GDP per capita in PPP (constant 2000 international $; available values 1990 to 2002)	World Development Indicators 2005 Database, World Bank (CD-ROM)
GDPCAPLN	LN (GDPCAP) = Natural logarithm of GDPCAP	
POPTOT	Average of total population in 1990 and total population in 2002; measured in persons	WHO and UNICEF Joint Monitoring Programme Database, http://www.wssinfo.org (accessed November 14, 2005)
LAAREA	Land Area (in 2002); measured in sq. km	World Development Indicators 2005 Database, World Bank (CD-ROM)
POPDENS	Division of POPTOT by LAAREA; measured in persons per sq. km	
POPDENSLN	LN (POPDENS) = Natural logarithm of POPDENS	

Variable	Description	Source
POPURB	Average of the population living in urban areas (1990 and 2002); percentage of total population	WHO and UNICEF Joint Monitoring Programme Database, http://www.wssinfo.org (accessed November 14, 2005)
WATRESCAP	Internal renewable water resources, long term average; measured in cubic meters per person per year	World Resources Institute Database http://earthtrends.wri.org/searchable_db/index.php?theme=2 (accessed January 31, 2006)
WATRESCAPLN	LN (WATRESCAP) = Natural logarithm of WATRESCAP	
ETHNIC	Index of ethnic fractionalisation; data measured between 1979 and 2001; range of values: 0 to 1 (greater values correspond to greater fractionalisation)	Data provided by William Easterly, http://www.nyu.edu/fas/institute/dri/fractionalization.xls (accessed February 16, 2006); Alesina et al. (2003)
CORRUPT	Index that measures control of corruption; original indicator "control of corruption;" average of available values 1996 to 2002; range of values –2.5 to 2.5 (higher scores correspond to "better" performance)	Database of the World Bank Institute, Governance & Anti-Corruption, http://www.worldbank.org/wbi/governance/pdf/2004kkdata.xls (accessed November 22, 2005); Kaufmann, Kraay, and Mastruzzi (2004)
PROPRIGHTS	Index that measures the integrity of the legal system and the security of private property rights; original indicator "Legal Structure and Security of Property Rights;" average of available values 1990 to 2002; range of values: 1 to 10 (higher scores correspond to "better" performance)	Economic Freedom of the World Database provided by the Fraser Institute. http://www.freetheworld.com/download.html#efw (accessed November 21, 2005); Gwartney, Lawson, and Gartzke (2005)
PSP	Sum of total investments with private sector participation in water and sewerage (1990 to 2002, US Dollars)	PPI Data Base, World Bank, and PPIAF, http://ppi.worldbank.org (accessed January 16, 2006)
PSPCAP	Sum of total investments with private sector participation in water and sewerage per capita (1990 to 2002, US Dollars): PSPCAP=PSP/POPTOT	

(continued)

Table A4.1 (continued)

Variable Name	Variable Description	Data Source; Additional Information
SUBSAFRICA	Variable = 1 if country belongs to the region "Africa, West" or "Africa, East" or "Africa, Central" or "Africa, South;" (otherwise variable = 0)	Penn World Tables Version 6.1
EASTSEASIA	Variable = 1 if country belongs to the regions "Asia, East" or "Asia, Southeast;" (otherwise variable = 0)	Penn World Tables Version 6.1
SOUTHWASIA	Variable = 1 if country belongs to the region "Asia, Southwest;" (otherwise variable = 0)	Penn World Tables Version 6.1
NAFRICAMEAST	Variable = 1 if country belongs to the region "North Africa and Middle East;" (otherwise variable = 0)	Penn World Tables Version 6.1
LAAMERCARI	Variable = 1 if country belongs to the region "America, North" (= Mexico) or "America, South" or "Caribbean;" (otherwise variable = 0)	Penn World Tables Version 6.1

WHO = World Health Organization. UNICEF = United Nations Children's Fund.

Table A4.2 Summary Statistics Variables Chapter 4

Variable	N	Mean	Std. Dev.	Min	Max
COV:					
WATTOT90	69	65.63768	19.09494	20	94
WATTOT02	69	74.97101	16.71647	22	98
SANTOT90	69	42.81159	22.99762	4	87
SANTOT02	69	51.24638	23.05582	6	99
GOV:					
POLITY	65	0.8396923	5.577878	−9	9
POLRIGHTS	69	3.542899	1.631842	1	6.38
POLCON	68	0.232222	0.173244	0	0.6617
CHECKS	66	2.543483	1.384287	1	8.384615
RULAW	69	− 0.4773913	0.5580709	− 1.87	1.27
CON:					
GDPCAP	69	2999.824	2449.342	509.4144	12166.89
POPDENS	69	93.74667	138.3943	2.046739	972.6168
POPURB	69	40.86232	18.78573	8	85
WATRESCAP	69	8725.596	13680.87	24.5	58620.8
ETHNIC	68	0.5491074	0.2464875	0	0.9302

Table A4.3   Countries Contained in the Sample

1.	Angola	24.	Ethiopia	47.	Oman
2.	Bangladesh	25.	Ghana	48.	Pakistan
3.	Benin	26.	Guatemala	49.	Paraguay
4.	Bolivia	27.	Guinea	50.	Peru
5.	Botswana	28.	Haiti	51.	Philippines
6.	Brazil	29.	Honduras	52.	Russian Federation
7.	Burkina Faso	30.	India	53.	Rwanda
8.	Burundi	31.	Indonesia	54.	Senegal
9.	Cameroon	32.	Iran	55.	South Africa
10.	Central African Republic	33.	Jamaica	56.	Sri Lanka
11.	Chad	34.	Kazakhstan	57.	Sudan
12.	Chile	35.	Kenya	58.	Syrian Arab. Republic
13.	China	36.	Madagascar	59.	Tanzania
14.	Colombia	37.	Malawi	60.	Thailand
15.	Comoros	38.	Mali	61.	Togo
16.	Cote d'Ivoire	39.	Mauritania	62.	Tunisia
17.	Democratic Republic of the Congo	40.	Mexico	63.	Turkey
18.	Djibouti	41.	Morocco	64.	Uganda
19.	Dominican Republic	42.	Namibia	65.	Uzbekistan
20.	Ecuador	43.	Nepal	66.	Vietnam
21.	Egypt	44.	Nicaragua	67.	Yemen**
22.	El Salvador	45.	Niger	68.	Zambia
23.	Eritrea*	46.	Nigeria	69.	Zimbabwe

*Missing data for POLCON; **Missing data for ETHNIC.

Table A5.1   Coverage 2003 by Income Quintiles

	Urban	*Rural*	*Total*
Water			
Quintile 1	97.5%	62.7%	83.5%
Quintile 2	98.1%	66.0%	86.3%
Quintile 3	98.2%	67.3%	90.3%
Quintile 4	98.8%	66.8%	94.2%
Quintile 5	98.3%	72.4%	96.8%
Total	98.2%	65.6%	90.2%
Sanitation			
Quintile 1	96.2%	63.4%	83.5%
Quintile 2	98.3%	71.2%	88.3%
Quintile 3	98.3%	78.9%	93.3%
Quintile 4	99.6%	80.8%	96.9%
Quintile 5	99.8%	88.6%	99.1%
Total	98.6%	72.2%	92.1%

Source: Meléndez (2004, 49).

Table A5.2 Corporate Form and Ownership of WS Service Providers Serving the Main Cities

City	Inhabitants 2003	WS Service Provider	Corporate Form	Coding of the Variable PRIVATE	% Private Shares	Year of PSP Engagement	Ownership According to Public Services Law Definition
Bogotá	6,865,997	Empresa de Acueducto y Alcantarillado de Bogotá	EICE	Public	0	—	Public
Cali	2,316,655	Empresas Municipales de Cali	EICE	Public	0	—	Public
Medellín	2,049,131	Empresas Públicas de Medellín	EICE	Public	0	—	Public
Barranquilla	1,332,454	Sociedad de Acueducto, Alcantarillado y Aseo de Barranquilla	ESP	Private	80	1991	Private
Cartagena	978,187	Aguas de Cartagena	ESP	Private	45	1994	Mixed
Cúcuta	702,325	Empresa Industrial y Comercial de Cúcuta	EICE	Public	0	—	Public
Bucaramanga	558,784	Cia. del Acueducto Metropolitano de Bucaramanga (*water*)	ESP	—	5	n.a.	Mixed
		Corp. de la Denfensa de la Meseta de Bucaramanga (*sewerage*)	ESP	—	5	n.a.	Mixed
Pereira	499,771	Aguas y Aguas de Pereira	ESP	Public	0	—	Public
Ibagué	439,785	Empresa Ibaguereña de Acueducto y Alcantarillado	ESP	Public	0	—	Public
Santa Marta	422,460	Cia. de Acueducto y Alcantarillado Metropolitano de Santa Marta	ESP	Private	65	1989/ 1997	Private
Pasto	413,557	Empresa de Obras Sanitarias de Pasto	ESP	Public	0	—	Public
Manizales	375,652	Aguas de Manizales	ESP	Public	1	1996	Mixed
Valledupar	362,816	Empresa de Servicios Públicos de Valledupar	ESP	Public	0	—	Public

Neiva	358,279	Empresas Públicas de Neiva	EICE	Public	0	—	Public
Villavicencio	349,374	Empresa de Acueducto y Alcantarillado de Villavicencio	EICE	Public	0	—	Public
Montería	339,080	Proactiva Aguas de Montería	ESP	Private	100	2000	Private
Armenia	311,000	Empresas Públicas de Armenia	EICE	Public	0	—	Public
Palmira	287,261	Acuaviva	ESP	Private	60	1997	Private
Sincelejo	255,122	Empresa de Acueducto y Aseo de Sincelejo	EICE	Public	0	—	Public
Popayán	233,100	Acueducto y Alcantarillado de Popayán	ESP	Public	1	n.a.	Mixed
Tuluá	186,882	Centroaguas Tuluá	ESP	Private	100	2000	Private
Sogamoso	158,647	Cia. de Servicios Públicos de Sogamoso	ESP	Public	n.a.	n.a.	Mixed
Florencia	142,681	Empresa de Servicios de Florencia	ESP	Private	51	1995	Private
Cartago	136,758	Empresas Municipales de Cartago	ESP	Public	0	—	Public
Buga	130,104	Aguas de Buga	ESP	Public	n.a.	n.a.	Mixed
Girardot	127,667	Empresa de Aguas de Girardot, Ricaurte y la Región	ESP	Private	70	1997	Private
Tunja	124,122	Sera Q.A. Tunja	ESP	Private	100	1996	Private
Fusagasugá	107,918	Empresa de Servicios Públicos de Fusagasugá	EICE	Public	0	—	Public
Piedecuesta	100,687	Empresa Municipal de Serv. Públ. Dom. de Piedecuesta	EICE	—	0	—	Public

(continued)

Table A5.2 (continued)

City	Inhabitants 2003	WS Service Provider	Corporate Form	Coding of the Variable PRIVATE	% Private Shares	Year of PSP Engagement	Ownership According to Public Services Law Definition
Ocaña	100,620	Empresa de Servicios Públicos de Ocaña	ESP	Private	100	1994	Private
Facatativa	97,673	Empresa de Acueducto, Alcantarillado y Aseo de Facatativa	EICE	—	0	—	Public
Ipiales	94,853	Empresa de Obras Sanitarias de la Provincia de Obando	EICE	Public	0	—	Public
Villa Del Rosario	64,210	EIC de Servicios Públicos Dom. de Villa del Rosario	EICE	Public	0	—	Public

Total inhabitants: 21,023,612*

* 47.2% of total population. EICE = Empresa Industrial y Comercial del Estado (State-owned corporation); ESP = Empresa de Servicios Públicos—Sociedad Anónima (Enterprise for Public Utility Services—Stock corporation); n.a. = not applicable; — = not available.
Sources: Inhabitants: DANE (www.dane.gov.co). Remaining data: SSPD; Fernández (2004). All information as of end of 2003.

Table A5.3 User Structure

User Class	Capitals With > 1 Million Habitants (4)	Districts With 70,000–1 Million Habitants (49)	Districts With 12,500–70,000 Habitants (171)	Districts With < 12,500 Habitants (858)
Residential stratum 1	7.8 %	11.0 %	16.2 %	13.8 %
Residential stratum 2	30.5 %	28.0 %	34.1 %	47.0 %
Residential stratum 3	31.1 %	31.8 %	37.8 %	31.9 %
Residential stratum 4	12.6 %	13.5 %	4.8 %	1.3 %
Residential stratum 5	7.3 %	4.5 %	0.4 %	0.1 %
Residential stratum 6	3.4 %	3.2 %	0.6 %	0.0 %
Commercial	6.5 %	4.7 %	2.2 %	3.7 %
Industrial	0.6 %	2.5 %	2.9 %	0.0 %
Official and Special	0.2 %	0.8 %	1.0 %	2.2 %
Total	*100 %*	*100 %*	*100 %*	*100 %*
Subsidees	*69.4 %*	*70.8 %*	*88.1 %*	*92.7 %*
Neutral	*12.8 %*	*14.3 %*	*5.8 %*	*3.5 %*
Contributors	*17.4 %*	*13.2 %*	*4.2 %*	*6.0 %*

Source: Domínguez Torres and Uribe Botero (2005, 45).

Table A5.4   Variables and Data Sources Used in the Statistical Analysis of Chapter 5

Variable Name	Variable Description	Data Source; Additional Information
WAT98	Coverage with piped water connections in 1998; if data for 1998 was not available, data for 1999 was taken (values are proportions between 0 and 1)	Information provided by SSPD and CRA in 2005; complemented with information taken from Fernández (2004) and SSPD (2002)
WAT98SQ	WAT98SQ = WAT98 * WAT98	
WAT03	Coverage with piped water connections in 2003; if data for 2003 was not available, data for 2002 was taken (values are proportions between 0 and 1).	Information provided by SSPD and CRA in 2005; complemented with information taken from Fernández (2004).
CHWAT	CHWAT = WAT03 / WAT98	
SEW98	Coverage with sewer connections in 1998; if data for 1998 was not available, data for 1999 was taken (values are proportions between 0 and 1).	Information provided by SSPD and CRA in 2005; complemented with information taken from Fernández (2004) and SSPD (2002).
SEW98SQ	SEW98SQ = SEW98 * SEW98	
SEW03	Coverage with sewer connections in 2003; if data for 2003 was not available, data for 2002 was taken (values are proportions between 0 and 1).	Information provided by SSPD and CRA in 2005; complemented with information taken from Fernández (2004).
CHSEW	CHSEW = SEW03 / SEW98	
PRIVATE	Ownership of the WS service provider; PRIVATE = 1 if shares held by the private sector ≥ 25%; PRIVATE = 0 if shares held by the private sector < 25%.	Information provided by SSPD in 2005; complemented with information taken from Fernández (2004).
UFW98	Proportion of unaccounted-for water in total drinking water produced in 1998; if data for 1998 was not available, data for 1999 was taken (values are proportions between 0 and 1).	Information provided by SSPD and CRA in 2005; complemented with information taken from Fernández (2004) and SSPD (2002).

UFW03	Proportion of unaccounted-for water in total drinking water produced in 2003; if data for 2003 was not available, data for 2002 was taken (values are proportions between 0 and 1).	Information provided by SSPD and CRA in 2005; complemented with information taken from Fernández (2004).
UFWAV	Proportion of unaccounted-for water in total drinking water produced; average for the years 1998 to 2003 for which data was available.	Information provided by SSPD and CRA in 2005; complemented with information taken from Fernández (2004) and SSPD (2002).
CR	Collection rate for water services; average for the years 1998 to 2003 for which data was available.	Information provided by SSPD and CRA in 2005; complemented with information taken from Fernández (2004).
VULWAT	Vulnerability of water resources of the district; conditions of a dry or average year; index takes values from 1 (very low vulnerability) to 5 (very high vulnerability).	Instituto de Hidrología, Meteorología y Estudios Ambientales (IDEAM): Estudio Nacional del Agua, Cuadro 5: Índice de escasez y vulnerabilidad por disponibilidad de agua en cabeceras municipales de Colombia. Condiciones hidrológicas de año medio y seco; www.ideam.gov.co (accessed September 21, 2006).
POV	Value of the Index of Unsatisfied Basic Needs in 1993; multidimensional index that measures the share of persons whose basic needs (housing, public services, education, income generation capacity) are not satisfied (values are percentages between 0 and 100).	Information provided by Departamento Nacional de Planeación (DNP) in 08/2005: Índice de Necesidades Básicas Insatisfechas.
POP	Change in the population of the district expressed as proportion: POP = population in 2003 / population in 1998.	Departamento Administrativo Nacional de Estadística (DANE): Series y proyecciones de población, proyecciones municipales; www.dane.gov.co (accessed September 10, 2006).

WS = Water and sanitation; SSPD = Superintendencia de Servicios Públicos Domiciliarios (Superintendency of Public Utility Services); CRA = Comisión de Regulación de Agua Potable y Saneamiento Básico (Regulatory Commission for Water and Sanitation).

Table A5.5 Summary Statistics Variables Chapter 5

Variable	N	Mean	Standard Deviation	Minimum	Maximum
WAT98	30	0.9102567	0.1039748	0.5778	1
WAT98SQ	30	0.8390176	0.1735711	0.3338528	1
CHWAT	30	1.050098	0.1107293	0.768	1.413984
SEW98	30	0.8390733	0.1635928	0.37	1
SEW98SQ	30	0.7299146	0.2407628	0.1369	1
CHSEW	30	1.02326	0.0973636	0.795	1.342032
PRIVATE	30	0.3333333	0.4794633	0	1
UFW98	29	0.4242931	0.1020432	0.2461	0.7
UFW03	29	0.4423621	0.10836	0.262	0.734
UFWAV	29	0.4427957	0.097011	0.3053667	0.71432
CR	29	0.8349455	0.1124618	0.462725	0.9883333
VULWAT	30	3.433333	0.727932	2	5
POV	30	27.623	9.071521	15.58	49.72
POP	30	1.108022	0.0408561	1.04794	1.178743

Table A5.6 List of Organisations Interviewed

City	Organisation	Date
Bogotá	German Agency for Technical Co-operation (GTZ): Prodespaz; Programa Ambiental	20/06/2005 22/06/2005 28/06/2005
Bogotá	Asociación Colombiana de Ingeniería Sanitaria y Ambiental (ACODAL)	21/06/2005
Bogotá	Superintendencia de Servicios Públicos Domiciliarios (SSPD): Superintendencia Delegada para Acueducto, Alcantarillado y Aseo	22/06/2005
Bogotá	Departamento Nacional de Planeación: Subdirectoría Agua y Ambiente	23/06/2005
Bogotá	B y P Servicios Ltda. (expert)	23/06/2005
Bogotá	Comisión de Regulación de Agua Potable y Sanemiento Básico (CRA)	24/06/2005 27/06/2005
Bogotá	Asociación Comunera Distrital de Comités de Desarrollo y Control Social de los Servicios Públicos Domicilarios y Vocales de Control	25/06/2005
Bogotá	Ministerio de Ambiente, Vivienda y Desarrollo Territorial (MAVDT): Directoría Agua Potable y Saneamiento Básico; Programa de Modernización Empresarial; Programa de Microempresas; Grupo Regulación y Normatividad	27/06/2005 28/06/2005 01/08/2005
Bogotá	Transparencia por Colombia	28/06/2005
Bogotá	Banco Interamericano de Desarrollo	29/06/2005
Bogotá	Asociación Nacional de Empresas de Servicios Públicos Domiciliaros y Actividades Complementarias e Inherentes (ANDESCO): Cámara de Agua Potable y Alcantarillado	30/06/2005
Manizales	Alcaldía de Manizales: Despacho del Alcalde	05/07/2005
Manizales	CDCS spokesman	05/07/2005
Manizales	Aguas de Manizales S.A.	06/07/2005
Manizales	Corporación Autónoma Regional de Caldas (CORPOCALDAS)	07/07/2005
Manizales	User representative, member of the CPE	07/07/2005
Manizales	Corporación Cívica de Caldas	08/07/2005
Santa Marta	Alcaldía de Santa Marta: Despacho del Alcalde	12/07/2005
Santa Marta	Metroagua S.A.	12/07/2005 13/07/2005
Santa Marta	Cámara de Comercio de Santa Marta	13/07/2005
Santa Marta	Corporación Autónoma Regional del Magdalena (CORPAMAG)	13/07/2005

(continued)

Table A5.6 (continued)

City	Organisation	Date
Santa Marta	CDCS spokesman; Asociación de Vocales de Control de Santa Marta y Magdalena	13/07/2005
Corregimiento de Bonda, Santa Marta	Junta de Acueducto de Bonda	14/07/2005
Santa Marta	Consultor particular (expert)	15/07/2005
Tunja	Sera Q.A. Tunja S.A.	21/07/2005 22/07/2005
Tunja	Alcaldía de Tunja: Secretaría de Desarrollo	21/07/2005
Tunja	Cámara de Comercio de Tunja	21/07/2005
Tunja	CDCS spokesman; Asociación de Comerciantes Mercados Móviles de Boyacá	21/07/2005
Tunja	Corporación Autónoma Regional de Boyacá (CORPOBOYACA)	22/07/2005
Villavicencio	Empresa de Acueducto y Alcantarillado de Villavicencio	27/07/2005
Villavicencio	Alcaldía de Villavicencio: Secretaría de Planeación; Secretaría de Medio Ambiente	27/07/2005
Villavicencio	Cámara de Comercio de Villavicencio	28/07/2005
Villavicencio	Corporación Autónoma Regional CORMACARENA	28/07/2005
Villavicencio	CDCS spokesman	28/07/2005
Bogotá	Económica Consultores (expert)	01/08/2005

Table A5.7 Ranking of 24 Cities According to the Overall Water and Sanitation Service Performance (Intermediate Cities)

	Good			Average			Bad	
Rank/Scores	City	Delivery Model	Rank/Scores	City	Delivery Model	Rank/Scores	City	Delivery Model
1/ 44	Palmira	Private	7/ 83	Pasto	Public	14/ 117	Popayán	Public
2/ 67	Buga	Public	8/ 92	Fusagasugá	Public	15/ 118	Ipiales	Public
3/ 69	Manizales	Public	9/ 95	Valledupar	Public	16/ 123	Santa Marta	Private
3/ 69	Girardot	Private	10/ 96	Armenia	Public	17/ 128	Neiva	Public
4/ 75	Ocaña	Private	10/ 96	Ibagué	Public	17/ 128	Florencia	Private
4/ 75	Pereira	Public	11/ 106	Montería	Private	18/ 130	V. del Rosario	Public
5/ 79	Cartago	Public	12/ 107	Sogamoso	Public	19/ 148	Villavicencio	Public
6/ 82	Tunja	Private	13/ 114	Cartagena	Private	20/ 159	Cúcuta	Public

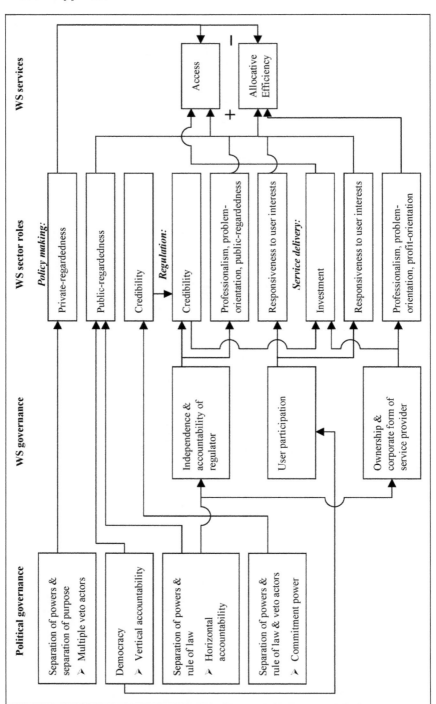

Figure A3.1 Expected influence of governance on water and sanitation services. Source: Author.

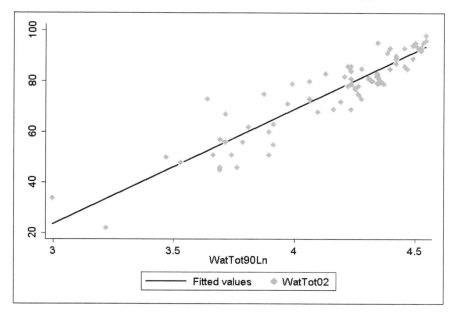

Figure A4.1 Bivariate regression of WATTOT02 on WATTOT90LN–fitted values.
Source: Author, elaborated with STATA/SE 9.0 for Windows.

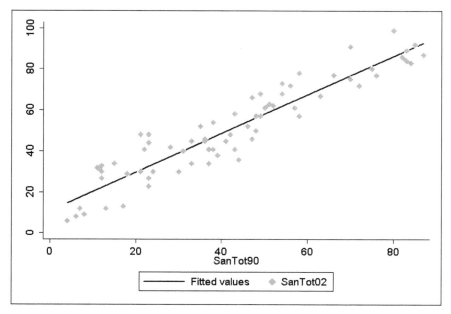

Figure A4.2 Bivariate regression of SANTOT02 on SANTOT90–fitted values.
Source: Author, elaborated with STATA/SE 9.0 for Windows

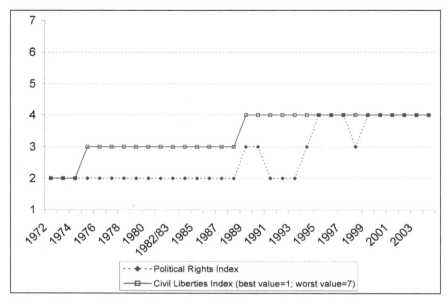

Figure A5.1   Political Rights and Civil Liberties Indexes Colombia (1972–2004). Source: Author; data source: Freedom of the World Database (www.freedomhouse. org; accessed November 16, 2005)

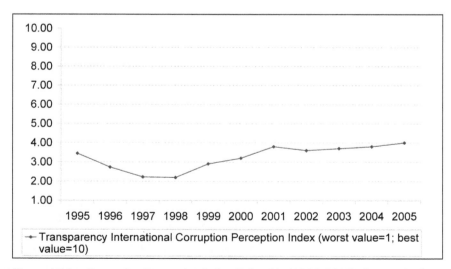

Figure A5.2   Corruption Perception Index Colombia (1995–2005). Source: Author; data source: Transparency International (www.transparency.org; accessed November 11, 2006)

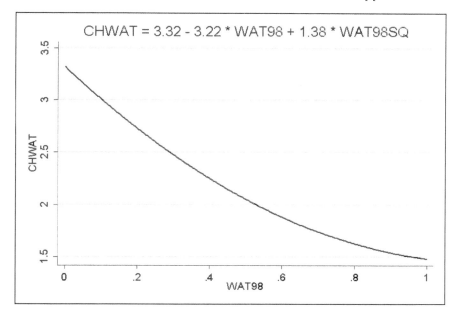

Figure A5.3 Estimated functional relation CHWAT → F(WAT98, WAT98SQ).
Source: Author, elaborated with STATA/SE 9.0 for Windows

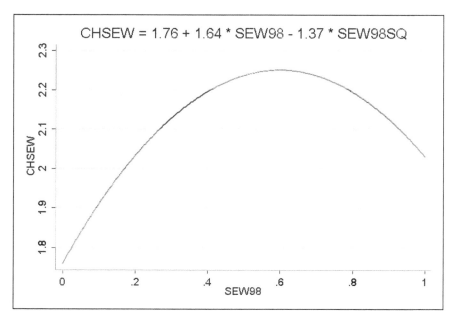

Figure A5.4 Estimated functional relation CHSEW → F(SEW98, SEW98SQ).
Source: Author, elaborated with STATA/SE 9.0 for Windows

Figure A5.5   Map of Colombia. Source: Elaborated by Gerd Storbeck for German Development Institute (DIE).

Notes

NOTES TO CHAPTER 1

1. The target is to "[h]alve by 2015 the proportion of people without sustainable access to safe drinking water and basic sanitation" with respect to the proportion in 1990 (Development Committee, International Monetary Fund, and World Bank 2004, xxii). See Table A2.1 in the appendix for an overview of the projected increase in coverage necessary to meet the target.

2. PSP means the involvement of private actors in the delivery of WS services. PSP can take a range of organisational forms (delivery models) that differ with respect to the scope of rights granted to and the scope of responsibilities borne by private actors. An extreme form of PSP is full divestiture, which means the complete transfer of ownership of assets—and consequently of the implied rights and responsibilities—to a private enterprise. Subsection 3.2.3.3 discusses, in more detail, different types of PSP delivery models in the WS sector. The term public–private partnership (PPP), which is often found in the literature, is a synonym for PSP.

3. Cf. Inkota-Netzwerk e.V. and Brot für die Welt (2004) for a critical perspective on PSP in WS services in developing countries. Generally, we can observe that the global political debate on water issues is marked by ideological polarisation; cf. Urquhart and Moore (2004) for a survey of the different positions in this debate. See Hall and Lubina (2002) for a survey of opposition to PSP in WS services in Latin America.

4. Cf. Izaguirre (2004) for the trend of private investments in WS services in developing countries, as compared to other infrastructure services.

5. Cf. e.g. Clarke, Kosec, and Wallsten (2004). See subsection 2.4.3 for a review of the empirical literature to this respect.

6. Cf. Basañes and Willig (2002) for a discussion of second-generation reforms in infrastructure policy. Cf. Pastor and Wise (1999) and González and Munar (2003) for the broader context of second-generation reform approaches in development policy. In contrast to first-generation reform approaches that were inspired by the Washington Consensus and concentrated on privatisation and liberalisation, these second-generation approaches are intended to tackle distributional and institutional problems.

7. For more details on the definition of governance see subsection 3.1.4.

8. According to Scharpf (1997, 38) institutions can be defined as "systems of rules that structure the courses of actions that a set of actors may choose." For more details concerning the term *institution*, cf. subsection 3.1.2.

9. Equity in this study basically means equality of opportunity and avoidance of absolute deprivation. For more details, see subsection 2.2.1.

10. In an econometric study Clarke, Kosec, and Wallsten (2004) find no statistically significant effect of PSP on coverage expansion. Moreover, the authors review the inconclusive empirical literature regarding the effect of PSP on internal efficiency. For more details, see subsection 2.4.3.
11. Cf. United Nations Development Programme (2003, 116–20); Shirley and Ménard (2002).
12. One of the few exceptions that focuses on the relation between governance and water services is the book authored by Rouse (2007).
13. For more details see the review of econometric literature in subsection 4.1.2.
14. This study distinguishes between two concepts of efficiency: the allocative efficiency of the whole WS sector (or even the whole economy) and the internal efficiency of a single WS service provider (see subsection 2.3.1 for the definition and discussion of these concepts). Internal efficiency is a subconcept of allocative efficiency, i.e., a situation of the economy that is allocatively efficient implies that the individual providers are internally efficient. When, in the following, the term *efficiency* is used without any attribute, it is meant to refer to the broad notion of allocative efficiency (which includes the internal efficiency of providers as one relevant aspect). Whenever it is referred to the subconcept of internal efficiency alone, this is made explicit by using the attribute *internal*.
15. For more details see section 3.1.
16. For an in-depth discussion of the characteristics, strengths and weaknesses of quantitative and qualitative approaches in empirical research, cf. King, Keohane, and Verba (1994); Creswell (1994); and Neubert (2003).

NOTES TO CHAPTER 2

1. For a brief discussion of normative and positive issues in general policy research cf. Scharpf (1997, 12–15).
2. These certain aspects are incomplete information and property rights (see discussion below, especially subsection 2.4.3). For an assessment of the school of new institutional economics contrasting it with neoclassical economics cf. Furubotn and Richter (1991).
3. When looking from an allocative efficiency perspective. Supplying a given urban settlement with a given service level (quantity and quality) at minimum social costs is typically achieved by choosing a network supply technology. For the details regarding the concepts of allocative efficiency and social costs, see 2.3.
4. An in-depth discussion of the pros and cons of different supply technologies for urban areas is provided by UN-HABITAT (2003, 1–8).
5. Often, besides collecting wastewater, urban service providers are also responsible for collecting storm water. Collection can be done by one combined sewer system or two separate systems for wastewater and storm water.
6. I.e., the costs that accrue to the WS service provider. For the distinction of private costs and external costs see subsection 2.3.4.
7. In general, capital costs (basically depreciation and payment of interests) are the largest components of the fixed costs in the WS industry. Other relevant components of fixed costs are maintenance of capital assets and administrative overheads.
8. Another relevant component of the variable costs are the materials required for drinking water treatment.
9. However, the share of fixed capital costs in total costs will vary across countries depending on the tax and business regulation. The annual capital costs of a WS service provider are driven, to a good extent, by the amount of

depreciation. The amount of depreciation varies according to the method of depreciation chosen, which, in turn, depends on the respective rules fixed in tax and business legislation.

10. The WHO (2004) has issued detailed guidelines concerning drinking-water quality. On other aspects of the adequacy of WS services (sufficient quantity, regularity, accessibility and affordability), cf. subsection 2.2.2.

11. The willingness to pay indicates the maximum price at which a household is willing to use the service in a setting in which the household chooses the bundle of goods (including water services) that maximizes its utility, given its preferences and given its budget constraint. There are two basic methodological approaches to measure the willingness to pay: (i) revealed preferences approaches that rely on information on observable economic behaviour (e.g. prices paid to water vendors by households that lack a service through the network); and (ii) stated preferences approaches that use information collected through household surveys based on constructed hypothetical scenarios (e.g. contingent valuation method). Cf. Komives et al. (2005, 37–38).

12. Komives et al. (2005, 37–45) provide a brief review of this body of literature.

13. Assuming a household size of 5 persons, this corresponds to ca. 53 litres per day and capita in the former case and to ca. 272 litres per day and capita in the latter case. In OECD-countries, water use per day and capita varies between 129 litres (Germany) and 382 litres (United States); cf. Levin et al. (2002, 44).

14. Assuming a household size of 5 persons this corresponds to ca. 10.7 litres per day and capita in the former case and to ca. 147 litres per day and capita in the latter case. These figures can be qualified by comparing them with normative benchmarks used in development co-operation. For instance, the guidelines used by German bilateral development agencies for the assessment of WS projects stipulate the following benchmarks for sound per capita consumptions: 40 litres per day (public standpipes), 60 litres per day (yard connections), and 120 litres per day (in-house connections); cf. KfW (2004, 5). See also subsection 2.2.2.

15. See subsection 2.2.2 for a definition of "improved" services.

16. See e.g. the newspaper coverage of the Fourth World Water Forum held from March 16 to 22, 2006 in Mexico City.

17. Cf. e.g. World Bank (2005, Chapter 4) and the quoted literature.

18. According to modern definitions of poverty, deprivations in well-being include the following dimensions: (i) material deprivation, (ii) low achievements in education, (iii) ill health, (iv) vulnerability, and (v) political voicelessness and powerlessness (World Bank 2001, Chapter 1).

19. For a definition of adequate WS services, see subsection 2.2.2.

20. The health and economic benefits for households from WS services are well documented, cf. Hutton and Haller (2004); UN-HABITAT (2003, Chapter 2); WHO and UNICEF (2000, 1–3); KfW (2004, 4); Fuest and Laube (2004, section 2.2). For an in-depth empirical analysis and discussion of health benefits from WS services, cf. e.g. Galdo and Briceño (2005); Jalan and Ravallion (2001); Esrey (1996).

21. Cf. UN-HABITAT (2003, 2); WHO and UNICEF (2000, annex A); Boland and Whittington (2000, 225); Komives et al. (2005, 40–41).

22. Such decisions will, however, typically depend on the individual willingness to pay (see previous discussion). The politically set affordability threshold may well lie above or below the willingness to pay of a particular household.

23. For a more in-depth discussion of the problems related to the definition and the measurement of adequate WS services, with some critical remarks concerning the concept of "improved" services, cf. UN-HABITAT (2003, 1–8).

24. According to Boland and Whittington (2000, 225), internationally cited standards for basic water needs are not 20, but 25–30 litres per person per day.
25. WHO and UNICEF do not use a standard definition to classify households in terms of rural or urban areas (WHO and UNICEF 2000, Annex A). Instead, the worldwide coverage statistics relies on the countries' own definitions for urban and rural. These definitions vary considerably between countries (Corbridge and Jones 2005, 21).
26. Water sold by public utilities is, however, commonly underpriced (with respect to the private costs of providing the services), which leads to a series of problems (water spillage, financially unsustainable firms that provide an unreliable and bad quality service, etc.—see the following discussion).
27. It shall be noted here that an increase in general coverage does not automatically imply an increase in the coverage among the income poor, because the increase might be due to the fact that, proportionally, more nonpoor than poor have gained access to WS services. According to empirical evidence from Latin America, this effect seems to depend on the initial coverage rate: when the initial rate is low, the poor benefit less than proportionally; when the initial rate is high, the poor benefit more than proportionally (de Ferranti et al. 2004, section 7.3).
28. The current annual investments amount to 15 billion US dollars.
29. The terminology used in the literature is not uniform. In this study, the term *internal efficiency* is used in the sense given by Vickers and Yarrow (1988, 67). However, Lundsgaard (2002, 47) uses the term *productive efficiency* and Shirley and Walsh (2000, 5) use the term *operational efficiency* for what here is called *internal efficiency*. Yet other authors use the term *technical efficiency* (e.g. Fraquelli and Erbetta 1999).
30. That is, the costs that accrue to the single firm. For the distinction of private costs and external costs, see subsection 2.3.4.
31. The term *X-(in)efficiency* has been coined by Leibenstein (1966).
32. I return to this issue in subsection 2.4.3, when discussing the consequences of private versus public ownership for the internal efficiency of a WS service provider.
33. This is true for Paretian social welfare functions (Atkinson and Stiglitz 1980, 339).
34. See subsection 2.3.4 for a definition of social cost.
35. For a more in-depth discussion cf. e.g. Atkinson and Stiglitz (1980, 336–50); Rosen (1992, Chapter 4).
36. The Kaldor-Hicks criterion builds the basis for economic cost-benefit analyses (e.g. Zerbe, Bauman, and Finkle 2006). On the application of cost-benefit-analyses for evaluation in development co-operation, cf. Hemmer (2002, 971–79).
37. A discussion of the relation between the Pareto criterion and different conceptualisations of equity is provided by Atkinson and Stiglitz (1980, 336–43).
38. For complete statements and proofs of Pareto-efficiency in a market economy cf. Arrow and Hahn (1971). Even a "pure market economy" presupposes certain state activities, such as the protection against violence, theft and fraud, the definitions of property rights and the enforcement of contracts, and thus entails taxation in order to finance these public goods (Atkinson and Stiglitz 1980, 336–37).
39. This statement does not imply that any specific sector policy necessarily will make things better as compared to a pure market allocation, cf., e.g. Noll's (1989, 1262–77) comments on "how regulation can make matters worse."

40. On the efficiency-related characteristics of the WS industry and policy implications cf. also Noll (2002); Vickers and Yarrow (1988, Chapter 11); Shirley (2000, 148–55); Kessides (2004, 219–27).
41. On the relation between (lacking) property rights and externalities, cf. the seminal paper by Coase (1960).
42. See especially subsection 2.4.3 on private versus public ownership.
43. For thorough discussions of natural monopoly characteristics and policy implications cf. Joskow (2007); Braeutigam (1989).
44. It is, however, not a necessary condition. The less restrictive condition for a natural monopoly according to the technology-oriented definition is subadditivity of the cost function. In the multiproduct case, cost subadditivity can arise from economies of scale or economies of scope, cf. Braeutigam (1989) for a thorough discussion of cost subadditivity.
45. Engineering economies of scale translate into organisational economies of scale if (i) there are no substantial diseconomies of scale at another stage of the production process and (ii) there are no substantial diseconomies of scale in organisational management.
46. For a more precise statement based on the concept of cost subadditivity, cf. Braeutigam (1989).
47. For a technical definition of sunk costs, cf. Braeutigam (1989, 1304) and for a general discussion of the importance of sunk costs in the context of natural monopolies, cf. Joskow (2007, 1232–48). Sunk costs result from investments in specific assets that have no alternative economic use (more precisely: for which the economic return from an alternative use is substantially lower than for the specific use). Sunk costs are, thus, irreversible. For a certain time period, they have to be incurred even if production ceases. In combination with imperfect information (uncertainty) sunk costs give rise to the hold-up problem in contractual settings (Grossman and Hart 1986). If no credible commitments among the parties (e.g. the municipality and the WS service provider) involved in the contract are feasible, this might imply that necessary investments in specific assets (like water and sewer pipes) are not carried out, cf. Spiller and Savedoff (1999) on this subject in the context of the WS industry, cf. Krause (2002, 13) for an illustrative example of the hold-up problem in the electricity industry.
48. For more in-depth discussions of these issues, cf. Joskow (2007); Tirole (1988, Chapter 8, 9). Further reasons that limit competition in the market for WS services are given by Kirkpatrick, Parker, and Zhang (2004, 17–18).
49. Cf. Demsetz (1968).
50. Noll (2002, 44) uses the terms *external costs* for what here is called *intratemporal external costs*, and *opportunity costs* for what here is called *intertemporal external costs*. Because the term *opportunity costs* in the economic literature commonly has a different meaning than the one intended by Noll, here the term *intertemporal external costs* is preferred.
51. For an in-depth theoretical analysis of externalities and public goods and their relation to property rights/a full set of markets, cf. Coase (1960), Cornes and Sandler (1996).
52. Standard marginal cost pricing leads to financial losses of the provider, as long as he produces in the range of falling average costs.
53. Cf. also Garcia and Reynaud (2004, 3–5); Komives et al. (2005, 30–32).
54. In systems that are fed by abundant sources nearby, the costs of metering and usage-based billing are typically high, compared to private marginal costs of supply. If intratemporal and intertemporal external costs can be neglected, it might be, therefore, preferable not to meter consumption but to rely exclusively on a fixed charge (Noll 2002, 48).

55. The asymmetric information regarding the "true" private costs between the utility and the regulator is indeed a problem which impedes a "perfect" price regulation in practice. Cf. e.g. Joskow (2007, 1285–86).
56. Cf. e.g. Siebert (2004); Perman et al. (2003); Baumol and Oates (1988).
57. Cf. also KfW (2004, 15).
58. Cf. Levy and Spiller (1996) for an analysis of this problem in the telecommunication sector.
59. For the following remarks cf. also KfW (2004, 7–13).
60. It is emphasized here, that tariff receipts do not only depend on average tariff height, but (among other things) also on collection performance.
61. Cf. Inkota-Netzwerk e.V. and Brot für die Welt (2004) for a critical perspective on privatisation in WS services in developing countries. Generally, we can observe that the political debate on privatisation in the WS industry is marked by ideological polarisation. See Urquhart and Moore (2004) and Budds and McGranahan (2003) for a survey of the different positions and arguments in this debate.
62. A classical work on this issue is Hayek (1945). Under conditions of perfect competition, perfect information and complete contracts, ownership does not matter (Shapiro and Willig 1990). These are the conditions underlying the first basic theorem of welfare economics (discussed previously).
63. For a critical perspective on the theoretical arguments for a superior internal efficiency of privately-owned firms in the WS sector, cf. Renzetti and Dupont (2004).
64. Whether ownership of public firms is highly diffuse and whether shares cannot be sold depends on whether it is, e.g. a government department governed primarily by public law or whether it is, e.g. a stock corporation governed by private-sector law with the government holding the majority of stocks (see subsection 3.2.3.3).
65. Things are different when looking at competitive markets. There is substantial empirical evidence that private firms perform better than state-owned firms in competitive markets (Shirley and Walsh 2000, Chapter 6).
66. See subsection 4.1.2 for a review of the econometric literature touching this issue.
67. Due to the sample selection bias, results from case studies cannot easily be generalised.

NOTES TO CHAPTER 3

1. For a characterisation of the term *actor*, see subsection 3.1.3.
2. Cf. Haggard and McCubbins (2001, 1) for a brief overview of this body of research.
3. Cf. Brown (2003); Cubbin and Stern (2006); Gutierrez (2003); Levy and Spiller (1996); Smith (2000); Stern and Holder (1999); Rouse (2007).
4. Erlei, Leschke, and Sauerland (1999) provide a good overview of new institutional economics and public choice approaches. For an overview in the English language, see Richter and Furubotn (1997). The term *political economics* refers to the work of a rather small group of scholars, most notably Alberto Alesina, Torsten Persson, and Guido Enrico Tabellini. Cf. Blankart and Koester (2006) and Alesina, Persson, and Tabellini (2006) for a debate on the characteristics and merits of the school of political economics as compared to the school of public choice.
5. The articles of Alt and Alesina (1996), Atkinson (1996), Grofman (1996), and Offe (1996), contained in the New Handbook of Political Science edited

by Goodin and Klingemann, give an excellent overview of the various meanings of political economy from different perspectives.

6. Major figures in classical political economy are, among others, James Mill, Adam Smith, and David Ricardo.

7. An influential contribution to the theory of institutions from an economic perspective is North (1990).

8. A more in-depth discussion of this aspect is developed by Scharpf (1997, 38–43).

9. On this issue, see Faust and Marx (2004), especially for a discussion of the problem of decreasing theoretical consistency that arises when a rational choice perspective is combined with a sociological institutionalism perspective.

10. On bounded rationality in this context, see Scharpf (1997, 19–22) and Esser (1990). Moreover, Esser (1990) presented a model of how the assumption of rational choice can be reconciled with the observation that actors often behave according to traditions.

11. For the purpose of policy analysis, it is meaningful to treat actors above the level of individuals similar to individual actors if they are capable of unified action, i.e., if "the individuals involved intend to create a joint product or to achieve a common purpose. Mere exchange relationships would not qualify, but a joint venture could" (Scharpf 1997, 54).

12. Cf. Faust (2004), Mkandawire (2004) and Haldenwang (2005, 35–36) for brief overviews of the use of the term (good) governance in the development community. For more in-depth discussions cf. e.g. United Nations Development Programme (1997); World Bank (1992).

13. When a company or organisation is the object of analysis, we speak of *corporate governance*.

14. With the limitation that competitive forces will not be at work, due to the natural monopoly characteristics of the WS industry.

15. For a more in-depth discussion on the distinction of policy making and regulation, cf. Brown (2003).

16. This classic question in political economy is treated, among others, by Cox and McCubbins (2001), Olson (1993), and Bueno de Mesquita et al. (2002).

17. The underlying general problem of time-inconsistency of government policies has been first discussed by Kydland and Prescott (1977) in the context of monetary policy. Keefer and Stasavage (2003) analyse the effect of political institutions on the credibility of monetary policy. Levy and Spiller (1996) treat the effect of political institutions on the credibility of regulatory policy in the infrastructure industries.

18. For an in-depth discussion of the attributes of democracies ("polyarchies") contrasting them to autocracies, cf. Dahl (1989).

19. Cf. Stasavage (2001, 5) for a similar argumentation.

20. For an empirical analysis that provides support to the hypothesis that democracies earn fewer monopoly rents and produce a higher level of services than autocracies, cf. Lake and Baum (2001).

21. Cf. also Olson (1965; 1982) who focuses on the welfare-diminishing role of interest groups and rent-seeking.

22. Cf. e.g. Goetz and Gaventa (2001, 2).

23. Cf. also Keefer and Stasavage (2003), who argue that an increasing number of veto players prevents political leaders from serving special interests.

24. See following discussion for a definition. Cf. Tsebelis (2002) for an in-depth discussion of the veto player concept.

25. Cf. Franzese (2002) for a similar argumentation.

26. Horizontal accountability depends on "the existence of state agencies that are legally empowered—and factually willing and able—to take actions

ranging from routine oversight to criminal sanctions or impeachments in relation to possibly unlawful actions or omissions by other agents or agencies of the state" (O'Donnell 1998, 117).

27. A thorough discussion of the veto player concept is provided by Tsebelis (2002). Cf. also Keefer and Stasavage (2003).

28. Provided it is a unicameral presidential system. In a bicameral presidential system, there would be three formal vetoes.

29. The underlying problem here is one of time-inconsistency of government policy. This problem has been first addressed in a seminal paper by Kydland and Prescott (1977) in the context of monetary policy.

30. On this issue, cf., e.g. Smith (1997; 2000); Stern and Holder (1999); Ugaz (2003).

31. Encroachment happens if "one state agency trespasses upon the lawful authority of another" (O'Donnell 1998, 121).

32. Users are not necessarily identical with citizens: so long as there is no universal coverage with WS services, the number of users is smaller than the number of citizens.

33. The terms short and long route of accountability in the context of public services have been coined by World Bank (2003b, Chapter 3).

34. Cf. Rouse (2007, 79–99) for a more differentiated discussion of the levels of participation in water services.

35. Due to the risk premium that private investors charge in order to compensate for the regulatory risk or the risk of policy change.

36. On the market concentration in the private international WS service industry and the role of multinational corporations, cf. Finger and Allouche (2002, ch. 4); Lobina (2005, 56–60); Kessides (2004, 234–35).

37. For more details concerning practical problems with regulatory governance, cf. Chapter 5 on Colombia.

38. In this case, the implicit regulatory contract between the regulatory body and service providers in the Anglo-american tradition would be complemented by an explicit contract which specifies e.g. appeals procedures, penalty clauses etc. (Bakovic, Tenenbaum, and Woolf 2003). However, such a combination requires a careful definition of the authority of the independent regulator for amending the conditions and responsibilities set in the concession contracts (Stern and Holder 1999, 37–40).

39. Especially if we consider *representation* and *influence*, which are stronger forms of participation (the weaker form is *consultation*—see subsection 3.2.3.1).

40. Cf. e.g. Inkota-Netzwerk e.V. and Brot für die Welt (2004) for a critical perspective on privatisation of WS services in developing countries. A survey of the positions and arguments in this polarised debate is provided by Urquhart and Moore (2004) and Budds and McGranahan (2003).

41. Cf. also Foster (1996); Irwin and Yamamoto (2004); Spiller and Savedoff (1999).

42. Cf. also Rouse (2007, 109–32) who described success stories of public providers. The author identified the separation between policy making and operations as common success factor.

43. For an in-depth discussion of regulatory instruments, including "price cap" and "cost-of-service regulation" cf. Joskow (2007, 1285–20).

44. Cf. Paul (1992) who applies the concepts of exit and voice coined by Hirschman (1970) to public service delivery.

45. Cf. Foster (2001a) for a thorough discussion of the case of La Paz–El Alto (Bolivia) where, thanks to consultations, households could opt for (cheaper) condominial systems instead of individual connections.

NOTES TO CHAPTER 4

1. Cf. Knack (2002) and Butkiewicz and Yanikkaya (2004) for overviews of this body of literature. Cf. Ahlfeld, Hemmer, and Lorenz (2005) for an assessment of the two competing hypotheses of (i) institutions versus (ii) geography being the driving forces for economic development.
2. For further information on the governance indicators touched in the following, cf. Knack (2002), as well as the World Bank Public Sector and Governance Webpage: http://web.worldbank.org/WBSITE/EXTERNAL/TOPICS/EXTPUBLICSECTORANDGOVERNANCE/0,,contentMDK:20773712~menuPK:433525~pagePK:210058~piPK:210062~theSitePK:286305,00.html
3. This index reflects perceptions based on surveys of business, households, public officials, and experts. It contains the following sub-indexes: (i) Regulatory quality, (ii) Government repudiation of contracts, (iii) Risk of expropriation of private property, (iv) Corruption in the political system, (v) Rule of law, and (vi) Quality of the bureaucracy.
4. This index reflects perceptions based on surveys of business, households, public officials, and experts. It contains—among others–the following sub-indexes: (i) Risk of nationalisation, (ii) Contract enforceability, (iii) Bureaucratic delays, and (iv) Policy stability.
5. On the data and indicators published by the Polity Project, see subsection 4.2.3.
6. Cf. also Dollar and Kraay (2001) who found a significant positive effect of rule of law on growth, but not so for democratic institutions. Acemoglu, Johnson, and Robinson (2002) analysed the patterns of wealth (and their reversal) in former European colonies between 1500 and today. They find that security of property rights and constraints on the executive are positively related to economic prosperity.
7. On the data and indicators published by Freedom House, see subsection 4.2.3.
8. Plümper (2001, 87) selected those countries that showed a mean value (for the years 1970 to 1998) of below 6 for the Polity 98 democracy index (0 = *least democratic*; 10 = *most democratic*).
9. The author does not provide an explanation for this unexpected result. In the regression model presented in this chapter the level of democracy is positively related with access to WS services (see the following sections).
10. See description of the variable POLCON in subsection 4.2.3.
11. The author's argument for explaining this effect is the following: More veto points (i) limit the discretion of the executive power to alter sectoral policies (e.g. regulated tariffs), increasing credibility and commitment of the government, and thus increasing investments in the telephone sector; and (ii) limit the profitability of rent-seeking behaviour, and thus provide incentives to invest in infrastructure assets (instead of investing in rent-seeking activities). This corresponds to the arguments given in subsection 3.2.2.2.
12. Unfortunately, the authors do not document the source and the characteristics of the corruption index and the governance index used, which is why it is not possible to judge which aspects of governance are measured.
13. For the methodology used cf. Gwartney, Lawson, and Gartzke (2005).
14. The aggregate economic freedom of the world index includes very diverse aspects of economic governance and neo-liberal macroeconomic policies in one single index. It is not suited to measure political governance as defined in this study.
15. Taken from the International Country Risk Guide provided by the PRS Group—see previous discussion.

16. Cf. also Gutiérrez (2003), who analyses the effects of regulatory governance aspects on the telecom sector in Latin America using a regulatory governance index similar to the one used by Cubbin and Stern (2006; actually, the methodology of the latter is inspired in the work of Gutiérrez). The author finds a positive impact of sound regulatory governance on network expansion and internal efficiency.
17. See e.g. the literature overview provided by Estache (2004).
18. Internal renewable water resources measure the average annual flow of rivers and the recharge of groundwater (aquifers) generated from endogenous (internal) precipitation. See also the definition of the variable WATRESCAP in Table A4.1 (Appendix).
19. Cf. www.wssinfo.org. See also WHO and UNICEF (2000; 2004). In December 2005, when the calculations for this chapter were made, information was available for the years 1990 and 2002.
20. For a description of definitions, data collection methods and coverage estimation procedures see WHO and UNICEF (2000, Annex A) and (2004, 22–23).
21. Cf. also Mainardi (2003, 244), who points out that, despite official definitions by WHO, the coverage information is liable to subjective judgement.
22. Cf. e.g. Müller and Pickel (2007) and Munck and Verkuilen (2002) for critical contributions to this debate.
23. Just as several other scholars whose work has been published in respected academic journals, e.g. Barro (1996), Alesina et al. (2003), Knack and Keefer (1995).
24. However, POLITY and CHECKS have been used to check for the sensitivity of the results obtained (see subsection 4.3.2).
25. See Table A4.1 for the exceptions to this rule.
26. This is true at least for pipe technologies that are marked by economies of scale.
27. This variable measures ethnic fractionalisation and can take values between 0 and 1. For more details, cf. Alesina et al. (2003).
28. Setting the threshold lower would have rendered the sample too small (would have left the model with too few degrees of freedom) in order to perform reliable multivariate regression analyses.
29. With the exception of Andorra, all countries with less than 500,000 inhabitant are small island states. These countries show very particular geographic and population patterns, which suggests that a joint analysis with the remaining countries in the sample is not meaningful.
30. All coverage values—water, sanitation, total, urban, rural, and household connections—were identical for the years 1990 and 2002.
31. On the advantages and disadvantages of informal regression models, as compared to formal regression models in the context of economic growth empirics, see Hemmer and Lorenz (2004, 173–98).
32. Because the dependent variable COV02 is a percentage (that always takes values between 0 and 100), some authors recommend a logit transformation that makes sure that the predicted values also fall between 0 and 100 (McDowell and Cox 2001). This is not necessary in this case for the sample analysed: All predicted values fall within the allowed range.
33. Simultaneity arises if one or more of the independent variables is jointly determined with the dependent variable (Wooldridge 2006, 552). In this case estimation with OLS is generally biased and inconsistent. For a thorough discussion of simultaneity, cf., e.g. Wooldridge (2006, Chapter 16).
34. On this quality of lagged dependent variables on the right-hand-side in cross-sectional models, cf. Wooldridge (2006, 315–17). Omitting a key variable

from the model can cause correlation between the error term (U) and some of the independent variables that will generally lead to bias and inconsistency of the OLS estimators.

35. This has been done by graphical analysis of the bivariate relation, as well as by running a bivariate regression of COV02 on the level of COV90 and then adding the square of COV90 to the model. If the (i) level and the (ii) square of COV90 show both significant (i) positive, and (ii) negative effects, then it is deduced that the relation COV02 → F(COV90) is one of diminishing returns. Cf. also Wooldridge (2006, 304–07).

36. We get decreasing returns of WATTOT90 if we assume increasing marginal costs of service coverage the closer countries move to 100%. This seems plausible as, in order to reach 100%, even remote and disperse settlements and, in general, areas with less favourable geographical and economic conditions have to be provided with improved WS services, implying typically higher costs than systems in (urban) areas with more favourable geographical and economic conditions.

37. WATTOT90LN = LN (WATTOT90).

38. In order to test the functional relation of these variables with COV02, the same procedure as for COV02 → F(COV90) was applied (as explained previously).

39. All calculations have been performed with the software STATA/SE 9.0 for Windows.

40. Heteroscedasticity means that the variance of the unobservable error U changes across different segments of countries as defined by different values of the independent variables (e.g. for the sample analysed residuals decrease with increasing values of WATTOT90LN and of GDPCAPLN). In the presence of heteroscedastidiy, OLS standard errors are not valid for constructing confidence intervals and t statistics. Cf., e.g. Wooldridge (2006, Chapter 8) for an introduction to this issue and for a description of estimation procedures with heteroscedasticity-robust standard errors.

41. This option is available in STATA with the *rreg* command. See Yaffee (2002) for a brief overview, and Hamilton (1991) for a detailed description of this procedure.

42. Using POLITY or CHECKS instead of POLRIGHTS or POLCON yields very similar results. The variable RULAW does not have any statistically significant effect on WATTOT02 in any model specification.

43. Regression with WATTOT90LN and an intercept alone yields an $\bar{R}^2$ of 0.850.

44. The same is true for adding RULAW or ETHNIC to model W1 (results not reported).

45. To be more precise: In model W3a the slope parameter of RULAW is positive, whereas in model W3b it is negative.

46. Cf. e.g. Wooldridge (2006, 241).

47. Confirming the results obtained here, UN-HABITAT (2003, 136) cites empirical work that does not find any statistically significant influence of the availability of water resources on access to water supply services and presents further descriptive statistics supporting these findings.

48. Regression with SANTOT90 and an intercept alone yields an $\bar{R}^2$ of 0.878.

49. The results have been checked by using POLCON, POLITY, or CHECKS instead of POLRIGHTS. The estimations obtained are similar to the ones reported.

50. Cf. Wooldridge (2006, 204–206) for a thorough description of this procedure.

51. Estimation with the RR procedure. Full estimation results are available from the author upon request.

52. The values of CORRUPT are taken from the original indicator "control of corruption" published by Kaufmann, Kraay, and Mastruzzi (2004). See also the description of variables in Table A4.1.

53. The values of PROPRIGHTS are taken from the original indicator "legal structure and security of property rights" published by the Fraser Institute. See also the description of variables in Table A4.1.
54. Estimation results are available from the author upon request.
55. The same is true when using POLCON, POLITY or CHECKS instead of POLRIGHTS.
56. Results are similar when using POLCON, POLITIY, or CHECKS instead of POLRIGHTS.
57. See Table A4.1 for the variable descriptions of PSP and PSPCAP and the data source used.
58. Coding has been done relying on the regional codes of the Penn World Tables Version 6.1. See also Table A4.1 (variable description).
59. Estimation results are available from the author upon request.
60. Author's calculations with data from the World Development Indicators 2005 (CD-ROM): Average of annual percentage change of GDP per capita in PPP (constant 2000 $) 1990 to 2002.

NOTES TO CHAPTER 5

1. For a worldwide overview of PSP in infrastructure, cf. Izaguirre (2004, Chapter 1). For an overview of PSP in the WS service industry in Latin America, cf. Foster (2005, 1–14).
2. Excludes on-site improved technologies. See Table 5.1.
3. Own calculation with the data reported by DANE (population estimate for 2003), www.dane.gov.co (accessed November 14, 2006).
4. Cities between 25,000 and 50,000 habitants: 78%; cities below 25,000 habitants: 88%.
5. Some WS service providers have called into question the quality of the information on drinking water quality reported by SSPD. See sub-section 5.4.4.
6. Technical and/or commercial water losses.
7. The maximum UFW recognised by CRA for tariff regulation is 30% (see sub-section 5.4.1).
8. Average of a sample of 7 cities above 500,000 habitants and 8 cities between 100,000 and 500,000 habitants.
9. Sample consisting of the 4 major capitals and 26 big and intermediate cities.
10. Average for a sample of 37 service providers from big, intermediate, and small cities.
11. Own calculation based on the data reported by Fernández (2004, 99–100). Big cities: above 500,000 habitants; intermediate cities: 100,000 to 500,000 habitants.
12. There are many small service providers that serve only a small number of users each (see sub-section 5.3.4).
13. In total, the author of this study conducted 38 interviews in Colombia. See Table A5.6 in the appendix for the organisations interviewed.
14. For an in-depth discussion of the characteristics, strengths, and weaknesses of quantitative and qualitative approaches in empirical research, cf. King, Keohane, and Verba (1994); Creswell (1994); Neubert (2003).
15. For details concerning Colombia's macroeconomic performance, as compared to other Latin American countries, cf. Edwards and Steiner (2000, 457, 461–62).
16. The homicide rate more than doubled between 1984 (40 per 100,000 inhabitants) and the peak in 1991 (90 per 100,000 inhabitants); cf. Cárdenas, Junguito, and Pachón (2004, figure 3, p. 83). According to another source

(Departamento Nacional de Planeación, www.dnp.gov.co, accessed October 10, 2006), the homicide rate rose from 32 (1984) to 78 (1991).

17. Paramilitary groups have developed from the drug cartels' private armies, cf. Cárdenas, Junguito, and Pachón (2004, 9–10).

18. Cf. Edwards and Steiner (2000, 461–62).

19. Cf. www.dnp.gov.co/paginas_detalle.aspx?idp=42 (accessed October 15, 2006).

20. There is a vast literature on "defective democracies," cf., e.g. Collier and Levitsky (1997); Merkel (2004); O'Donnell (1994); and Zakaria (1997). In this context, cf. also the economic rent-seeking literature: Krueger (1974) and Olson (1965; 1982).

21. This subsection draws on Cárdenas, Junguito, and Pachón (2006) and Departamento Nacional de Planeación (2005a).

22. Before 1991, presidents widely used their extraordinary legislative powers to pass legislation. This has dramatically changed with the greater restrictions contained in the 1991 Constitution, cf. Cárdenas, Junguito, and Pachón (2006, 30–32).

23. Cf. Roland and Zapata (2000) and Cárdenas, Junguito, and Pachón (2006, 17–19) for a detailed description and analysis of the Colombian electoral rules and their effects.

24. I.e., state employees or advisors with a technical or academic profile, typically trained in the United States or Europe, who usually do not embark on successful political careers but stay within the state administration or return to an academic organisation after their employment.

25. Cf. e.g. Fox (1994); Keefer (2002); Roniger (1990).

26. On this issue, cf., Carey and Shugart (1995); Leal and Dávila (1990); Maldonado Copello (2002); Martz (1997); Robinson (2005); Urrutia (1991).

27. A legalistic definition of corruption is given by O'Donnell (1998, 121): "a public official obtains illegal advantages, whether for personal use or for the benefit of associates." Cf. Robinson (1998) for a compilation of work on corruption in developing countries. A discussion of the concept of corruption in the Colombian context is provided by Wills Herrera (2002, 374–79).

28. On the prevalence of clientelistic practices of local governments in Colombia, cf. also Maldonado Copello (2002, 293).

29. For more details, see the empirical investigation in section 5.6 and Krause (2008).

30. Unlike the mayor and the councillors, the members of the Local Administrative Councils (*ediles*) are not remunerated.

31. The assessment of the freedom of the press has changed from "free" (1980–1990) to "partially free" (1991–2002) to "non free" (2003–2006), cf. www.freedomhouse.org (accessed October 20, 2006).

32. The literature typically does not distinguish between regulation on the one hand and control (and sanctioning) on the other hand. However, because Colombian legislation makes this distinction, it is maintained here.

33. The CARs are not part of the provincial administration, but are autonomous. Their jurisdiction is not always identical to provinces: some CARs have supra-provincial jurisdictions (Fernández 2004, 27).

34. In urban areas, these are the common three delivery models. In rural areas, services are predominantly delivered through community organisations (Fernández 2004, 9–11).

35. The Procurator General is a peculiarity of the Colombian Constitution that is not commonly found in other countries. The Procurator's functions are distinct from those of the Prosecutor General (*Fiscal General*). The latter

belongs to the judiciary branch of government and is responsible for criminal prosecution before the court.

36. The Public Services Law applies to the following services: WS services, waste disposal services, telecommunication services, electricity, and gas services.

37. Legal regulations: (i) Board of directors of EICEs: One third of the board members have to be spokesmen whom the mayor has to elect among the registered spokesmen within the district (Maldonado and Vargas Forero 2001, 312). (ii) The CPE consists by equal parts of representatives (a) of the local service providers and (b) of the service users (not spokesmen!). In addition, one spokesman of the local CDCSs shall participate in the CPE, however, without the right to vote (Departamento Nacional de Planeación without year-b).

38. Information provided by SSPD at the public hearing "Rendición de Cuentas," in Bogotá on June 29, 2005.

39. Information gained in interviews with representatives of service providers and with spokesmen in Manizales, Santa Marta, Tunja, and Villavicencio.

40. For the role of JACs in the organisation of civil society in Colombia, cf. Villar (2001).

41. Information gained in interviews with spokesmen in Manizales, Tunja, Villavicencio, Santa Marta; cf. also Buitrago Restrepo (2001).

42. Asociación Nacional de Empresas de Servicios Públicos Domiciliarios y Actividades Complementarias e Inherentes.

43. Recently, some committed user representatives are making efforts to build up national user associations that, in the future, may enhance participation on the national level, provided that they obtain the necessary resources. By the end of 2005, there existed at least two incipient national user associations: (i) *Asociación Comunera Distrital de Comités de Desarrollo y Control Social de los Servicios Públicos Domiciliarios y Vocales de Control* (ASCOM); (ii) *Confederación Nacional de Vocales de Control.*

44. The present sub-section draws on the following sources: Araque (2004); Fernández (2004, 79–85); interviews with representatives of CRA, SSPD, experts.

45. In addition to water and sewerage, CRA is responsible for regulating solid waste disposal.

46. SSPD is responsible for control and sanctioning with respect to all public services regulated in the Public Services Law: water, sewerage, solid waste disposal, electricity, telecommunication, and liquefied petroleum gas.

47. For more details, see sub-section 5.4.1.

48. Information gained in an interview with a representative of SSPD.

49. Information provided by SSPD at the public hearing "Audiencia Pública de Rendición de Cuentas", in Bogotá on June 29, 2005.

50. This applies, above all, to districts with intermediate or small urban centres, because the big cities had been generally served by district-owned public enterprises even before decentralisation. The respective transition period ended in January 1998 (SSPD 2001, 11). The Public Services Law defines exceptions for which direct service delivery through the district administration can be maintained.

51. These definitions of "public," "mixed," and "private" are the ones established in the Public Services Law (Congreso de Colombia 1994, article 14).

52. The number of inhabitants actually served depends on the coverage level.

53. There is no uniform criterion for the distinction between big and intermediate cities in the context of analyses of the Colombian WS industry. Fernández (2004) uses the threshold of 500,000 inhabitants whereas SSPD (2002) draws the line at 600,000 inhabitants.

54. These two groups consist of 60 cities in total (SSPD 2002, 39). From the 30 cities of these groups for which data on the corporate form was available, all are either served by a EICE or a ESP, cf. also CRA (2006, 69).
55. CRA and SSPD have begun to implement simplified procedures to regulate and control small providers (< 2,500 connections/points of service).
56. Translation by the author.
57. In the case of EICEs, legal regulations prescribe that one-third of the board members have to be spokesmen of the local CDCSs (see sub-section 5.3.2).
58. Cf. Fernández (2004, 76).
59. Debt overload and generous but onerous wage and pension agreements are common for Colombian public enterprises. The cases of Cúcuta and Cali are examples from the WS industry; cf. the information provided by SSPD on its Web page, www.superservicios.gov.co (accessed November 11, 2006).
60. Information gained in interviews with experts and representatives from service providers; cf. also Beato and Díaz (2003), who describe the model of lease and management contract in Cartagena.
61. Includes waste disposal.
62. Exchange rate 1 US Dollar = 2,276 Colombian Pesos (November 29, 2006).
63. Cf. also Beato and Díaz (2003, 3–4); Ángel Gómez and Aguilera (2002, 13–14).
64. By "economic efficiency," Congreso de Colombia (1994, article 87) seems to refer to the concept of allocative efficiency, however implicitly to a scenario without externalities (cf. "Optimal tariff policy if external costs equal zero," sub-section 2.3.4). In this respect, it shall be noted that environmental regulation with the objective to internalise external costs lies in the responsibility of the CARs and is not touched in the Public Services Law. However, according to the new tariff formula, applied by CRA since 2005 (explained in the following), the fees charged by the CARs are recognised. This means that tariff regulation, de facto, accounts for external costs.
65. The concept of "financial sufficiency" referred to in Congreso de Colombia (1994, article 87) is similar to the long-term version of the concept of financial sustainability discussed in sub-section 2.4.2. However, in addition to replacement investments, the concept used in the Public Services Law includes expansion investments (expansion investments were not considered in sub-section 2.4.2 because demand was set fix). This means that the necessary tariff level needs to be even higher.
66. For the sake of comparison: In OECD-countries, water use per day and capita varies between 129 litres (Germany) and 382 litres (United States); cf. Levin et al. (2002, 44). The normative benchmark used in German development co-operation for assessing sound water use per day and per capita is 120 litres (in-house connections); cf. KfW (2004, 5).
67. The period since 2005 is not discussed in detail here. The new tariff formula contains upper limits for comparable cost components. These limits were estimated by using a data envelope analysis (cost frontier approach); cf. CRA (2004). For the terms cost-of-service regulation and incentive regulation, cf. Joskow (2007, 1285–1320).
68. Here, only the calculation of the tariffs for water is illustrated. The sewerage tariff is calculated similarly.
69. Cf. CRA (2001); Beato and Díaz (2003, 3–4); Congreso de Colombia (1994). Here, a simplified version of the process of tariff calculation is presented. For more details, cf. the sources indicated.
70. Share of technical or commercial water losses. For a precise definition, see sub-section 5.1.2.

71. With 20 m³ per month per connection, the level of "basic consumption" defined by CRA seems to be relatively high. It is more or less equal to the actual national average consumption (SSPD 2005b, section 1.1).
72. At least as of December 2005, the end of the tariff transition period (SSPD 2005a, 8). With regard to the legal norms that require a balance in the Solidarity Funds, cf. MAVDT (2005).
73. However, a recent decree of MAVDT contradicts this law by setting *minimum* surcharges for the contributing user classes (see previous discussion).
74. This could be an explanation for the fact that surcharges levied on the fixed part of the tariff usually are considerably higher than those levied on the variable part of the tariff. In Bogotá, the actual tariff surcharge for the fixed part of the tariff is 305% (water) and 368% (sewerage) for residential users of the stratum 6. For the variable part of the tariff, the surcharge is 38% (water) and 43% (sewerage). Cf. Concejo de Bogotá (2006). http://www.alcaldiabogota.gov.co/sisjur//normas/Norma1.jsp?i=21496 (accessed November 6, 2006).
75. 575.86 million US Dollars; exchange rate: 1 US Dollar = 2,276 Col. Pesos (November 29, 2006).
76. 4% for the period 1993 to 2004, cf. Departamento Nacional de Planeación (2004, 11).
77. See sub-section 2.2.2.
78. 19.77 US Dollars; exchange rate: 1 US Dollar = 2,276 Col. Pesos (November 29, 2006).
79. Cf. Ministerio de Desarrollo Económico (2000).
80. It may, however, be related to major investments for the WS service provider e.g. in dams or in drinking water treatment plants in order to increase the drinking water production capacity in case production capacity is a limiting factor. This depends on the relation between the installed production capacity and the growth of demand.
81. The term *public funds*, here, refers to funds from general income sources like taxes, royalties, and loans. The term excludes WS tariff receipts of public service providers.
82. Departamento Nacional de Planeación (2004) provides a description of the fiscal transfer system from national to district governments with a focus on the WS sector.
83. Own calculation with the figures reported by Departamento Nacional de Planeación (2004, 8).
84. Not to cover deficits means to extract quasi-rents (see 2.4.1 and 2.4.2) from service providers, with the likely consequence that reposition and expansion investments are not undertaken.
85. Corruption has repeatedly been an issue in the awarding of construction contracts in the WS sector. This seems to hold for both mixed ESPs (case of Cartagena; information gained in an interview with a representative from Transparencia por Colombia) and EICEs (case of Villavicencio; see sub-section 5.6.5).
86. Criticism refers to the way of taking samples. Samples have to be taken directly from the water distribution network (and not from inside the dwelling); health authorities do not always seem to comply with this, cf. Empresas Públicas de Medellín E.S.P. (2006); ANDESCO (2006).
87. For the Chilean WS subsidy system cf. Gómez-Lobo and Contreras (2003) and Serra (2000).
88. For more details concerning the estimation techniques, cf. the previously cited sources.
89. See sub-section 5.1.2 for the definition of this indicator.
90. See sub-section 5.1.2 for the definition of this indicator.
91. "Índice de necesidades básicas insatisfechas". For more details, see the following sections, as well as Table A5.4.

92. See the next section, 5.6, that investigates four cases in more detail. The two PSP models analysed are the one in Tunja and the one in Santa Marta. The former is a concession contract, and the latter is a combination of lease and management contract.

93. I.e., the higher cash flow (internal financing) is not exclusively used to increase the short-term profit of private shareholders but is reinvested.

94. All calculations have been performed with the software STATA/SE 9.0 for Windows.

95. Because COV03 is a proportion (that always takes values between 0 and 1), it is desirable that the predicted values also fall between 0 and 1. With the data used in Chapter 4, it was no problem to use the coverage level directly as dependent variable because all predicted values actually fell into the allowed range (see sub-section 4.3.1). This was like this because the values of the initial coverage level used as independent variable lay all considerably below 1 (or 100%). In the data sample used here, by contrast, some providers present initial coverage levels of 1. This implies that the predicted values would lie above 1 when using COV03 as dependent variable. In order to avoid this, instead of COV03, CHCOV is used as dependent variable—which is an equivalent procedure.

96. Just like in sub-section 4.3.1, the functional form of the relation CHCOV → F(COV98) has been explored by graphical analysis and by running a bivariate regression of CHCOV on the level of COV98 and then adding the square of COV98 to the model. For both water and sewer connections, the results suggest that the relation is not linear. This is modelled by including both COV98 (level) and COV98SQ (square) on the right-hand side of the model. For a discussion of such a procedure, cf. Wooldridge (2006, 304–07).

97. Apart from the independent variables mentioned, the influence of the size of the system (number of connections) was tested for all models discussed here. This variable proved to have no significant effects (results not reported).

98. For a description and discussion of this index, cf. Rodríguez del Gallego and Carvajal (2004).

99. This is largely due to the influential case of "Villavicencio," which shows an extremely high value for UFW03 (0.73) and a low vulnerability of water resources (VULWAT = 2). Dropping "Villavicencio" from the OLS estimation renders the effect of VULWAT statistically not significant (the results for the remaining independent variables remain largely the same).

100. This strong decrease in coverage is due to a change in the definition of how to measure coverage in Villavicencio—see section 5.6.2.

101. Regressing CHWAT on WAT98, WAT98SQ, and an intercept yields an $\bar{R}^2$ of 0.734.

102. On the effect of multicollinearity on estimation results, cf. Wooldridge (2006, 101–04).

103. If the causes of good provider performance are to be explained, there have to be chosen good, as well as bad, cases. If only good cases are investigated, the sample chosen presents a selection bias. On the problem of selection bias in the context of intentional selections of small samples, cf. King, Keohane, and Verba (1994, 128–49).

104. I.e., all 30 cities contained in the sample (see Table A5.2) except the four capitals above 1 million habitants (Bogotá, Barranquilla, Cali, Medellín). Moreover, due to missing values, the cases of Sincelejo and Tuluá have not been considered for the selection procedure. This means that the four cases have been selected amongst a sample of 24 cities.

105. See also Table A5.4 for the data sources.

106. The difference between Sera QA Tunja and EAA Villavicencio with respect to the collection rate is only moderate.

107. The only exception is coverage with sewer connections, which has slightly fallen from 98.8% to 98.2%.
108. Annual growth rate corresponding to the increase of water connections from 76,637 (2000) to 80,737 (2004).
109. Installed drinking water production capacity is 2,066 litres per second, whereas the actual water production is 950 litres per second.
110. The values of the ordinally scaled indicator are: very low, low, middle, high, very high.
111. Annual growth rate corresponding to the increase of water connections from 25,353 (1998) to 30,993 (2004).
112. The coverage figures by 2001 according to the "new" coverage definition (see the following) were estimated by the author based on the available coverage figures for 2004, the number of water and sewer connections (2001, 2004) and population (2001, 2004).
113. According to the information gained from EAA Villavicencio, there are 57 private water companies in the city.
114. Annual growth rate corresponding to the increase of water connections from 53,547 (2001) to 63,922 (2004).
115. The commercial water losses are related to the low coverage with meters. Residential users without meters are billed based on an assumed monthly consumption of 20 m^3. There are indications that many users without meters consume considerably more water.
116. Cf., "Conclusiones de visita fiscal realizada a la planta de tratamiento de aguas de La Esmeralda," www.contraloriavillavicencio.gov.co (accessed November 29, 2006).
117. 102.53 million US Dollars; exchange rate 1 US Dollar = 2,276 Col. Pesos (November 29, 2006). On the wastewater investment project, cf. also BRC Investor Services S.A. (2004).
118. Unfortunately the indicators collection rate, continuity, and coverage with meters were not available for 1999.
119. Annual growth rate corresponding to the increase of water connections from 56,724 (1999) to 69,231 (2004).
120. Another explanation given by the management of Metroagua is that many users in Santa Marta are not used to pay for WS services because they rarely had to do it in the past. This is why their willingness to pay for these services is low.
121. The term *displaced people*, in Colombia, refers to those persons that have to leave their home (and possibly their land) due to threats by non-state armed groups or due to conflicts among these groups or between these groups and the state security forces.
122. The biggest portion of the receipts corresponds to transfers from the national government.
123. Cf. "Acuerdo de reestructuración de pasivos celebrado entre el Distrito Turístico, Cultural e Histórico de Santa Marta (Magdalena) y sus acreedores con base en la Ley 550 de 1999", http://www.minhacienda.gov.co/pls/portal30/docs/PAGE/DAF/ACUERDOSLEY550/ACUERDOS_MUNICIPIOS/SANTA%20MARTA.ZIP (accessed November 30, 2006).
124. I.e., raw water extraction, treatment, drinking water distribution and wastewater collection, *excluding* water body rehabilitation activities: construction of interceptor sewers and wastewater treatment plant.
125. The accumulated deficit (sum of annual deficits 2000 to 2004) amounts to 20,131 million Col. Pesos (8.85 million US Dollars; exchange rate 1 US Dollar = 2,276 Colombian Pesos; November 29, 2006). By July 2005, the district government has transferred a total amount of 2,500 million Col. Pesos in order to compensate for this deficit.

126. *Federación Nacional de Comerciantes.*
127. 2.55 million US Dollars; exchange rate 1 US Dollar = 2,276 Colombian Pesos (November 29, 2006).
128. For more details, cf. BRC Investor Services S.A. (2004).
129. 7 million US Dollars; exchange rate 1 US Dollar = 2,276 Colombian Pesos (November 29, 2006).
130. Proactiva Medioambiente SA is owned 50% by Veolia Environnement (France) and 50% by Fomento de Construcciones y Contratas (FCC–Spain).
131. 3.08 million US Dollars; exchange rate 1 US Dollar = 2,276 Colombian Pesos (November 29, 2006).
132. 4.83 million US Dollars; exchange rate 1 US Dollar = 2,276 Colombian Pesos (November 29, 2006).
133. 1.76 million US Dollars; exchange rate 1 US Dollar = 2,276 Colombian Pesos (November 29, 2006).
134. 7.24 million US Dollars; exchange rate 1 US Dollar = 2,276 Colombian Pesos (November 29, 2006).
135. Which is the operator of the WS system of Barranquilla.
136. 6.59 million US Dollars; exchange rate: 1 US Dollar = 2,276 Col. Pesos (November 29, 2006).
137. 1.42 million US Dollars; exchange rate: 1 US Dollar = 2,276 Col. Pesos (November 29, 2006).
138. 32.37 million US Dollars; exchange rate: 1 US Dollar = 2,276 Col. Pesos (November 29, 2006).
139. 4.39 million US Dollars; exchange rate: 1 US Dollar = 2,276 Col. Pesos (November 29, 2006).
140. 7.75 million US Dollars; exchange rate: 1 US Dollar = 2,276 Col. Pesos (November 29, 2006).
141. The *Personero Municipal* is a decentralised agent of the Procurator General. He is elected by the district assembly and his function is to protect the human rights and the public interest (Departamento Nacional de Planeación 2005a, 55).
142. Asociación Nacional de Industriales, Asociación Colombiana de Pequeñas y Medianas Industrias, Comité Departamental de Cafeteros de Caldas, Comité Intergremial de Caldas.
143. The spokesman interviewed in Santa Marta was, in addition, President of the National Association of CDCS spokesmen (*Confederación Nacional de Vocales de Control*).
144. On the relation of violence, the presence of non-state armed groups, democratic participation and extortion in Colombia, cf. Sarmiento and Becerra (1998); Observatorio del Programa Presidencial de Derechos Humanos y DIH (2006b).
145. Fundación Seguridad y Democracia (2004); Observatorio del Programa Presidencial de Derechos Humanos y DIH (2005; 2006b; 2006a); República de Colombia (2004; 2005).
146. An example for this influence is the practice of extortion of the local business in Santa Marta by paramilitary groups; Observatorio del Programa Presidencial de Derechos Humanos y DIH (2006b, 39).
147. Cf. article without author "El Meta, a la deriva," published in *El Espectador*, November 14, 2005, available at www.acnur.org/index.php?id_pag=4296 (accessed November 11, 2006).
148. Cf. communication of the Procuraduría General de la República from March 14, 2006, available at www.procuraduria.gov.co/html/noticias_2006/noticias_095.htm (accessed September 18, 2006).
149. On the methodological aspects of this index cf. the cited sources.

150. Still, it cannot be precluded that, in the remaining cases, clientelism and corruption have occurred. Such practices are quite common in the whole country (United States Department of State 2006; Wills Herrera 2002) and collecting information on these matters is difficult.

151. Cf. article without author "El Meta, a la deriva," published in *El Espectador*, November 14, 2005, available at www.acnur.org/index.php?id_pag=4296 (accessed November 11, 2006).

152. Cf. Boletín 353 of the Procuraduría General de la República from October 26, 2005, available at www.procuraduria.gov.co/html/noticias_2005/noticias_353.htm (accessed September 18, 2006).

153. 7.54 million US Dollars; exchange rate: 1 US Dollar = 2,276 Col. Pesos (November 29, 2006).

154. 754 thousand US Dollars; exchange rate: 1 US Dollar = 2,276 Col. Pesos (November 29, 2006).

155. 782 thousand US Dollars; exchange rate: 1 US Dollar = 2,276 Col. Pesos (November 29, 2006).

156. Information gained in interviews. Cf. also Instituto Prensa y Sociedad, "Corrupción en la alcaldía de Santa Marta," available at www.ipys.org/investigaciones/investigacion.php?id =154 (accessed November 11, 2006).

157. 6.59 million US Dollars; exchange rate: 1 US Dollar = 2,276 Col. Pesos (November 29, 2006).

158. Cf. e.g. charges against an ex-mayor of Tunja: Boletín 125 of the Procuraduría General de la Nación from April 27, 2006 available at www.procuraduria.gov.co/html/noticias_2005/noticias_ 125.htm (accessed November 11, 2006).

159. The irregularity in the awarding of contracts in 2003 by Aguas de Manizales can be considered a minor issue when compared to Villavicencio.

Bibliography

Acemoglu, D., S. Johnson, and J. A. Robinson. 2002. Reversal of fortune: Geography and institutions in the making of the modern world income distribution. *Quarterly Journal of Economics* 17 (4):1231–94.

Ahlfeld, S., H.-R. Hemmer, and A. Lorenz. 2005. *The economic growth debate— Geography versus institutions: Is there anything really new?* Discussion Papers in Development Economics 34. Giessen: Justus-Liebig-Universität.

Alesina, A. et al. 2003. Fractionalization. *Journal of Economic Growth* 8 (2):155–94.

Alesina, A., T. Persson, and G. E. Tabellini. 2006. Reply to Blankart and Koester's political economics versus public choice: Two views of political economy in competition. *Kyklos* 59 (2):201–08.

Alt, J. E., and A. Alesina. 1996. Political economy: An overview. In: *A new handbook of political science*, eds. R. E. Goodin and H.-D. Klingemann, 645–74. Oxford: Oxford University Press.

ANDESCO. 2006. *Comentarios de ANDESCO al informe de calidad del agua en Colombia–Resultados 2005*. Bogotá. http://www.andesco.com (accessed November 21, 2006).

Ángel Gómez, J. E., and J. C. Aguilera. 2002. El problema tarifario en los servicios de acueducto, alcantarillado y aseo en Colombia. *Revista Regulación de Agua Potable y Saneamiento Básico* (8):13–57.

Araque, L. A. 2004. *Agencias reguladoras en los sectores agua, electricidad y telecomunicaciones en Colombia, Ecuador, Peru y Venezuela*. Unpublished paper. Washington, DC.

Arrow, K. J., and F. H. Hahn. 1971. *General competitive analysis*. Edinburgh: Oliver and Boyd.

Asamblea Nacional Constituyente. 1991. Constitución Política de Colombia. *Gaceta Constitucional* 116 (20 July 1991). Online version made available by Secretaría del Senado. República de Colombia. http://www.secretariasenado.gov.co/.

Atkinson, A. B. 1996. Political economy, old and new. In *A new handbook of political science*, eds. R. E. Goodin and H.-D. Klingemann, 702–13. Oxford: Oxford University Press.

Atkinson, A. B., and J. E. Stiglitz. 1980. *Lectures in public economics*. London: McGraw-Hill.

Bakovic, T., B. Tenenbaum, and F. Woolf. 2003. *Regulation by contract: A new way to privatize electricity distribution?* World Bank Working Paper 14. Washington, DC: World Bank.

Barrera-Osorio, F., and M. Olivera. 2007. *Does society win or lose as a result of privatization? Provision of public services and welfare of the poor: The case of water sector privatization in Colombia*. Research Network Working Paper #R-525. Washington, DC: Inter-American Development Bank.

Barro, R. J. 1996. Democracy and growth. *Journal of Economic Growth* 1 (1):1–27.

Basañes, F., and R. Willig, eds. 2002. *Second-generation reforms in infrastructure services*. Washington, DC: Inter-American Development Bank.

Baumol, W. J., and W. E. Oates. 1988. *The theory of environmental policy*. 2nd ed. Cambridge, MA: Cambridge University Press.

Beato, P., and J. Díaz. 2003. *La participación del sector privado en los servicios de agua y saneamiento en Cartagena de Indias*. Informe de trabajo. Washington, DC: Inter-American Development Bank.

Beck, T. et al. 2001. New tools in comparative political economy: The database of political institutions. *The World Bank Economic Review* 15 (1):165–76.

Blankart, C. B., and G. B. Koester. 2006. Political economics versus public choice: Two views of political economy in competition. *Kyklos* 59 (2):171–200.

Boland, J. J., and D. Whittington. 2000. The political economy of water tariff design in developing countries: Increasing block tariffs versus uniform price with rebate. In *The political economy of water pricing reforms*, ed. A. Dinar, 215–35. Washington, DC: World Bank.

Bollen, K. A., and P. Paxton. 2000. Subjective measures of liberal democracy. *Comparative Political Studies* 33 (1):58–86.

Braeutigam, R. R. 1989. Optimal policies for natural monopolies. In Vol. 2 of *Handbook of industrial organization*, eds. R. Schmalensee and R. D. Willig, 1289–346. Amsterdam: Elsevier.

BRC Investor Services S.A. 2004. *Empresa de Acueducto y Alcantarillado de Villavicencio—E.S.P.: Revisión Anual*. Bogotá: BRC Investor Services S.A.

Brown, A. C. 2003. Regulators, policy-makers, and the making of policy: Who does what and when do they do it? *International Journal of Regulation and Governance* 3 (1):1–11.

Budds, J., and G. McGranahan. 2003. Are the debates on water privatization missing the point? Experiences from Africa, Asia and Latin America. *Environment & Urbanization* 15 (2):87–113.

Bueno de Mesquita, B. et al. 2002. Political institutions, policy choice and the survival of leaders. *British Journal of Political Science* 32 (4):559–90.

Buitrago Restrepo, C. M. 2001. El control social en los servicios públicos domiciliarios: Expresión del principio de soberanía popular. *Revista Univerciudad Online 9*. http://univerciudad.redbogota.com/ediciones/indice009.htm (accessed April 5, 2006).

Butkiewicz, J. L., and H. Yanikkaya. 2004. *Institutional quality and economic growth: Maintenance of the rule of law or democratic institutions, or both?* Department of Economics Working Paper 2004–03. Newark: University of Delaware.

Cárdenas, M., R. Junguito, and M. Pachón. 2004. *Political institutions, policy making processes, and policy outcomes: The case of Colombia*. Second Draft. April 30, 2004. Unpublished paper.

Cárdenas, M., R. Junguito, and M. Pachón. 2006. *Political institutions and policy outcomes in Colombia: The effects of the 1991 Constitution*. Research Network Working Paper R-508. Washington, DC: Inter-American Development Bank.

Carey, J. M., and M. S. Shugart. 1995. Incentives to cultivate a personal vote: A rank-ordering of electoral formulas. *Electoral Studies* 14 (4):417–39.

Clarke, G. R. G., K. Kosec, and S. J. Wallsten. 2004. *Has private participation in water and sewerage improved coverage? Empirical evidence from Latin America*. World Bank Policy Research Working Paper 3445. Washington, DC: World Bank.

Coase, R. H. 1960. The problem of social cost. *Journal of Law and Economics* 3:1–44.

Collier, P., and S. Levitsky. 1997. Democracies with adjectives: Conceptual innovation in comparative research. *World Politics* 49 (2):430–51.

Comisión de Regulación de Agua Potable y Saneamiento Básico. 2001. *Resolución CRA No. 151 de 2001: Regulación integral de los servicios de Acueducto, Alcantarillado y Aseo.* Bogotá. http://www.cra.gov.co/ (accessed March 7, 2008).

———. 2004. *Resolución CRA No. 287 de 2004: Por la cual se establece la metodología tarifaria para regular el cálculo de los costos de prestación de los servicios de acueducto y alcantarillado.* Bogotá. http://www.cra.gov.co/ (accessed March 7, 2008).

———. 2005. *Informe de gestión Marzo 2004—Marzo 2005.* Bogotá: CRA.

———. 2006. *Impactos regulatorios en los sectores de acueducto, alcantarillado y aseo.* Bogotá: CRA.

Concejo de Bogotá. 2006. *Proyecto de Acuerdo 378 de 2006.* Bogotá. http://www.alcaldiabogota.gov.co/sisjur//normas/Norma1.jsp?i=21496 (accessed November 6, 2006).

Congreso de Colombia. 1994. Ley 142 de 1994: Por la cual se establece el Régimen de los Servicios Públicos Domiciliarios y se dictan otras disposiciones. *Diario Oficial* 41433 (July 11, 1994). Updated and commented edition made available by Comisión de Regulación de Agua Potable y Saneamiento Básico on its Web page. http://www.cra.gov.co/ (accessed March 12, 2007).

———. 1996. Ley 286 de 1996: Por la cual se modifican parcialmente las leyes 142 y 143 de 1994. *Diaro Oficial* 42824 (July 5, 1996).

———. 2000. Ley 632 de 2000: Por la cual se modifican parcialmente las leyes 142, 143 de 1994, 223 de 1995 y 286 de 1996. *Diaro Oficial* 44275 (December 29, 2000).

———. 2001. Ley 715 de 2001: Por la cual se dictan normas orgánicas en materia de recursos y competencias de conformidad con los artículos 151, 288, 356 y 357 (Acto Legislativo 01 de 2001) de la Constitución Política y se dictan otras disposiciones para organizar la prestación de los servicios de educación y salud, entre otros. *Diaro Oficial* 44654 (December 21, 2001).

Consultoría para los Derechos Humanos y el Desplazamiento. 2005. *Número de personas desplazadas por municipio de llegada por trimestre desde 1999 a 2005.* July 19, 2005. Bogotá: CODHES.

Consumidores Colombia. 2005. *Informe final: Servicio público domiciliario de agua potable en Colombia.* Bogotá: Consumidores Colombia.

Contraloría Municipal de Villavicencio. 2006. *Informe de gestión 2005.* Villavicencio, Colombia: Contraloría Municipal de Villavicencio.

Corbridge, S., and G. A. Jones. 2005. *The continuing debate about urban bias: The thesis, its critics, its influence, and implications for poverty reduction.* Research Papers in Environmental and Spatial Analysis 99. London: London School of Economics.

Cornes, R., and T. Sandler. 1996. *The theory of externalities, public goods and club goods.* 2nd ed. Cambridge, MA: Cambridge University Press.

Cox, G. W., and M. D. McCubbins. 2001. The institutional determinants of economic policy outcomes. In *Presidents, parliaments, and policy,* eds. S. Haggard and M. D. McCubbins, 21–63. Cambridge, UK: Cambridge University Press.

Creswell, J. W. 1994. *Research design: Qualitative and quantitative approaches.* Thousand Oaks, CA: Sage Publications.

Cubbin, J., and J. Stern. 2006. The impact of regulatory governance and privatization on electricity industry generation capacity in developing economies. *The World Bank Economic Review* 20 (1):115–41.

Cuéllar, M. M. 2005. La prueba de razonabilidad y la estabilidad de las reglas de juego. *Revista de Economía Institucional* 7 (12):13–42.

Dahl, R. A. 1989. *Democracy and its critics.* New Haven, CT: Yale University Press.

de Ferranti, D. et al. 2004. *Inequality in Latin America: Breaking with history?* Washington, DC: World Bank.

Demsetz, H. 1968. Why regulate utilities? *Journal of Law and Economics* 11 (1):55–65.

Departamento Administrativo de la Función Pública. 2003. *Mecanismos jurídicos para el control social: Plan Nacional de Formación para el Control Social a la Gestión Pública*. Serie Documentos de Consulta 2. Bogotá: Departamento Administrativo de la Función Pública.

Departamento Nacional de Planeación. 2002. *Marco conceptual y resultados de progreso municipal*. Vol 1 of *Evaluación de la descentralización municipal en Colombia: Balance de una década*. Bogotá: Departamento Nacional de Planeación.

———. 2004. *El sistema general de participaciones en el sector de agua potable y saneamiento básico*. Bogotá: Departamento Nacional de Planeación.

———. 2005a. *El estado y su organización*. Bogotá: Departamento Nacional de Planeación.

———. 2005b. *Gestión pública local*. Bogotá: Departamento Nacional de Planeación.

———. 2005c. *Inversión privada en infraestructura 1993–2003. Actualizado: Junio 2005*. Bogotá: Departamento Nacional de Planeación.

———. 2005d. *Plan de desarrollo del sector de acueducto y alcantarillado*. Documento CONPES 3383. Bogotá: Departamento Nacional de Planeación.

———. without year-a. *Empresas descentralizadas del orden nacional. Estudio de sostenibilidad*. Bogotá: Departamento Nacional de Planeación.

———. without year-b. *Modelo de Reglamento del Comité Permanente de Estratificación Socioeconómica*. Bogotá: Departamento Nacional de Planeación.

Development Committee, International Monetary Fund, and World Bank. 2004. *Global Monitoring Report 2004*. Washington, DC: International Monetary Fund, World Bank.

Dollar, D., and A. Kraay. 2001. *Growth is good for the poor*. Policy Research Working Paper 2587. Washington, DC: World Bank.

Domínguez Torres, C., and E. Uribe Botero. 2005. *Evolución del servicio de acueducto y alcantarillado durante la última década*. Documento CEDE 2005–19. Bogotá: Universidad de los Andes.

Dworkin, R. 1981a. What is equality? Part 1: Equality of welfare. *Philosophy and Public Affairs* 10 (3):185–246.

———. 1981b. What is equality? Part 2: Equality of resources. *Philosophy and Public Affairs* 10 (3):283–45.

Echeverri, J. C. Palabras del Departamento Nacional de Planeación. In *Seminario Internacional de Regulación en Agua Potable y Saneamiento Básico: Memorias y Lecturas Complementarias*, ed. Ministerio de Desarrollo Económico, 285–91. Bogotá: Ministerio de Desarrollo Económico.

Edwards, S., and R. Steiner. 2000. On the crises hypothesis of economic reform: Colombia 1989–91. *Cuadernos de Economía* 37 (112):445–93.

Empresas Públicas de Medellín E.S.P. 2006. *Comunicado a la opinión pública sobre el informe de calidad del agua en Colombia 2005 de la Superintendencia de Servicios Públicos Domiciliarios*. Medellín. http://www.eeppm.com/epmcom/contenido/boletinesprensa/boletines2006.htm (accessed November 11, 2006).

Erlei, M., M. Leschke, and D. Sauerland. 1999. *Neue Institutionenökonomik*. Stuttgart: Schäffer-Poeschel Verlag.

Esrey, S. A. 1996. Water, waste, and well-being: A multicountry study. *American Journal of Epidemiology* 143 (6):608–23.

Esser, H. 1990. "Habits", "Frames" und "Rational Choice". *Zeitschrift für Soziologie* 19 (4):231–47.

Estache, A. 2004. *A selected survey on recent economic literature on emerging infrastructure policy issues in developing countries.* First draft August 2004. Background paper for the October 2004 Berlin meeting of the POVNET Infrastructure Working Group. http://www. ecd.org/dataoecd/34/21/36568195.pdf (accessed June 23, 2008).

Estache, A., and E. Kouassi. 2002. *Sector organization, governance, and the inefficiency of African water utilities.* World Bank Policy Research Working Paper 2890. Washington, DC: World Bank.

Estache, A., and M. A. Rossi. 2002. How different is the efficiency of public and private water companies in Asia? *The World Bank Economic Review* 16 (1):139–48.

Estache, A., B. Speciale, and D. Veredas. 2005. How much does infrastructure matter to growth in Sub-Saharan Africa? Draft 5 June 2005. http://www. ecare.ulb.ac.be/ecare/people/members/veredas/veredas/David%20Veredas%20African%20Infrastructures%20Version%201.pdf (accessed June 23, 2008).

Faust, J. 2004. Good Governance, Transformationsprobleme und Entwicklungszusammenarbeit. *Nord-Süd Aktuell* 18 (3):486–98.

———. 2006. Die Dividende der Demokratie: Politische Herrschaft und gesamtwirtschaftliche Produktivität. *Politische Vierteljahresschrift* 47 (1):62–83.

Faust, J., and J. Marx. 2004. Zwischen Kultur und Kalkül? Vertrauen und Sozialkapital im Kontext der neoinstitutionalistischen Wende. *Swiss Political Science Review* 10 (1):29–55.

Federación Colombiana de Municipios. 2005. *Superintendencia de Servicios revela fallas en la reestratificación. Artículo del rubro "noticias": February 22, 2005.* http://www.fcm.org.co. (accessed April 12, 2005).

Fernández, D. 2004. *Sector agua potable.* Informes de base: Colombia; Desarrollo económico reciente en infraestructura (REDI). Washington, DC: World Bank.

Finger, M., and J. Allouche. 2002. *Water privatisation: Trans-national corporations and the re-regulation of the water industry.* London: SPON Press.

Foster, V. 1996. *Policy issues for the water and sanitation sectors.* Washington, DC: Inter-American Development Bank.

———. 2001a. *Condominial water and sewerage systems: Costs of implementation of the model: El Alto–Bolivia pilot project.* Lima: Water and Sanitation Program.

———. 2001b. Opciones para el marco regulador del servicio de agua y alcantarillado: Principios fundamentales y preguntas claves. In *Seminario internacional de regulación en agua potable y saneamiento básico: Memorias y lecturas complementarias,* ed. Ministerio de Desarrollo Económico, 295–360. Bogotá: Ministerio de Desarrollo Económico.

———. 2005. *Ten years of water service reform in Latin America: Toward an Anglo-French model.* Water Supply and Sanitation Sector Board Discussion Paper 3. Washington, DC: World Bank.

Fox, J. 1994. Difficult transition from clientelism to citizenship: Lessons from Mexico. *World Politics* 46 (2):151–84.

Franzese, R. 2002. *Macroeconomic policies of developed democracies.* Cambridge, MA: Cambridge University Press.

Fraquelli, G., and F. Erbetta. 1999. *Privatization in Italy: An analysis of factors productivity and technical efficiency.* Working Paper 5/1999. Turin, Italy: Ceris-CNR.

Freedom House. 2002. *Freedom in the world: The annual survey of political rights and civil liberties 2001–2002.* New York: Freedom House.

———. various years. *Freedom in the world: The annual survey of political rights and civil liberties.* New York: Freedom House.

Fuest, V., and W. Laube. 2004. *Konzept einer armutsorientierten Entwicklungszusammenarbeit im Wassersektor.* Teilgutachten 1 im Rahmen des Forschungsprojekts des Bundesministeriums für wirtschaftliche Zusammenarbeit und Entwicklung: Wasser und Armut; Schlussfolgerungen für die Umsetzung des Aktionsprogramms 2015 und das Erreichen der Millennium Development Goals. Bonn: German Development Institute (DIE).

Fundación Seguridad y Democracia. 2004. *Informe especial: Colombia: Balance de seguridad 2001–2004.* Bogotá: Fundación Seguridad y Democracia.

———. 2006. *Informe especial: La seguridad en los últimos tres períodos presidenciales 1994–2006.* Bogotá: Fundación Seguridad y Democracia.

Furubotn, E., and R. Richter. 1991. The new institutional economics: An assessment. In *The New Institutional Economics: A collection of articles from the Journal of Institutional and Theoretical Economics,* eds. E. Furubotn and R. Richter, 1–32. Tübingen: Mohr Siebeck.

Galdo, V., and B. Briceño. 2005. *Evaluating the impact on child mortality of a water supply and sewerage expansion in Quito: Is water enough?* Office of Evaluation and Oversight Working Paper. Washington, DC: Inter-American Development Bank.

Garcia, S., and A. Reynaud. 2004. Estimating the benefits of efficient water pricing in France. *Resource and Energy Economics* 26 (1):1–25.

Gleick, P. H. 2002. *Dirty water: Estimated deaths from water-related diseases 2000–2020.* Oakland, CA: Pacific Institute.

Goetz, A. M., and J. Gaventa. 2001. *Bringing citizens voice and client focus into service delivery.* IDS Working Paper 138. Brighton, UK: Institute of Development Studies.

Gómez-Lobo, A., and D. Contreras. 2003. Water subsidy policies: A comparison of the Chilean and Colombian schemes. *World Bank Economic Review* 17 (3):391–407.

Gómez-Lobo, A., and M. Meléndez. 2007. Social policies and private sector participation in water supply—the case of Colombia. Draft working document. April 2007. Prepared for the UNRISD project on "Social Policy, Regulation and Private Sector Involvement in Water Supply". http://www.unrisd.org/unrisd/website/document.nsf/ab82a6805797760f8025 6b4f005da1ab/bed05be0c8f15b69 c12572b300429f09/$FILE/Colombia_web.pdf (accessed November 24, 2007).

González, A., and W. Munar. 2003. *The political economy of social sector reforms: Economic and sector study series.* Washington, DC: Inter-American Development Bank.

González Salas, E. 2002. Evaluación de la descentralización: Componente de capacidad institucional. In Vol. 2 of *Evaluación de la Descentralización Municipal en Colombia: Balance de Una Década,* ed. Departamento Nacional de Planeación, 325–63. Bogotá: Departamento Nacional de Planeación.

Groenewegen, P. 1991. "Political economy" and "economics". In *The new palgrave: The world of economics,* eds. J. Eatwell, M. Milgate, and P. Newman, 556–62. London: Macmillan.

Grofman, B. 1996. Political economy: Downsian perspectives. In *A new handbook of political science,* eds. R. E. Goodin and H.-D. Klingemann, 691–701. Oxford: Oxford University Press.

Grossman, S., and O. Hart. 1986. The costs and benefits of ownership: A theory of vertical and lateral integration. *Journal of Political Economy* 94 (4):691–719.

Gutierrez, L. H. 2003. The effect of endogenous regulation on telecommunications expansion and efficiency in Latin America. *Journal of Regulatory Economics* 23 (3):257–86.

Gwartney, J., R. Lawson, and E. Gartzke. 2005. *Economic freedom of the world: Annual Report 2005.* Vancouver, Canada: Fraser Institute.

Haggard, S., and M. D. McCubbins. 2001. Introduction: Political institutions and the determinants of public policy. In *Presidents, Parliaments, and Policy*, eds. S. Haggard and M. D. McCubbins, 1–20. Cambridge, UK: Cambridge University Press.

Haldenwang, C. v. 2005. Systemic governance and development in Latin America. *CEPAL Review* 85 (April):33–49.

Hall, D., and E. Lubina. 2002. *Water privatisation in Latin America. 2002*: PSIRU Reports. London: Public Services International Research Unit: University of Greenwich.

Hamilton, L. C. 1991. srd1: How robust is robust regression? *Stata Technical Bulletin* 2:21–26.

Hansson, L. 2004. *Water as an economic and social good: Some socio-economic principles for Indian water management.* IIIEE Reports 2004:1. Lund: IIIEE: Lund University.

Hayek, F. A. 1945. *The road to serfdom.* Chicago: Chicago University Press.

Hemmer, H.-R. 2002. *Wirtschaftsprobleme der Entwicklungsländer.* 3rd. ed. Munich: Vahlen.

———., and A. Lorenz. 2004. *Grundlagen der Wachstumsempirie.* Munich: Vahlen.

Henisz, W. J. 2002. The institutional environment for infrastructure investment. *Industrial and Corporate Change* 11 (2):355–89.

———, and B. A. Zelner. 2001. The institutional environment for telecommunications investment. *Journal of Economics and Management Strategy* 10 (1):123–47.

———, and B. A. Zelner. 2004. *Interest groups, veto points and electricity infrastructure deployment.* William Davidson Institute Working Paper 711. Ann Arbor: University of Michigan Business School.

Hirschman, A. O. 1970. *Exit, voice and loyalty: Responses to decline in firms, organizations and states.* Cambridge, MA: Harvard University Press.

Horrall, J. 2002. *Institutions, political regime and access to telecommunications infrastructure in Africa.* Public Utilities Research Center Working Paper. Gainesville: University of Florida.

Hutton, G., and L. Haller. 2004. *Evaluation of the costs and benefits of water and sanitation improvements at the global level.* Geneva: World Health Organization.

Instituto de Hidrología, Meteorología y Estudios Ambientales. without year. *Estudio nacional del agua.* Bogotá: IDEAM.

Inkota-Netzwerk e.V. and Brot für die Welt. 2004. *Wasser—Öffentliche Kontrolle statt Kommerz.* Berlin: Brot für die Welt.

Irwin, T., and C. Yamamoto. 2004. *Some options for improving the governance of state-owned electricity utilities.* Energy and Mining Sector Board Discussion Paper 11. Washington, DC: World Bank.

Izaguirre, A. K. 2004. Private infrastructure: Activity down by 30 percent in 2002. *Public Policy for the Private Sector* No. 267. http://rru.worldbank.org/publicpolicyjournal (accessed May 24, 2008).

Jaggers, K., and T. Gurr. 1995. Tracking democracy's third wave with Polity III data. *Journal of Peace Research* 32 (4):469–82.

Jalan, J., and M. Ravallion. 2001. *Does piped water reduce diarrhea for children in rural India?* Policy Research Working Paper 2664. Washington, DC: World Bank.

Joskow, P. L. 2007. Regulation of natural monopoly. In Vol 2 of *Handbook of law and economics*, eds. A. M. Polinsky and S. Shavell, 1227–348. Amsterdam: Elsevier.

———, and N. L. Rose. 1989. The effects of economic regulation. In *Handbook of industrial organization*, eds. R. Schmalensee and R. D. Willig, 1449–506. Amsterdam: Elsevier.

Jouravlev, A. S. 2000. *Water utility regulation: Issues and options for Latin America and the Caribbean*. Santiago de Chile: United Nations Economic Commission for Latin America and the Caribbean.

Kahn, A. E. 1971. *The economics of regulation: Principles and institutions* Vol. 2. New York: Wiley.

Kaufmann, D., and A. Kraay. 2002. Growth without governance. *Economia* 3 (1):169–229.

Kaufmann, D., A. Kraay, and M. Mastruzzi. 2004. *Governance matters III: Governance indicators for 1996–2002*. World Bank Policy Research Working Paper 3106. Revised version 5 April 2004. Washington, DC: World Bank.

Keefer, P. 2002. *Clientelism, credibility, and democracy*. Development Research Group Working Paper. Washington, DC: World Bank.

———. 2005. *Database of political institutions: Changes and variable definitions*. Washington, DC: World Bank.

Keefer, P., and S. Knack. 1997. Why don't poor countries catch up? A cross-national test of an institutional explanation. *Economic Inquiry* 35 (3):590–602.

Keefer, P., and D. Stasavage. 2003. The limits of delegation: Veto players, central bank independence and the credibility of monetary policy. *American Political Science Review* 47 (3):389–403.

Kessides, I. N. 2004. *Reforming infrastructure: Privatization, regulation, and competition*. World Bank Policy Research Report. Washington, DC: World Bank.

King, G., R. O. Keohane, and S. Verba. 1994. *Designing social inquiry: Scientific inference in qualitative research*. Princeton: Princeton University Press.

Kirkpatrick, C., D. Parker, and Y.-F. Zhang. 2004. *State versus private sector provision of water services in Africa: An empirical analysis*. Paper presented at Centre on Regulation and Competition 3rd International Conference: Pro-poor regulation and competition: Issues, policies and practices. Cape Town, South Africa, 7–9 September 2004. http://www. competition-regulation.org. uk/conferences/southafrica04/kirkpatrick&parker&zhang.pdf (accessed June 23, 2008).

Knack, S. 2002. *Governance and growth: Measurement and evidence*. IRIS Discussion Papers on Institutions and Growth 02/05. College Park, MD: Center for Institutional Reform and the Informal Sector.

Knack, S., and P. Keefer. 1995. Institutions and economic performance: Cross-country tests using alternative institutional measures. *Economics and Politics* 7 (3):207–27.

Komives, K. et al. 2005. *Water, electricity, and the poor: Who benefits from utility subsidies?* Washington, DC: World Bank.

Komives, K., D. Whittington, and X. Wu. 2003. Infrastructure coverage and the poor: A global perspective. In *Infrastructure for poor people: Public policy for private provision*, eds. P. J. Brook and T. Irwin, 77–124. Washington, DC: World Bank.

Krause, M. 2002. *Restrukturierung der Stromwirtschaft: Aufgaben für Staat und Entwicklungszusammenarbeit*. Berichte und Gutachten 8/2002. Bonn: German Development Institute (DIE).

———. 2008. The political economy of water and sanitation services in Colombia. In *Water politics and development cooperation: Local power plays and global governance*, eds. W. Scheumann, S. Neumann and M. Kipping, 237–58. Berlin: Springer.

Kreditanstalt Für Wiederaufbau. 2004. *Zur Berücksichtigung der Nachhaltigkeit durch die KfW in Schlussprüfungen von Projekten der Siedlungswasserwirtschaft*. Diskussionsbeiträge. Frankfurt am Main: KfW.

Krueger, A. 1974. The political economy of the rent-seeking society. *American Economic Review* 64 (3):291–303.

Kugler, M., and H. Rosental. 2000. *Checks and balances: An assessment of the institutional separation of political powers in Colombia.* Working Paper 17. Bogotá: Fedesarrollo.

Kydland, F., and E. Prescott. 1977. Rules rather than discretion: The inconsistency of optimal plans. *Journal of Political Economy* 85 (3):473–90.

Lake, D. A., and M. A. Baum. 2001. The invisible hand of democracy: Political control and provision of public services. *Comparative Political Studies* 34 (6):587–621.

Leal, F., and A. Dávila. 1990. *Clientelismo en Colombia: El sistema político y su expresión regional.* Bogotá: Tercer Mundo.

Leibenstein, H. 1966. Allocative efficiency versus X-efficiency. *American Economic Review* 56:392–415.

Levin, R. B. et al. 2002. U.S. drinking water challenges in the twenty-first century. *Environmental Health Perspectives* 110 (Suppl 1: Febr 2002):43–52.

Levy, B., and P. T. Spiller. 1996. A framework for resolving the regulatory problem. In *Regulations, institutions and commitment: Comparative studies of telecommunications,* eds. B. Levy and P. T. Spiller, 1–35. Cambridge, MA: Cambridge University Press.

Lobina, E. 2005. Problems with private water concessions: A review of experiences and analysis of dynamics. *Water Resources Development* 21 (1):55–87.

Lundsgaard, J. 2002. *Competition and efficiency in publicly funded services.* Economics Department Working Papers 331. Paris: OECD.

Mainardi, S. 2003. Water availability and infrastructure development: Cross-country econometric and neural network estimates. *Desalination* 158 (1–3):241–54.

Maldonado Copello, A. 2002. Avances y resultados de la descentralización política en Colombia. In Vol. 2 of *Evaluación de la descentralización municipal en Colombia: Balance de una década,* ed. Departamento Nacional de Planeación, 259–321. Bogotá: Departamento Nacional de Planeación.

Maldonado, M. M., and G. Vargas Forero. 2001. *Evaluación de la descentralización municipal en Colombia: La descentralización en el sector de agua potable y saneamiento básico.* Archivos de Economía Documento 166. Bogotá: Departamento Nacional de Planeación.

Marshall, M. G., and K. Jaggers. 2000. *Polity IV Project: Political regime characteristics and transitions 1800–1999; Dataset users manual.* College Park, MD: University of Maryland.

Martz, J. D. 1997. *The politics of clientelism: Democracy and the state in Colombia.* New Brunswick, NJ: Transaction Publishers.

Mauro, P. 1995. Corruption and growth. *Quarterly Journal of Economics* 110 (3):681–712.

McDowell, A., and N. J. Cox. 2001. How do you estimate a model when the dependent variable is a proportion? Webresource Stata Corporation: Frequently asked questions. http://www.stata.com/support/faqs/stat/logit.html (accessed February 24, 2006).

McIntosh, A. C. 2003. *Asian water supplies: Reaching the urban poor.* Manila: Asian Development Bank/IWA Publishing.

Media Analytics Ltd. 2004. Tariffs: Half way there. *Global Water Intelligence* 5 (9):8–9.

Meléndez, M. 2004. *Subsidios al consumo de los servicios públicos en Colombia: Hacia dónde movernos?* Informes de base: Colombia; Desarrollo económico reciente en infraestructura (REDI). Washington, DC: World Bank.

Merkel, W. 2004. Embedded and defective democracies. *Democratization* 11 (5):33–58.

Ministerio de Ambiente, Vivienda y Desarrollo Territorial. 2005. Decreto Número 1013 de 2005: Por el cual se establece la metodología para la determinación del equilibrio entre los subsudios y las contribuciones para los servicios públicos domiciliarios de acueducto, alcantarillado y aseo. *Diario Oficial* 45871 (April 6, 2005).

——. 2006. Decreto 57 de 2006: Por el cual de establecen unas reglas para la aplicación del factor de aporte solidario para los servicios públicos domiciliarios de acueducto, altantarillado y aseo. *Diario Oficial* 46150 (January 13, 2006).

Ministerio de Desarrollo Económico. 2000. *Resolución No. 1096 de 17 de Noviembre de 2000: Por la cual se adopta el Reglamento Técnico para el sector de Agua Potable y Saneamiento Básico—RAS.* Bogotá. http://www.cra.gov.co/.

Ministerio de Salud. 1998. Decreto Número 475 de 1998: Por el cual se expiden normas técnicas de calidad del agua potable. *Diario Oficial* 43259 (March 16, 1998).

Mkandawire, T. 2004. Good governance: The itinerary of an idea. *D+C Development Cooperation* 31 (10/2004):380–81.

Munck, G. L., and J. Verkuilen. 2002. Conceptualizing and measuring democracy. *Comparative Political Studies* 35 (1):5–34.

Müller, T., and S. Pickel. 2007. Wie lässt sich Demokratie am besten messen? Zur Konzeptqualität von Demokratie-Indizes. *Politische Vierteljahresschrift* 48 (3):511–39.

Neubert, S. 2003. *Methodological orientation for short-term and practical research projects in developing countries.* Bonn: German Development Institute (DIE).

Nickson, A. 2001. *Establishing and implementing a joint venture: Water and sanitation services in Cartagena, Colombia.* Working paper 442 03. London: GHK International.

Noll, R. 2002. The economics of urban water systems. In *Thirsting for efficiency: The economics and politics of urban water system reform,* ed. M. M. Shirley, 43–63. Amsterdam: Pergamon.

Noll, R. G. 1989. Economic perspectives on the politics of regulation. In Vol. 2 of *Handbook of industrial organization,* eds. R. Schmalensee and R. D. Willig, 1253–87. Amsterdam: Elsevier.

North, D. C. 1990. *Institutions, institutional change and economic performance: The political economy of institutions and decisions.* Cambridge, MA: Cambridge University Press.

O'Donnell, G. 1994. Delegative democracy. *Journal of Democracy* 5 (1):55–69.

——. 1998. Horizontal accountability in new democracies. *Journal of Democracy* 9 (3):112–26.

Observatorio del Programa Presidencial de Derechos Humanos y DIH. 2005. *Algunos indicadores sobre la situación de los derechos humanos en el departamento de Meta.* Bogotá: Vicepresidencia de la República.

——. 2006a. *Dinámica reciente de la confrontación armada en Caldas.* Bogotá: Vicepresidencia de la República.

——. 2006b. *Dinámica reciente de la confrontación armada en la Sierra Nevada de Santa Marta.* Bogotá: Vicepresidencia de la República.

Ochoa, F. 1996. Evaluación de la participación del sector privado en acueducto y alcantarillado: Enseñanzas. Noviembre de 1996. Unpublished study. Bogotá.

Offe, C. 1996. Political economy: Sociological perspectives. In *A new handbook of political science,* eds. R. E. Goodin and H.-D. Klingemann, 675–90. Oxford: Oxford University Press.

Olson, M. 1965. *The logic of collective action: Public goods and the theory of groups.* Cambridge, MA: Harvard University Press.

——. 1982. *The rise and decline of nations: Economic growth, stagflation, and social rigidities.* New Haven, CT: Yale University Press.

——. 1993. Dictatorship, democracy and development. *American Political Science Review* 87 (3):567–76.

Pastor, M., and C. Wise. 1999. The politics of second-generation reform. *Journal of Democracy* 10 (3):34–48.

Paul, S. 1992. Accountability in public services: Exit, voice and control. *World Development* 20 (7):1047–60.

Perman, R. et al. 2003. *Natural resource and environmental economics.* 3rd ed. Harlow, UK: Pearson.

Plümper, T. 2001. Die Politik wirtschaftlichen Wachstums in autoritären Staaten. *Politische Vierteljahresschrift* 42 (1):79–100.

Rawls, J. 1971. *A theory of justice.* Cambridge, MA: Harvard University Press.

Renzetti, S. 2000. An empirical perspective on water pricing reforms. In *The political economy of water pricing reforms,* ed. A. Dinar, 123–40. Washington, DC: World Bank.

Renzetti, S., and D. Dupont. 2004. Ownership and performance of water utilities. *Greener Management International* 42:9–19.

República de Colombia. 2004. *Informe anual de Derechos Humanos y Derecho Internacional Humanitario 2003.* Bogotá: Vicepresidencia de la República.

———. 2005. *Informe anual de Derechos Humanos y Derecho Internacional Humanitario 2004.* Bogotá: Vicepresidencia de la República.

Richter, R., and E. Furubotn. 1997. *Institutions and economic theory: An introduction to and assessment of the new institutional economics.* Ann Arbor: University of Michigan Press.

Robinson, J. A. 2005. A normal Latin American country? A perspective on Colombian development. Cambridge, MA. http://www.people.fas.harvard.edu/~jrobins/researchpapers/ unpublishedpapers/index.htm (accessed March 20, 2008).

Robinson, M. 1998. Corruption and development: An introduction. *European Journal of Development Research* 10 (1):1–14.

Rodríguez del Gallego, A., and J. C. Carvajal. 2004. *Conceptos y medición del índice de necesidades básicas insatisfechas NBI (II).* Maestría en Gestión Urbana. Papeles de Coyuntura 2. Bogotá: Universidad Piloto de Colombia.

Roemer, J. E. 1998. *Equality of opportunity.* Cambridge, MA: Harvard University Press.

Roland, G., and J. G. Zapata. 2000. *Colombia's electoral and party system: Proposals for reforms.* Working Paper. Berkeley: University of California.

Roniger, L. 1990. *Hierarchy and trust in modern Mexico and Brazil.* New York: Praeger Publishers.

Rosen, H. S. 1992. *Public finance.* 3rd ed. Homewood, IL: Irwin.

Rouse, M. J. 2007. *Institutional governance and regulation of water service: The essential elements.* London: IWA Publishing.

Sappington, D. 1996. Principles of regulatory policy design. In *Infrastructure delivery: Private initiative and the public good,* ed. A. Mody, 79–105. Washington, DC: World Bank.

Sarmiento, A., and L. M. Becerra. 1998. *Análisis de las relaciones entre violencia y equidad.* Archivos de Macroeconomía Documento 93. Bogotá: Departamento Nacional de Planeación.

Sauer, J. 2003. The efficiency of rural infrastructure—Water supply in rural areas of transition. ERSA Conference Papers ersa03p463. http://www.ersa.org/ersa-confs/ersa03/ cdrom/papers/463.pdf (accessed March 19, 2008).

———. 2005. Economies of scale and firm size optimum in rural water supply. *Water Resources Research* 41 (11):1–13.

Scharpf, F. W. 1997. *Games real actors play: Actor-centered institutionalism in policy research.* Boulder, CO: Westview Press.

Sen, A. 1985. *Commodities and capabilities.* Amsterdam: North-Holland.

Serra, P. 2000. *Subsidies in Chilean public utilities.* Serie Economía del Centro de Economía Aplicada 70. Santiago de Chile: Universidad de Chile.

Shapiro, S., and R. Willig. 1990. Economic rationales for the scope of privatization. In *The political economy of public sector reform and privatization*, eds. E. N. Suleiman and J. Waterbury, 55–87. Boulder, CO: Westview Press.

Shirley, M. M., and P. Walsh. 2000. *Public versus private ownership: The current state of the debate*. Working Paper 2420. Washington, DC: World Bank.

Shirley, M. M. 2000. Reforming urban water systems: A tale of four cities. In *Regulatory policy in Latin America: Post-privatization realities*, ed. L. Manzetti, 147–70. Miami: North-South Center Press.

———, and C. Ménard. 2002. Cities awash: A synthesis of the country cases. In *Thirsting for efficiency: The economics and politics of urban water system reform*, ed. M. M. Shirley, 1–41. Amsterdam: Pergamon.

Siebert, H. 2004. *Economics of the environment*. 6th ed. Berlin: Springer.

Smith, W. 1997. Utility regulators: The independence debate. *Public Policy for the Private Sector* 12 (Dec 1997):9–12.

———. 2000. *Regulating Infrastructure for the Poor: Perspectives on regulatory system design*. Paper Presented at "Infrastructure for development: Private solutions and the poor". May 31–June 2, 2000. London.

Spiller, P. T., and W. Savedoff. 1999. Government opportunism and the provision of water. In *Spilled water: Institutional commitment in the provision of water services*, eds. W. Savedoff and P. T. Spiller, 1–34. Washington, DC: Inter-American Development Bank.

Stasavage, D. 2001. *Electoral competition and public spending on education: Evidence from African countries*. The Centre for the Study of African Economies Working Paper 155. London: London School of Economics.

Stern, J., and S. Holder. 1999. Regulatory governance: Criteria for assessing the performance of regulatory systems: An application to infrastructure industries in the developing countries of Asia. *Utilities Policy* 8 (1):33–50.

Superintendencia de Servicios Públicos Domiciliarios. 2001. *Gestión integral para los servicios públicos domiciliarios de agua potable y saneamiento básico: Deberes y responsabilidades de alcaldes y concejales*. Bogotá: SSPD.

———. 2002. Acueducto, alcantarillado y aseo 1998–2001. *Supercifras en m3* 6:1–143.

———. 2004a. Concepto SSPD-OJ-2004–272. Bogotá: SSPD.

———. 2004b. *Informe control de la calidad del agua en Colombia—2003*. Bogotá: SSPD.

———. 2004c. *Manual de comités de desarrollo y control social: Participación Cuidadana en Servicios Públicos Domiciliarios* Vol I. Bogotá: SSPD.

———. 2004d. *Manual del vocal de control de servicios públicos domiciliarios: Participación Cuidadana en Servicios Públicos Domicilarios* Vol II. Bogotá: SSPD.

———. 2005a. *Balance entre asignaciones municipales, contribuciones y subsidios aplicados a los servicios de acueducto, alcantarillado y aseo: Colombia—2001–2004*. Bogotá: SSPD.

———. 2005b. *Boletín tarifario 01 de 2005: Servicios públicos de acueducto, altancarillado y aseo*. Bogotá: SSPD.

———. 2005c. *Informe de calidad del agua en Colombia 2004*, Bogotá: SSPD.

———. 2006. *Estudio sectorial servicios públicos de acueducto y alcantarillado 2002–2005*. Documento de trabajo. Bogotá: SSPD.

Tirole, J. 1988. *The theory of industrial organization*. Cambridge, MA: MIT Press.

Torres, M., and C. J. Morrison Paul. 2006. Driving forces for consolidation or fragmentation of the US water utility industry: A cost function approach with endogenous output. *Journal of Urban Economics* 59 (1):104–20.

Transparencia por Colombia. 2004. *El control social de la administración pública en Colombia*. Cuadernos de Transparencia 8. Bogotá: Transparencia por Colombia.

———. 2005. *Índice de transparencia departamental: Resultados 2004–2005.* Bogotá: Transparencia por Colombia.

———. Without year. *Índice de integridad de los gobiernos, asambleas y contralorías departamentales. Resultados 2003–2004.* Bogotá: Transparencia por Colombia.

Tsebelis, G. 2002. *Veto players: How political institutions work.* Princeton: Princeton University Press.

Ugaz, C. 2003. Consumer participation and pro-poor regulation in Latin America. In *Utility privatization and regulation: A fair deal for consumers?* eds. C. Ugaz and C. Waddams Price, 80–98. Cheltenham: Edward Elgar Publishing.

United Nations Development Programme. 1997. *Reconceptualising governance.* Management Development and Governance Division Discussion Paper No. 2. New York: United Nations Development Programme.

———. 2003. *Human development report 2003: Millennium development goals; A compact among nations to end human poverty.* New York: Oxford University Press.

United Nations Economic and Social Council. 2002. *Substantive issues arising in the implementation of the International Covenant on Economic, Social and Cultural Rights.* Draft. General comment 15: The right to water. Geneva: Office for the UN High Commissioner for Human Rights.

United Nations Human Settlements Programme. 2003. *Water and sanitation in the world's cities: Local action for global goods.* London: Earthscan.

United Nations Office on Drugs and Crime. Without year. Línea base para una política trasparente. Unpublished document. Manizales, Colombia.

United States Department of State. 2006. *Country report on Human Rights practices—Colombia.* Washington, DC: United States Department of State.

Urquhart, P., and D. Moore. 2004. *Global water scoping process. Is there a case for a multistakeholder review of private sector participation in water and sanitation?* Scoping report: Executive summary. Brasilia: Associação Nacional dos Serviços Municipais de Saneamento.

Urrutia, M. 1991. The absence of populism in Colombia. In *The macro-economics of populism in Latin America*, eds. S. Edwards and R. Dornbusch, 369–87. Chicago: University of Chicago Press.

Veeduría de Servicios Públicos. 2003. Calidad en la prestación de los servicios públicos en la ciudad de Villavicencio: Presentación Octubre de 2003. Unpublished. Villavicencio, Colombia.

Vickers, J., and G. Yarrow. 1988. *Privatization: An economic analysis.* Cambridge, MA: MIT Press.

Villar, R. 2001. La institucionalidad política y el tercer sector en Colombia: Notas para una reflexión. Paper preseted at 'Tercer Encuentro de ISTR-LAC'. September 12–14, 2007. Buenos Aires.

Wallsten, S. J. 2001. An econometric analysis of telecom competition, privatization, and regulation in Africa and Latin America. *The Journal of Industrial Economics* 49 (1):1–19.

Weiss, T. G. 2000. Governance, good governance and global governance: Conceptual and actual challenges. *Third World Quarterly* 21 (5):795–814.

Whittington, D. et al. 1992. *Household demand for improved sanitation services: A case study of Kumasi, Ghana.* Water and Sanitation Discussion Paper. Washington, DC: World Bank.

Wills Herrera, E. 2002. La relación entre la corrupción y el proceso de descentralización en Colombia. In Vol. 2 of *Evaluación de la descentralización municipal en Colombia: Balance de una década*, ed. Departamento Nacional de Planeación, 368–415. Bogotá: Departamento Nacional de Planeación.

Winpenny, J. 2003. Financing water for all: Report of the World Panel on Financing Water Infrastructure. Marseille: World Water Council.

Wolff, G., and E. Hallstein. 2005. *Beyond privatization: Restructuring water systems to improve performance.* Oakland, CA: Pacific Institute.

Wooldridge, J. M. 2006. *Introductory econometrics: A modern approach.* 3rd ed. Mason, OH: South-Western.

World Bank. 1992. *Governance and development.* Washington, DC: World Bank.

———. 1994. *World Development Report 1994: Infrastructure for Development.* Washington, DC: World Bank.

———. 2001. *World Development Report 2000/2001: Attacking Poverty.* Washington, DC: World Bank.

———. 2003a. *Efficient, sustainable service for all? An Operation Evaluation Department review of the World Bank's assistance to water supply and sanitation.* Washington, DC: World Bank.

———. 2003b. *World Development Report 2004: Making Services Work for Poor People.* Washington, DC: World Bank.

———. 2004. *Public and private sector roles in water supply and sanitation services: Operational guidance for World Bank Group staff.* Washington, DC: World Bank.

———. 2005. *World Development Report 2006: Equity and Development.* Washington, DC: World Bank

World Health Organization. 2004. *Guidelines for drinking-water quality: Recommendations* Vol. 1. 3rd ed. Geneva: WHO.

World Health Organization and United Nations Children's Fund. 2000. *Global water supply and sanitation assessment 2000 report.* Geneva: WHO and UNICEF.

———. 2004. *Meeting the MDG drinking water and sanitation target: A midterm assessment of progress.* Geneva: WHO and UNICEF.

———. 2005. *Water for life: Making it happen.* Geneva: WHO and UNICEF.

———. 2006. *Meeting the MDG drinking water and sanitation target: The urban and rural challenge of the decade.* Geneva: WHO and UNICEF.

Yaffee, R. A. 2002. *Robust regression analysis: Some popular statistical package options.* Paper of the Statistics, Social Science, and Mapping Group. New York: New York University.

Zakaria, F. 1997. The rise of illiberal democracy. *Foreign Affairs* 76 (6):22–43.

Zerbe, R. O., Y. Bauman, and A. Finkle. 2006. An aggregate measure for benefit-cost-analysis. *Ecological Economics* 58 (3):449–61.

Zhang, Y.-F., and C. Kirkpatrick. 2002. *Electricity sector reform in developing countries: An econometric assessment of the effects of privatisation, competition and regulation.* Centre on Regulation and Competition Working Paper 31. Manchester: University of Manchester.

Index

For Product Safety Concerns and Information please contact our EU
representative GPSR@taylorandfrancis.com
Taylor & Francis Verlag GmbH, Kaufingerstraße 24, 80331 München, Germany

www.ingramcontent.com/pod-product-compliance
Ingram Content Group UK Ltd.
Pitfield, Milton Keynes, MK11 3LW, UK
UKHW021607240425
457818UK00018B/424